Reader's Digest

# Fast Healthy
# Food

Reader's Digest
# Fast Healthy Food

Published by
The Reader's Digest Association Limited
London • New York • Sydney • Montreal

# Contents

# Introduction

Fast food need not be unhealthy food. With today's quick cooking methods you don't have to sacrifice goodness and taste. The wide variety of delicious and nutritious dishes in this collection can be prepared and cooked in 30 minutes or less. The recipes offer a balance of different foods that will supply all the nutrients your body requires.

## Getting it into proportion

Current guidelines are that most people in the UK should eat more starchy foods, more fruit and vegetables, and less fat, meat products and sugary foods. It is almost impossible to give exact amounts that you should eat, as every person's requirements vary, depending on size, age and the amount of energy expended during the day.

However, nutrition experts have suggested an ideal balance of the different foods that provide us with energy (calories) and the nutrients needed for health. The number of daily portions of each of the food groups will vary from person to person – for example, an active teenager might need to eat up to 14 portions of starchy carbohydrate foods every day, whereas a sedentary adult would only require 6 or 7 portions – but the proportions of the food groups in relation to each other should ideally stay the same.

## Food on the plate

A simple way to get the balance right, however, is to imagine a daily 'plate' divided into the different food groups. On the imaginary 'plate', starchy carbohydrate foods fill at least a third of the space, thus constituting the main part of your meals. Fruit and vegetables fill the same amount of space. The remaining third of the 'plate' is divided mainly between protein foods and dairy foods, with just a little space allowed for foods containing fat and sugar. These are the proportions to aim for.

It isn't essential to eat the ideal proportions on the 'plate' at every meal, or even every day – balancing them over a week or two is just as good. This will ensure that the body receives the steady supply of vitamins, minerals and phytochemicals required to stay well. The healthiest diet for you and your family is one that is generally balanced and sustainable in the long term.

## Daily energy requirements in adult life

Daily calorie needs vary according to age, sex and lifestyle. To maintain an ideal body weight, we need to balance the calories we consume with the energy we expend.

| Men | | | Women | | |
|---|---|---|---|---|---|
| 18-34 years | sedentary | 2510 kcal | 18-54 years | sedentary | 1940 kcal |
| | active | 2900 kcal | | active | 2150 kcal |
| | very active | 3350 kcal | | very active | 2500 kcal |
| 35-64 years | sedentary | 2400 kcal | | pregnant | 2400 kcal |
| | active | 2750 kcal | | breastfeeding | 2750 kcal |
| | very active | 3350 kcal | 55-74 years | sedentary | 1900 kcal |
| 65-74 years | sedentary | 2330 kcal | | active | 2000 kcal |
| 75+ years | sedentary | 2100 kcal | 75+ years | sedentary | 1810 kcal |

# Our daily plate

## Fruit and vegetables:

### eat at least 5 portions a day

Nutrition experts are unanimous that we would all benefit from eating more fruit and vegetables each day – a total of at least 400 g (14 oz) of fruit and vegetables (edible part) is the target. Fruit and vegetables provide vitamin C for immunity and healing, and other 'antioxidant' vitamins and minerals for protection against cardiovascular disease and cancer. They also offer several 'phytochemicals' that help protect against cancer, and B vitamins, especially folate, which is important for women planning a pregnancy, to prevent birth defects. All of these, plus other nutrients, work together to boost well-being.

Antioxidant nutrients (e.g. vitamins C and beta-carotene, which are mainly derived from fruit and vegetables) and vitamin E help to prevent harmful free radicals in the body initiating or accelerating cancer, heart disease, cataracts, arthritis, general ageing, sun damage to skin, and damage to sperm. Free radicals occur naturally as a by-product of normal cell function, but are also caused by pollutants such as tobacco smoke and over-exposure to sunlight.

## What is a portion of fruit or vegetables?

Some examples are:

1 medium-sized portion of
   vegetables or salad
1 medium-sized piece of
   fresh fruit
6 tbsp (about 140 g/5 oz) stewed
   or canned fruit
1 small glass (100 ml/3½ fl oz)
   fruit juice

## Starchy carbohydrate foods:

### eat 6–14 portions a day

At least 50% of the calories in a healthy diet should come from carbohydrates, and most of that from starchy foods – bread, potatoes and other starchy vegetables, pasta, rice and cereals. For most people in the UK this means doubling current intake. Starchy carbohydrates are the best foods for energy. They also provide protein and essential vitamins and minerals, particularly those from the B group. Eat a variety of starchy foods, choosing wholemeal or wholegrain types whenever possible, because the fibre they contain helps to prevent constipation, bowel disease, heart disease and other health problems.

## What is a portion of starchy food?

Some examples are:

3 tbsp breakfast cereal
2 tbsp muesli
1 slice of bread or toast
1 bread roll, bap or bun
1 small pitta bread, naan bread
   or chapatti
3 crackers or crispbreads
1 medium-sized potato
1 medium-sized plantain or
   small sweet potato
2 heaped tbsp boiled rice
2 heaped tbsp boiled pasta

## Dairy foods:

### eat 2–3 portions a day

Dairy foods, such as milk, cheese, yogurt and fromage frais, are the best source of calcium for strong bones and teeth, and important for the nervous system. They also provide some protein for growth and repair, vitamin $B_{12}$, and vitamin A for healthy eyes. They are particularly valuable foods for young children, who need full-fat versions at least up to age 2. Dairy foods are also especially important for adolescent girls to prevent the development of osteoporosis later in life, and for women throughout life generally.

To limit fat intake, wherever possible adults should choose lower-fat dairy foods, such as semi-skimmed milk and low-fat yogurt.

## What is a portion of dairy food?

Some examples are:

1 medium-sized glass
   (200 ml/7 fl oz) milk
1 matchbox-sized piece
   (40 g/1½ oz) Cheddar cheese
1 small pot of yogurt
125 g (4½ oz) cottage cheese or
   fromage frais

## Foods containing fat:

### 1–5 portions a day

Unlike fruit, vegetables and starchy carbohydrates, which can be eaten in abundance, fatty foods should not exceed 33% of the day's calories in a balanced diet, and only 10% of this should be from saturated fat. This quantity of fat may seem a lot, but it isn't – fat contains more than twice as many calories per gram as either carbohydrate or protein.

Overconsumption of fat is a major cause of weight and health problems. A healthy diet must contain a certain amount of fat to provide fat-soluble vitamins and essential fatty acids, needed for the development and function of the brain, eyes and nervous system, but we only need a small amount each day – just 25 g is required, which is much less than we consume in our Western diet. The current recommendations from the Department of Health are a maximum of 71 g fat (of this, 21.5 g saturated) for women each day and 93.5 g fat (28.5 g saturated) for men. The best sources of the essential fatty acids are natural fish oils and pure vegetable oils.

## What is a portion of fatty food?

Some examples are:

1 tsp butter or margarine
2 tsp low-fat spread
1 tsp cooking oil
1 tbsp mayonnaise or vinaigrette (salad dressing)
1 tbsp cream
1 individual packet of crisps

## Foods containing sugar:

### 0–2 portions a day

Although many foods naturally contain sugars (e.g. fruit contains fructose, milk lactose), health experts recommend that we limit 'added' sugars. Added sugars, such as table sugar, provide only calories – they contain no vitamins, minerals or fibre to contribute to health, and it is not necessary to eat them at all. But, as the old adage goes, 'a little of what you fancy does you good' and sugar is no exception. Denial of foods, or using them as rewards or punishment, is not a healthy attitude to eating, and can lead to cravings, binges and yo-yo dieting. Sweet foods are a pleasurable part of a well-balanced diet, but added sugars should account for no more than 11% of the total daily carbohydrate intake.

In assessing how much sugar you consume, don't forget that it is a major ingredient of many processed and ready-prepared foods.

## What is a portion of sugary food?

Some examples are:

3 tsp sugar
1 heaped tsp jam or honey
2 biscuits
half a slice of cake
1 doughnut
1 Danish pastry
1 small bar of chocolate
1 small tube or bag of sweets

## Protein foods:

### eat 2–4 portions a day

Lean meat, fish, eggs and vegetarian alternatives provide protein for growth and cell repair, as well as iron to prevent anaemia. Meat also provides B vitamins for healthy nerves and digestion, especially vitamin $B_{12}$, and zinc for growth and healthy bones and skin. Only moderate amounts of these protein-rich foods are required. An adult woman needs about 45 g of protein a day and an adult man 55 g, which constitutes about 11% of a day's calories. This is less than the current average intake. For optimum health, we need to eat some protein every day.

## What is a portion of protein-rich food?

Some examples are:

3 slices (85–100 g/3–3½ oz) of roast beef, pork, ham, lamb or chicken
about 100 g (3½ oz) grilled offal
115–140 g (4–5 oz) cooked fillet of white or oily fish (not fried in batter)
3 fish fingers
2 eggs (up to 7 a week)
about 140 g/5 oz baked beans
60 g (2¼ oz) nuts, peanut butter or other nut products.

## Too salty

Salt (sodium chloride) is essential for a variety of body functions, but we tend to eat too much through consumption of salty processed foods, 'fast' foods and ready-prepared foods, and by adding salt in cooking and at the table. The end result can be rising blood pressure as we get older, which puts us at higher risk of heart disease and stroke. Eating more vegetables and fruit increases potassium intake, which can help to counteract the damaging effects of salt.

## Alcohol in a healthy diet

In recent research, moderate drinking of alcohol has been linked with a reduced risk of heart disease and stroke among men and women over 45. However, because of other risks associated with alcohol, particularly in excessive quantities, no doctor would recommend taking up drinking if you are teetotal. The healthiest pattern of drinking is to enjoy small amounts of alcohol with food, to have alcohol-free days and always to avoid getting drunk. A well-balanced diet is vital because nutrients from food (vitamins and minerals) are needed to detoxify the alcohol.

## Water – the best choice

Drinking plenty of non-alcoholic liquid each day is an often overlooked part of a well-balanced diet. A minimum of 8 glasses (which is about 2 litres/3½ pints) is the ideal. If possible, these should not all be tea or coffee, as these are stimulants and diuretics, which cause the body to lose liquids, taking with them water-soluble vitamins. Water is the best choice. Other good choices are fruit or herb teas or tisanes, fruit juices – diluted with water, if preferred – or semi-skimmed milk (full-fat milk for very young children). Fizzy sugary or acidic drinks such as cola are more likely to damage tooth enamel than other drinks.

As a guide to the vitamin and mineral content of foods and recipes in the book, we have used the following terms and symbols, based on the percentage of the daily RNI provided by one serving for the average adult man or woman aged 19–49 years:

| ✓✓✓ | *or* excellent | at least 50% (half) |
| ✓✓ | *or* good | 25–50% (one-quarter to one-half) |
| ✓ | *or* useful | 10–25% (one-tenth to one-quarter) |

Note that recipes contribute other nutrients, but the analyses only include those that provide at least 10% RNI per portion. Vitamins and minerals where deficiencies are rare are not included.

**V** denotes that a recipe is suitable for vegetarians.

# Soups and starters

Wake up your taste buds with this delicious collection of recipes. From vibrant Garden of Eden soup to Quail's eggs with asparagus and Parmesan shavings, these dishes look impressive, taste great, and can be prepared easily and quickly. Whether you are looking for something traditional, such as Potato and bacon chowder, or for the novel taste combination of Melon, feta and orange salad for instance, you will find plenty of suggestions in this chapter.

# Garden of Eden soup

An assortment of vegetables cooked in tomato juice and stock makes a simple, satisfying soup that tastes terrific. Take advantage of frozen vegetables, such as broccoli and peas. They reduce the preparation time and are just as nutritious as fresh vegetables.

**Serves 4**

300 ml (10 fl oz) boiling water

1 vegetable stock cube, crumbled, or 2 tsp vegetable bouillon powder or paste

1 litre (1¾ pints) tomato juice

2 garlic cloves, crushed

4 spring onions, finely chopped

1 large potato, scrubbed and diced

1 large carrot, diced

100 g (3½ oz) frozen broccoli florets

100 g (3½ oz) white cabbage, finely shredded or coarsely chopped

55 g (2 oz) frozen cut green beans

55 g (2 oz) frozen peas

55 g (2 oz) frozen broad beans

8 large sprigs of fresh basil

salt and pepper

Preparation time: 10 minutes

Cooking time: about 20 minutes

**1** Pour the boiling water into a saucepan. Stir in the stock cube, powder or paste, the tomato juice, garlic, spring onions, potato and carrot. Bring to the boil, then reduce the heat and cover the pan. Simmer the soup for about 10 minutes, stirring occasionally.

**2** Use a sharp knife to cut any large frozen broccoli florets into smaller pieces, then add them to the soup with the cabbage, green beans, peas and broad beans. Bring the soup back to the boil, then reduce the heat slightly, but keep the soup simmering rapidly. Cook for about 5 minutes or until the vegetables are just tender but still crisp.

**3** Taste and season the soup, then ladle it into 4 warm bowls. Use scissors to snip half the basil into shreds and scatter over the soup, discarding the tough ends of the sprigs. Add a whole sprig of basil to each portion and serve at once.

**Some more ideas**

• Instead of weighing out 4 types of frozen vegetables, use 250 g (8½ oz) frozen mixed vegetables. There are many different mixtures for simmering or stir-frying and all are great for making quick soups.

• For a hearty soup, add 1 can borlotti beans, about 400 g, drained and rinsed, with the frozen vegetables. Before serving, swirl 1 tsp pesto into each bowl of soup and sprinkle with 1 tsp lightly toasted pine nuts.

• The soup can be varied according to the fresh or frozen vegetables you have in the house. For example, try 1 peeled sweet potato with, or instead of, the ordinary potato and add 1 peeled and diced turnip for a hearty root-vegetable soup.

**Plus points**

• This is a good example of a 'cold-start' recipe, in which the vegetables are added straight to the liquid without being cooked in fat. The resulting soup is virtually fat free.

• Different fruit and vegetables contain different phytochemicals, so it is important to eat a variety. This soup includes a good mixture of vegetables.

**Each serving provides**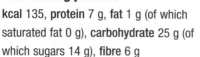

kcal 135, **protein** 7 g, **fat** 1 g (of which saturated fat 0 g), **carbohydrate** 25 g (of which sugars 14 g), **fibre** 6 g

| | |
|---|---|
| ✓✓✓ | A, C |
| ✓✓ | B₆ |
| ✓ | iron |

# Chilled leek and avocado soup

Coriander and lime juice accentuate the delicate avocado flavour in this refreshing soup. It is simple, quick and ideal for summer. Do not add the avocado too soon – not only will it discolour slightly, but its flavour will mellow and lose the vital freshness.

**Serves 4**

1 tbsp extra virgin olive oil

450 g (1 lb) leeks, halved lengthways and thinly sliced

1 garlic clove, finely chopped

750 ml (1¼ pints) vegetable or chicken stock, bought chilled or made with a stock cube or bouillon powder

1 large ripe avocado

125 g (4½ oz) plain low-fat yogurt

1 tbsp lime juice

2 tbsp chopped fresh coriander

salt and pepper

**To garnish**

8–12 ice cubes (optional)

slices of lime

sprigs of fresh coriander

Preparation and cooking time: 30 minutes, plus cooling and chilling

---

**Each serving provides** Ⓥ

kcal 170, **protein** 5 g, **fat** 14 g (of which saturated fat 3 g), **carbohydrate** 7 g (of which sugars 5 g), **fibre** 4 g

| ✓✓ | B₆, C, E, potassium |
| ✓ | A, B₁, folate |

1 Heat the oil in a saucepan, add the leeks and garlic, and cook for 10 minutes, stirring frequently, until the leeks are slightly softened but not coloured. Pour in the stock and bring to the boil. Cover the pan, reduce the heat and simmer for 10 minutes or until the leeks are cooked.

2 Remove the soup from the heat and let it cool slightly, then purée it in a blender or food processor. Alternatively, the soup can be puréed in the saucepan with a hand-held blender. Pour the soup into a bowl and leave it to cool, then chill well.

3 Just before serving the soup, prepare the avocado. Halve the avocado and discard the stone. Scoop the flesh from the peel and press through a fine stainless steel or nylon sieve. The avocado can also be puréed in a blender or food processor until smooth, adding a little of the chilled soup to thin the purée and ensure it is completely smooth.

4 Stir the avocado purée into the soup together with the yogurt, lime juice and coriander. Add seasoning to taste, then ladle the soup into 4 bowls. Float 2–3 ice cubes in each bowl, if you wish, then add slices of lime and sprigs of coriander. Serve at once.

**Plus points**

● Half an avocado provides a quarter of the recommended daily intake of vitamin B₆ and useful amounts of vitamin E and potassium. Other substances in avocados are good for the skin.

● Leeks provide useful amounts of folate, which is important for proper blood cell formation and development of the nervous system in an unborn baby.

**Some more ideas**

● This soup is also good hot. Purée the hot soup with the avocado and stir in crème fraîche instead of yogurt.

● For a soup with Mexican flavours, cook 1–2 seeded and finely chopped fresh green chillies with the leeks.

● For a simple no-cook avocado soup, blend 2 avocados with 450 ml (15 fl oz) vegetable stock, then add the yogurt and lime juice, and season to taste.

● To make vichyssoise, the classic chilled leek and potato soup, increase the stock to 1 litre (1¾ pints) and cook 2 peeled and sliced potatoes with the leeks. Omit the avocado, lime juice and coriander, and serve sprinkled with snipped fresh chives.

# Teriyaki-style noodles with tofu

This rich, fresh-tasting Japanese-style broth, flavoured with vibrant herbs, ginger and garlic, peps up firm cubes of tofu and long strands of earthy buckwheat noodles. It is a delicious low-fat vegetarian recipe for protein-rich tofu.

### Serves 2

150 g (5½ oz) soba (Japanese buckwheat noodles)

225 g (8 oz) mixed vegetables, such as asparagus tips, broccoli, carrots, cauliflower, green beans or mange-tout

100 ml (3½ fl oz) light soy sauce

300 ml (10 fl oz) vegetable stock

4 tbsp rice wine (sake or mirin) or dry sherry

280 g (10 oz) firm tofu, diced

2 spring onions, chopped

1 fresh red chilli, seeded and chopped

1 heaped tbsp chopped fresh mint

1 heaped tbsp chopped fresh coriander

1 large garlic clove, crushed

½ tsp grated fresh root ginger

2 tsp toasted sesame oil (optional)

Preparation time: 15 minutes
Cooking time: 10 minutes

1 Bring a large saucepan of water to the boil and cook the soba noodles for about 6 minutes, or according to the packet instructions, until al dente.

2 Meanwhile, cut all the mixed vegetables into bite-sized pieces. Add them to the simmering pasta for the final 3–4 minutes of cooking.

3 Drain the pasta and vegetables in a large colander. Place all the remaining ingredients in the empty saucepan and return it to the heat. Heat until simmering, then reduce the heat to the minimum setting. Return the pasta and vegetables to the pan, and cook very briefly until they are reheated.

4 Serve in deep soup bowls, with a spoon to drink the tasty broth and a fork or chopsticks for picking up the solid ingredients.

### Plus points

● Evidence is accumulating from around the world to suggest that eating soya beans and soya products, such as tofu, may help to reduce the risk of certain cancers, heart disease and osteoporosis, as well as helping to alleviate symptoms associated with the menopause.

### Some more ideas

● Replace the tofu with 225 g (8 oz) peeled cooked prawns or diced, skinned, cooked chicken or turkey.

● Fresh basil can be used in place of, or in addition to, the mint and coriander, and pumpkin seed oil or walnut oil can be added instead of sesame oil.

● Wheat-flour or rice noodles such as rice sticks can be used in place of soba noodles, but adjust the cooking time according to the instructions on the packet.

**Soups and starters**

### Each serving provides    Ⓥ

kcal 495, **protein** 30 g, **fat** 14.5 g (of which saturated fat 1 g), **carbohydrate** 65 g (of which sugars 4.5 g), **fibre** 5 g

✓✓✓ C, calcium, iron

✓✓   B₁, E, niacin, folate, copper, potassium

# Potato and bacon chowder

It's easy to make a nourishing supper based on ingredients you are likely to have on hand, such as onion, potatoes, bacon and milk. Here they're turned into a hearty and satisfying soup, which is finished with spinach and parsnip. Serve with crusty brown bread.

**Serves 4**

1 litre (1¾ pints) whole/creamy milk

1 tbsp extra virgin olive oil

55 g (2 oz) lean smoked back bacon, rinded and finely chopped

1 large onion, finely chopped

2 tbsp plain flour

400 g (14 oz) smooth thin-skinned potatoes, such as Desiree, scrubbed and finely diced

1 parsnip, about 150 g (5½ oz), grated

freshly grated nutmeg

115 g (4 oz) baby spinach leaves

salt and pepper

Preparation and cooking time: about 30 minutes

1 Bring the milk just to the boil in a saucepan. Meanwhile, in another large saucepan heat the oil over a moderately high heat. Add the bacon and onion and cook for 2 minutes, stirring frequently. Add the flour and stir to combine, then slowly add about one-quarter of the hot milk, stirring and scraping the bottom of the pan to mix in the flour. When the mixture thickens, stir in the remaining hot milk.

2 Add the potatoes and parsnip. Season with salt, pepper and nutmeg to taste and bring just to the boil, stirring occasionally. Adjust the heat so the soup bubbles gently. Half cover the pan and continue cooking for about 10 minutes or until the vegetables are nearly tender, stirring occasionally.

3 Stir in the spinach and continue cooking for 1–2 minutes or until the spinach has wilted. Taste the soup and adjust the seasoning, if necessary. Ladle into a warm tureen or individual bowls and serve at once.

**Some more ideas**

• Substitute 85 g (3 oz) rocket leaves or 150 g (5½ oz) cavolo nero (a leafy cabbage), thinly shredded, for the spinach. Cavolo nero will need 3–4 minutes cooking.

• Instead of bacon, use 150 g (5½ oz) frozen sweetcorn kernels, adding them with the potatoes and parsnip.

• For a smoked haddock chowder, omit the bacon and add 115 g (4 oz) skinless smoked haddock fillet with the potatoes and parsnip.

• Use a large carrot instead of the parsnip.

**Plus points**

• Dark green, leafy vegetables such as spinach and cavolo nero are a good source of several important phytochemicals, including indoles which some studies suggest may help to protect against breast cancer by inhibiting the action of the oestrogens that trigger the growth of tumours. They also contain sulphoraphane which is believed to stimulate the liver to produce cancer-fighting enzymes.

• Parsnips are a useful source of fibre, vitamin C and folate.

**Each serving provides**

kcal 355, **protein** 15 g, **fat** 14 g (of which saturated fat 7 g), **carbohydrate** 43 g (of which sugars 17 g), **fibre** 4 g

| | |
|---|---|
| ✓✓✓ | B₆ |
| ✓✓ | A, B₁, B₁₂, C, folate, calcium |
| ✓ | B₂, E, iron, potassium, zinc |

*Soups and starters*

# Quick chicken soup

This easy recipe is perfect for a quick lunch or supper. Red pepper, sweetcorn and fresh greens bring colour and texture to a simple chicken soup base, and adding sherry makes it taste just that bit more special. With seeded bread rolls it makes a tasty light meal.

**Serves 4**

900 ml (1½ pints) boiling water

2 chicken stock cubes, crumbled

1 red pepper, seeded and cut into fine strips

125 g (4½ oz) frozen sweetcorn

225 g (8 oz) skinless boneless chicken breasts (fillets), cut into short 1 cm (½ in) strips

125 g (4½ oz) purple sprouting broccoli, cut into small pieces, or spring greens, finely shredded

2 tbsp medium sherry

3 tbsp snipped fresh chives

3 tbsp chopped fresh tarragon

salt and pepper

Preparation time: 10 minutes

Cooking time: about 15 minutes

**Each serving provides**

kcal 140, **protein** 16 g, **fat** 4 g (of which saturated fat 1 g), **carbohydrate** 10 g (of which sugars 5 g), **fibre** 2 g

| | |
|---|---|
| ✓✓ | A, C |
| ✓ | B₆, niacin |

1 Pour the water into a large saucepan. Add the stock cubes and whisk over a high heat until the stock boils. Add the red pepper strips and sweetcorn. Bring back to the boil, then add the chicken strips and immediately reduce the heat to low. Cover and simmer gently for 5 minutes.

2 Uncover the pan and bring the soup back to the boil. Sprinkle the sprouting broccoli or spring greens into the soup, but do not stir them in. Leave the broccoli or greens to cook on the surface of the soup, uncovered, for 3–4 minutes or until just tender.

3 Take the pan off the heat. Stir in the sherry, chives, tarragon and seasoning to taste. Serve at once.

**Some more ideas**

● A generous amount of fresh tarragon gives this soup a powerful flavour. For a delicate result reduce the quantity of tarragon to 1 tbsp or use chervil instead.

● Use Savoy cabbage or curly kale instead of the greens. Trim off any very thick stalks before shredding the cabbage or kale.

● To give the soup a Chinese flavour, marinate the chicken strips in a mixture of 2 tbsp soy sauce, 2 tbsp rice wine or dry sherry and 2 tsp grated fresh root ginger for 10 minutes while you prepare the vegetables. Use pak choy instead of purple sprouting broccoli or spring greens. Slice the thick white stalks lengthways and the green tops across into ribbon strips. Add the white strips in step 2 and cook for 1 minute before adding the green tops. Add 2 chopped spring onions with the shredded pak choy tops. Cook for 2–3 minutes.

● Fine strips of lean boneless pork can be used instead of chicken.

● Add 75 g (2½ oz) dried thin egg noodles to make the soup more substantial. Crush the noodles and stir them into the soup in step 2 and bring to the boil before adding the greens.

**Plus points**

● Sweetcorn adds carbohydrate and dietary fibre to the soup. Green vegetables are also a good source of fibre, which is thought to reduce the risk of cancer of the colon.

● In this fast recipe, cutting fresh broccoli in small pieces and greens in fine strips means they cook quickly to retain as much of their vitamin C as possible.

● Red pepper is an excellent source of vitamin C, as well as beta-carotene and bioflavonoids.

Soups and starters

# Cauliflower cheese soup

A classic combination as a vegetable dish, cauliflower and Cheddar cheese are equally good partners in a soup. Here the cauliflower is gently simmered, then puréed to a velvety-smooth texture. Serve this warming soup with crusty rolls.

**Serves 4**

15 g (½ oz) butter

1 onion, chopped

¼ tsp mustard powder

1 large cauliflower, about 900 g (2 lb),
   broken into small florets

600 ml (1 pint) semi-skimmed milk

150 ml (5 fl oz) vegetable stock

1 bay leaf

2 tsp sunflower oil

100 g (3½ oz) mature Cheddar cheese, grated

salt and pepper

chopped fresh flat-leaf parsley to garnish

Preparation and cooking time: 30 minutes

1 Melt the butter in a large saucepan. Add the onion and cook over a moderate heat for 3 minutes, stirring frequently, until soft. Sprinkle over the mustard and stir it in.

2 Reserve about 85 g (3 oz) of the cauliflower florets; add the rest to the saucepan together with the milk, stock and bay leaf. Bring to the boil, then reduce the heat. Cover and simmer for 10 minutes or until the cauliflower is tender.

3 Meanwhile, heat the oil in a non-stick frying pan. Break the reserved cauliflower into tiny florets and fry for 4–5 minutes or until lightly browned, stirring frequently. Set aside.

4 Remove the bay leaf from the soup. Purée in the pan with a hand-held blender, or in a blender or food processor. Season with salt and pepper to taste, then reheat until just bubbling.

5 Remove from the heat, add the grated cheese and stir until melted. Ladle into 4 warmed soup bowls and sprinkle with the sautéed cauliflower florets and parsley. Serve immediately.

**Plus points**

● Cheddar cheese, like most other cheeses, is a good source of protein and an excellent source of calcium, but it is high in fat. Reducing the amount of cheese that would normally be used in a dish like this, and choosing a mature cheese with a strong taste, keeps fat levels healthy, and the cheese still makes a valuable nutritional contribution.

● Cauliflower is a member of the brassica family of cruciferous vegetables. Its distinctive sulphurous compounds are believed to play a part in protecting against certain forms of cancer and heart disease.

● Onions are not only believed to help reduce the risk of cancer but also to help lower blood cholesterol levels.

**Each serving provides** Ⓥ

kcal 303, **protein** 20 g, **fat** 18 g (of which saturated fat 10 g), **carbohydrate** 17 g (of which sugars 15 g), **fibre** 5 g

| | |
|---|---|
| ✓✓✓ | C, calcium |
| ✓✓ | A, B$_1$, B$_6$, B$_{12}$, folate, potassium, zinc |
| ✓ | B$_2$, E, niacin, iron |

## Some more ideas

● Use all the cauliflower in the soup. For the garnish, mix together 4 tbsp plain low-fat yogurt and 2 tbsp chopped parsley or snipped fresh chives. Swirl a spoonful of this herb yogurt on top of each bowl of soup.

● For a spiced parsnip and cheese soup to serve 6, soften 1 finely chopped onion in 15 g (½ oz) butter. Stir in 550 g (1¼ lb) finely diced parsnips, 1 tsp cumin seeds and ½ tsp ground coriander. Cook for 2 minutes, then add 600 ml (1 pint) semi-skimmed milk, 450 ml (15 fl oz) vegetable stock and a bay leaf. Bring to the boil, then cover and simmer for 10 minutes or until the parsnips are tender. Remove the bay leaf and purée the soup with a hand-held blender, or in a blender or food processor. Reheat until piping hot. Ladle into warmed bowls and sprinkle with 115 g (4 oz) grated Red Leicester or Double Gloucester cheese. Garnish with a few torn fresh coriander leaves and serve hot.

# Wild mushroom broth with herby ciabatta croutons

Mixtures of fresh wild mushrooms are good for making a quick soup that tastes really special. Instead of thickening or puréeing the soup, serving it as a light broth allows the individual flavours of the mushrooms, vegetables and herbs to be fully appreciated.

**Serves 6**

3 tbsp extra virgin olive oil

1 small onion, finely chopped

1 small bulb of fennel, finely chopped

1 garlic clove, chopped

500 g (1 lb 2 oz) mixed fresh mushrooms, such as chanterelles (girolles), horns of plenty, oysters and chestnuts, roughly chopped

900 ml (1½ pints) boiling water

1½ vegetable stock cubes, crumbled, or 1 tbsp vegetable bouillon powder or paste

8 thin slices ciabatta bread

2 tbsp chopped parsley

2 tbsp chopped fresh mint

salt and pepper

Preparation time: 10 minutes

Cooking time: about 20 minutes

**Each serving provides** Ⓥ

kcal 95, **protein** 3 g, **fat** 5 g (of which saturated fat 1 g), **carbohydrate** 10 g (of which sugars 1 g), **fibre** 1 g

| | |
|---|---|
| ✓✓✓ | B₁, copper |
| ✓✓ | B₆, C, niacin |
| ✓ | folate |

1 Heat 2 tbsp of the oil in a large saucepan. Add the onion and fennel and cook over a high heat for 5 minutes, stirring frequently, until slightly softened. Stir in the garlic and mushrooms. Continue to cook, stirring frequently, for a further 5 minutes. Pour in the boiling water and stir in the stock cubes, powder or paste. Bring back to the boil, then reduce the heat and simmer the soup, uncovered, for 10 minutes.

2 Meanwhile, preheat the grill. Brush the slices of ciabatta bread lightly on both sides with the remaining 1 tbsp oil and toast them under the grill for about 1 minute on each side or until golden. Cut the bread into cubes and place in a bowl. Add the parsley and mint and toss well.

3 Taste the soup and add seasoning if necessary. Ladle the soup into bowls. Sprinkle with the parsley and mint croutons and serve at once.

## Some more ideas

● For a rich and creamy version of this soup, thicken with a yolk and cream liaison. Whisk 1 egg yolk with 4 tbsp single cream until lightly mixed. When the soup is cooked and croutons prepared, remove the pan from the heat and stir a ladleful of the soup into the liaison. Pour the mixture into the pan and stir over a low heat for about 30 seconds. Do not allow the soup to get too hot and start to simmer or the egg yolk will curdle. Serve at once.

● Use 3 diced celery sticks instead of fennel.

● Dried wild mushrooms can be used for this soup, although it will take a bit longer to make. Use 1 packet of dried porcini, about 15 g, and 225 g (8 oz) chestnut mushrooms. Soak the porcini in some of the boiling water for 15 minutes and add them to the soup with the water. Cook the chestnut mushrooms in step 1 with the garlic.

### Plus points

● In Asian cultures mushrooms are renowned for their ability to boost the immune system, and the Chinese have put them to medicinal use for over 6000 years. Mushrooms are a useful source of the B vitamins B₆, folate and niacin, as well as copper.

● Brushing slices of bread with oil and toasting under the grill before cutting them into cubes is a good way to make low-fat, crisp croutons.

Soups and starters

# Mixed seafood and noodle broth

In China soups are served between courses or dishes. This is why they are made with a light stock, so they are more appropriate as a starter in a Western meal. You can prepare the stock ahead of time, then add the scallops, vegetables and noodles when you re-heat.

**Serves 6**

55 g (2 oz) fine stir-fry rice noodles, broken into 10 cm (4 in) lengths

2 tsp groundnut oil

2.5 cm (1 in) piece fresh root ginger, finely chopped

75 g (2½ oz) shiitake mushrooms, stalks discarded and caps thinly sliced

1.2 litres (2 pints) chicken stock

1 tbsp dry sherry

2 tbsp light soy sauce

125 g (4½ oz) cooked mixed seafood, such as prawns, squid and queen scallops

75 g (2½ oz) Chinese leaves, shredded

4 spring onions, thinly sliced

75 g (2½ oz) beansprouts

fresh coriander leaves to garnish

chilli sauce to serve

Preparation and cooking time: 25 minutes

1 Put the noodles in a bowl and pour over plenty of boiling water. Set aside to soak for 4 minutes.

2 Meanwhile, heat the groundnut oil in a large saucepan, add the ginger and mushrooms, and cook for about 2 minutes to soften slightly. Add the stock, sherry and soy sauce, and bring to the boil.

3 Halve the scallops if they are large. Add the mixed seafood to the boiling stock together with the Chinese leaves, spring onions and beansprouts. Bring back to the boil and cook for 1 minute or until the seafood is heated through.

4 Drain the noodles and add to the soup. Bring back to the boil, then ladle into large soup bowls. Scatter over a few fresh coriander leaves and serve with chilli sauce, to be added to taste.

**Another idea**

• For a crab and noodle broth, use 1 can white crab meat, about 170 g, drained, instead of the mixed seafood. Replace the mushrooms with 100 g (3½ oz) thinly sliced baby corn and 100 g (3½ oz) diced courgettes, cooking them with the ginger for 1 minute. In step 3, omit the Chinese leaves. After adding the rice noodles in step 4, bring to the boil and season with 1 tbsp fish sauce.

**Plus points**

• Seafood provides an excellent source of low-fat protein and a range of other nutrients. Scallops are an excellent source of selenium and $B_{12}$, and a useful source of phosphorus and potassium. Prawns provide calcium, while squid is an excellent source of $B_{12}$.

• Shiitake mushrooms contain the B vitamins $B_2$, niacin and pantothenic acid. They also provide potassium and good quantities of copper.

• Rice noodles are gluten-free and wheat-free, making them useful for people with gluten intolerances or wheat allergies.

**Each serving provides**

kcal 80, **protein** 5 g, **fat** 1.5 g (of which saturated fat 0.3 g), **carbohydrate** 9 g (of which sugars 1 g), **fibre** 0.5 g

| | |
|---|---|
| ✓✓ | $B_{12}$ |
| ✓ | copper, selenium |

Soups and starters

# Butter bean dip with crudités

This quick and tasty dip is made from canned butter beans puréed with sun-dried tomato paste, garlic and fresh basil leaves. Served with sesame seed breadsticks, pitta bread and a selection of crunchy vegetables for dipping, it makes a nutritious starter.

## Serves 8

1 can butter beans, about 410 g, drained and rinsed

150 g (5½ oz) Greek-style yogurt

1–2 garlic cloves, crushed

2 tbsp sun-dried tomato paste

few drops of Tabasco sauce

1 tsp lemon juice

10 g (¼ oz) fresh basil leaves

salt and pepper

**To serve**

225 g (8 oz) baby carrots

250 g (8½ oz) baby corn, blanched for 1 minute and drained, then halved lengthways, if wished

1 small red pepper, seeded and cut into strips

1 small yellow pepper, seeded and cut into strips

4 celery sticks, cut into 7.5 cm (3 in) strips

4 pitta breads

125 g (4½ oz) sesame seed breadsticks

Preparation time: about 15 minutes

## Each serving provides

**V**

kcal 379, protein 16.5 g, fat 6 g (of which saturated fat 3 g), carbohydrate 68 g (of which sugars 11 g), fibre 7.5 g

| | |
|---|---|
| ✓✓✓ | A, C |
| ✓✓ | B₁, B₆, folate, copper, iron |
| ✓ | B₂, E, niacin, potassium, zinc |

1 Place the butter beans, yogurt, garlic, tomato paste, Tabasco sauce and lemon juice in a food processor or blender. Reserve one basil leaf for garnishing, and add the rest to the food processor or blender. Blend to a smooth purée, scraping down the sides of the container once or twice. Season with salt and pepper to taste. Spoon into a bowl and garnish with the reserved basil leaf. Cover and chill while preparing the crudités.

2 Preheat the grill. Prepare all the vegetables and arrange them on a large serving platter. Warm the pittas under the grill for 1–2 minutes, then cut into wedges. Add to the vegetable platter with the sesame breadsticks. Serve with the dip.

## Some more ideas

• Use deliciously creamy 0%-fat Greek-style yogurt for a lower-fat dip.

• For a saffron and lime dip, pour 1 tsp boiling water over a small pinch of saffron threads and leave to soak for 5 minutes. Stir the liquid into 200 g (7 oz) fromage frais (virtually fat-free, if you prefer) and add 3 tbsp mayonnaise, 1 tsp fresh lime juice, ½ crushed garlic clove and ½ tsp coarsely ground mixed red and black peppercorns. Serve with the vegetable crudités and bread.

## Plus points

• Using yogurt in a dip, rather than oil or mayonnaise, helps to boost the calcium content – all dairy products are an excellent source of calcium. Because calcium is contained in the non-creamy portion of milk, it remains in reduced-fat dairy products after the fat has been removed, so using 0%-fat Greek-style yogurt will still provide calcium.

• Butter beans and raw vegetables are full of dietary fibre, essential for a healthy digestive system.

• Some studies have shown that eating raw garlic can help to reduce the cholesterol level in the blood.

• Colourful vegetables such as red and yellow peppers, tomatoes and sweetcorn contain plenty of beta-carotene, which the body can convert to vitamin A, and vitamin C, needed for healthy bones and tissues. Beta-carotene and vitamin C are also powerful antioxidants, which means they help to protect the body's cells from the damaging effects of free radicals.

Soups and starters

# Naan bread with lentil caviar

Yogurt spiced with garlic and mint, then mixed with raw vegetables and high-protein lentils, is delicious on warmed naan bread. A few coriander and mint leaves add a touch of freshness, and a dab of chutney or pickle on the side gives texture and extra flavour.

**Serves 4**

**Lentil 'caviar'**

340 g (12 oz) plain low-fat yogurt

2 garlic cloves, chopped

1 can green lentils, about 300 g, drained

½ cucumber, finely chopped

½ green pepper, seeded and cut into fine dice

1 ripe tomato, finely chopped

1 tbsp chopped fresh mint

¼ tsp ground cumin, or to taste

large pinch of curry powder

juice of ½ lemon

2 tbsp extra virgin olive oil

salt and cayenne pepper

**To serve**

4 individual plain naans, cut into wedges

leaves from 3–4 sprigs of fresh mint

3 tbsp fresh coriander leaves

few rocket leaves

2 carrots, grated

2 tbsp chutney of choice or lime pickle

Preparation time: 15 minutes

---

**Each serving provides**   Ⓥ

kcal 420, **protein** 17 g, **fat** 14 g (of which saturated fat 1 g), **carbohydrate** 60 g (of which sugars 20 g), **fibre** 6 g

| | |
|---|---|
| ✓✓✓ | A, C |
| ✓✓ | B₁, B₂, B₆, folate, calcium, copper, iron, selenium, zinc |
| ✓ | B₁₂, E, potassium |

1 Preheat the grill. Mix together all the ingredients for the lentil 'caviar' and season with salt and cayenne pepper to taste.

2 Sprinkle the naans with water, then place under the grill and toast for 1 minute on each side. Transfer them to individual plates.

3 Spoon the lentil 'caviar' over the warm breads, dividing it equally among them. Sprinkle with the fresh mint, coriander and rocket leaves and the grated carrots. Serve at once, with the chutney or lime pickle on the side.

**Some more ideas**

● You can use garlic naan or peshwari naan, although these have a higher fat and calorie content than plain naan.

● Keep some pre-cooked lentils in your freezer; that way, even if plain cooked lentils in a can are not readily available, you can still make this tasty snack. Lentils thaw easily, especially in a microwave, or heated on the hob, or simply left out at room temperature.

● Use 100 g (3½ oz) shredded red cabbage instead of the grated carrot.

● For chickpea and spinach naans, make the 'caviar' with 1 can chickpeas, about 400 g, drained, instead of lentils, and omit the cucumber, green pepper and tomato. Cook 225 g (8 oz) spinach leaves, either by steaming or boiling for 3 minutes, or microwave in the cellophane bag if using ready-prepared spinach.

Squeeze dry, then chop coarsely. Divide the spinach among the naans, top with spoonfuls of the chickpea 'caviar' and garnish with the mint, coriander and rocket. Serve with wedges of lemon to squeeze over the top.

● Fill pitta breads with the lentil or chickpea 'caviar'. Warm 4 pitta breads in a toaster or under the grill until they puff up, then slash open to form a pocket. Fill each one with 'caviar' and add a handful of grated carrot or cabbage and a dab of chutney or lime pickle.

**Plus points**

● Like all beans and pulses, lentils are a good source of soluble fibre – the type that can help to reduce high blood cholesterol levels. Unlike other beans, lentils don't need to be soaked overnight, but they do take about 20 minutes to cook, so when time is short canned lentils are a good alternative. The canning process does not reduce the fibre content.

● Yogurt is a useful source of calcium, phosphorus and vitamins B₂ and B₁₂.

● The large amount of beta-carotene and other carotenoids in carrots makes them an excellent source of vitamin A. Carrots also contain some vitamin C and niacin and a small amount of vitamin E.

Soups and starters

31

# Grilled oysters with fennel and spinach topping

For some people, the only way to eat oysters is raw, but if you prefer them cooked, this is a great recipe. Topped with potato, fennel and spinach, they make a substantial starter. Ask the fishmonger to open the oysters for you. Serve with warm pitta bread slices.

**Serves 4**

16 oysters in the shell, opened and top shell discarded

30 g (1 oz) butter

1 shallot, finely chopped

100 g (3½ oz) potato, peeled and finely diced

100 g (3½ oz) bulb of fennel, finely diced

100 g (3½ oz) spinach, torn into pieces

1 tbsp lemon juice

2 tbsp chopped parsley

salt and pepper

lemon wedges to serve

Preparation time: 25 minutes
Cooking time: about 3 minutes

**Each serving provides**

kcal 101, protein 4 g, fat 7 g (of which saturated fat 4 g), carbohydrate 6 g (of which sugars 1 g), fibre 2 g

| | |
|---|---|
| ✓✓✓ | B₁, B₆, B₁₂, niacin, copper, zinc |
| ✓✓ | A, iron |
| ✓ | C, folate, calcium, potassium |

*Soups and starters*

**1** Check the oysters to make sure there are no bits of shattered shell on them. Arrange them, on their half shells, in four individual flameproof dishes, or on one large dish, and season with salt and pepper to taste. (Propping the shells with crumpled foil will prevent them from tipping.)

**2** Preheat the grill to moderate. Heat the butter in a frying pan, add the shallot and cook over a gentle heat for 2 minutes or until beginning to soften. Add the diced potato and fennel and cook gently for 10 minutes or until tender, stirring occasionally.

**3** Stir in the spinach and cook for 1–2 minutes or until the spinach has just wilted. Add the lemon juice, parsley and seasoning to taste. Spoon 1 tbsp of the mixture over each oyster.

**4** Cook the oysters under the grill for 3 minutes or until the topping is tinged brown. Serve immediately, with lemon wedges.

**Some more ideas**

● For a spicy almond topping, use 55 g (2 oz) slivered almonds instead of potatoes. Roughly chop the nuts in a blender or food processor, or by hand, and mix with 1–2 garlic cloves, finely chopped, 2 tbsp chopped fresh coriander, ½ small red chilli, seeded and finely chopped, 1 tsp ground cumin, 1 tsp paprika and 1 tbsp extra virgin olive oil. Add this mixture to the cooked shallot and fennel, together with 55 g (2 oz) white breadcrumbs and the juice of ½ lemon. Mix well, then add the spinach and finish as in the main recipe.

● Replace the fennel and spinach with 55 g (2 oz) smoked back bacon, finely chopped, and 100 g (3½ oz) Savoy cabbage, finely shredded. Add some toasted cumin seeds or caraway seeds for extra flavour.

**Plus points**

● Oysters have long been linked with aphrodisiac powers, probably because they are an excellent source of zinc which is essential for growth and sexual maturity.

● Although spinach appears to be an excellent source of iron, the iron isn't easily absorbed by the body. However, the vitamin C from the lemon juice in this recipe will help the absorption.

# Dolcelatte and pear toasts

Slices of fresh juicy pear, tasty blue cheese and pecan nuts on toasted bread make a lovely flavour combination in this starter. Cut generous slices of bread – for a lighter starter, limit each portion to 1 slice per plate. Cherry tomatoes are the perfect accompaniment.

**Serves 4**

2 ripe pears, preferably red-skinned

lemon juice

200 g (7 oz) wedge of Dolcelatte cheese

30 g (1 oz) pecan nuts

8 large slices of baguette, about 2 cm (¾ in) thick

4 tbsp mango chutney

30 g (1 oz) watercress sprigs

30 g (1 oz) rocket

pepper

cherry tomatoes to serve

Preparation time: about 15 minutes

1 Preheat the grill. Core and quarter or slice the pears, then toss with a squeeze of lemon juice to prevent the pears from discolouring. Cut the cheese down the length of the wedge to make 8 thin, triangular slices.

2 Lightly toast the pecan nuts under the grill, watching carefully to make sure they don't burn, then roughly chop them. Set aside. Spread out the bread slices on the grill pan and toast lightly on both sides.

3 Spread the mango chutney on the toasted bread and top with the watercress and rocket. Arrange a slice of cheese and a quarter of the pears on each piece of toast and scatter over the pecan nuts. Season with pepper. Serve at once, with halved cherry tomatoes.

**Some more ideas**

● Use Granary or wholemeal bread instead of baguette to increase fibre content.

● Substitute thin slices of Stilton cheese for the Dolcelatte, and replace the pecan nuts with walnuts.

● Replace the pears with 2 star fruit, cut into thin slices.

● To make Cheddar, date and apple open sandwiches, use 8 slices of walnut bread, toasting it, if liked. Top each slice with a small leaf of cos lettuce and a little watercress. Cover with thin slices of Cheddar cheese and apple slices, then scatter over 4 stoned and chopped fresh dates, preferably Medjool from California, which are deliciously moist.

**Each serving provides**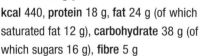

kcal 440, **protein** 18 g, **fat** 24 g (of which saturated fat 12 g), **carbohydrate** 38 g (of which sugars 16 g), **fibre** 5 g

| | |
|---|---|
| ✓✓ | A, B$_1$, B$_2$, B$_{12}$, C, folate, calcium, copper, iron, selenium, zinc |
| ✓ | B$_6$, niacin |

**Plus points**

● Cheese is a good source of protein, calcium, phosphorus and the vitamins B$_2$ and B$_{12}$. Although Dolcelatte is high in fat, its strong flavour means a little goes a long way.

● Slicing the bread thickly will increase the ratio of starchy carbohydrate to fat, thus helping to make this a healthy balanced dish.

Soups and starters

# Melon, feta and orange salad

Here, the classic starter of melon and Parma ham is transformed into a tempting and speedy salad with the addition of feta cheese, cherry tomatoes, cucumber and oranges. Serve with pieces of warm ciabatta bread to mop up the juices.

**Serves 6**

2 oranges

½ honeydew melon, peeled, seeded and sliced

115 g (4 oz) cherry tomatoes, halved

85 g (3 oz) stoned black olives

½ small cucumber, diced

4 spring onions, thinly sliced

6 slices of Parma ham, about 80 g (2¾ oz) in total, trimmed of all fat and cut into strips

100 g (3½ oz) feta cheese, roughly broken into pieces

**Orange and basil dressing**

½ tsp grated orange zest

4 tbsp orange juice

2 tbsp extra virgin olive oil

1 tsp toasted sesame oil

6 fresh basil leaves, shredded

salt and pepper

Preparation time: 20–25 minutes

**1** Make the dressing first. Mix the orange zest and juice with the olive oil, sesame oil and basil in a large salad bowl. Season with salt and pepper to taste.

**2** Cut the peel and pith away from the oranges with a sharp knife. Holding them over the salad bowl to catch the juice, cut between the membrane to release the orange segments. Add the segments to the bowl.

**3** Add the melon, tomatoes, olives, cucumber, spring onions and Parma ham. Toss until the ingredients are well blended and coated in dressing. Scatter the feta cheese over the top and serve.

**Some more ideas**

● To make a melon and fresh pineapple salad with cottage cheese, mix the melon, tomato and cucumber with ½ pineapple, peeled, cored and chopped, and 3 shallots, thinly sliced. Make a lime dressing by mixing ½ tsp grated lime zest and 2 tbsp lime juice with 2 tbsp sunflower oil and 1 tsp clear honey. Season to taste. Stir the dressing into the melon mixture and pile onto 4 plates. Spoon 75 g (2½ oz) plain cottage cheese on top of each salad and scatter over roasted, chopped macadamia nuts, 50 g (1¾ oz) in total. Garnish generously with small sprigs of watercress.

● Substitute Serrano ham from Spain or smoky Black Forest ham for the Parma ham.

● As an alternative to honeydew melon, try other varieties such as Ogen or Charentais or a wedge of watermelon.

**Plus points**

● Although feta cheese is high in fat and salt, it is an excellent source of calcium and because it has a strong flavour a little goes a long way. Calcium in dairy products is much more easily absorbed by the body than calcium from other foods.

● Only 1 in 4 people in the UK drink enough water or other fluid. Foods that have a high water content, such as melon and cucumber, are an easy way of increasing fluid intake.

**Each serving provides**

kcal 173, **protein** 9 g, **fat** 11 g (of which saturated fat 4 g), **carbohydrate** 11 g (of which sugars 11 g), **fibre** 2 g

| | |
|---|---|
| ✓✓✓ | C |
| ✓✓ | B₆, B₁₂, calcium |
| ✓ | A, B₁, E, folate, potassium |

Soups and starters

# Ciabatta with garlic mushrooms

Garlic mushrooms make a delightful starter but many recipes use generous quantities of butter. This version is deliciously buttery without being over-indulgent. A salad of finely shredded white cabbage and chopped spring onion would be a good accompaniment.

### Serves 4

1 part-baked ciabatta loaf

1 tbsp extra virgin olive oil

30 g (1 oz) unsalted butter

2 garlic cloves, crushed

450 g (1 lb) button mushrooms, halved

1 tbsp wholegrain mustard

dash of Worcestershire sauce

30 g (1 oz) Parmesan cheese shavings

salt and pepper

sprigs of fresh flat-leaf parsley to garnish

Preparation time: about 20 minutes

1 Preheat the oven to 200°C (400°F, gas mark 6). Cut the ciabatta diagonally into eight 2.5 cm (1 in) thick slices – they should be long and oval in shape. Place the slices of bread on a baking sheet and brush them lightly with oil. Bake the bread for 8–12 minutes or until crisp and golden.

2 Meanwhile, melt the butter in a frying pan. When the butter starts to sizzle, add the garlic and cook for 1 minute. Add the mushrooms and cook over a moderately high heat, stirring occasionally, for 4–5 minutes or until the mushrooms are lightly cooked.

3 Stir in the mustard. Reduce the heat slightly and add the Worcestershire sauce and seasoning to taste. Cook for a further 1 minute, then remove the pan from the heat.

4 Place 2 slices of ciabatta bread on each plate. Spoon the mushrooms and their cooking juices over the bread. Scatter on the Parmesan shavings and garnish with sprigs of parsley. Serve immediately.

### Some more ideas

● Instead of part-baked ciabatta you can use part-baked French bread. Alternatively, use fully baked ciabatta or French bread and simply brush the slices with oil and toast under the grill.

● To make a roasted pepper bruschetta, preheat the grill to the hottest setting. Quarter and seed 2 red and 2 yellow peppers, then grill them, cut sides down, for about 10 minutes or until the skin is charred. Place the peppers in a polythene bag and set aside until cool enough to handle. Peel the skin off the peppers using a small sharp knife and coarsely chop them. Mix the peppers with 10 large fresh basil leaves in a bowl. Drizzle 2 tbsp balsamic vinegar and 3 tbsp extra virgin olive oil over the peppers and mix well. Divide the peppers and their dressing among the bread slices and serve immediately.

### Each serving provides

kcal 290, protein 11 g, fat 14 g (of which saturated fat 6 g), carbohydrate 34 g (of which sugars 2 g), fibre 2 g

| | |
|---|---|
| ✓✓✓ | copper |
| ✓✓ | B₂, folate, niacin, selenium |
| ✓ | A, B₁, B₆, calcium, iron, potassium, zinc |

### Plus points

● Mushrooms contain the water-soluble B vitamins $B_2$, niacin and $B_6$, all of which are important for the efficient metabolism of other nutrients. Mushrooms also contain copper, an essential component of many enzyme systems. Copper helps the body to absorb iron from food.

● The small quantity of Parmesan cheese here contributes useful calcium as well as a wonderful flavour.

# Quail's eggs with asparagus and Parmesan shavings

Make this lovely, warm salad in late spring with the new season's asparagus. The lightly steamed spears are topped with poached quail's eggs, then finished with Parmesan shavings and a crisp salad. Accompany with a crusty baguette for an easy, quick dish.

**Serves 4**

125 g (4½ oz) lamb's lettuce

2 heads chicory, about 170 g (6 oz) in total

15 g (½ oz) fresh chives, snipped

750 g (1 lb 10 oz) asparagus

1 tsp vinegar

12 quail's eggs

50 g (1¾ oz) Parmesan cheese, cut into fine shavings

**Mustard vinaigrette**

2 tbsp extra virgin olive oil

2 tsp red wine vinegar

1 garlic clove, crushed

½ tsp wholegrain mustard

salt and pepper

Preparation and cooking time: about 25 minutes

**Each serving provides** Ⓥ

kcal 233, **protein** 17 g, **fat** 16 g (of which saturated fat 5 g), **carbohydrate** 6 g (of which sugars 5 g), **fibre** 4 g

| | |
|---|---|
| ✓✓✓ | folate |
| ✓✓ | A, B₁, C, E, calcium, zinc |
| ✓ | B₂, B₆, niacin, copper, iron, potassium |

1 Break up any large bunches of lamb's lettuce, then put into a mixing bowl. Thinly slice the chicory on the diagonal, discarding the last 1 cm (½ in) of the base. Add to the lamb's lettuce together with the chives and toss together. Set aside.

2 Put all the ingredients for the dressing in a screw-top jar and season with salt and pepper to taste. Shake together to mix.

3 Steam the asparagus for about 4 minutes or until barely tender. Alternatively, cook the asparagus in a wide pan of simmering water for 3–4 minutes. To test, pierce the thickest part of the stalk with a thin, sharp knife. If cooked in simmering water, carefully lift out the asparagus spears with a draining spoon and drain thoroughly on kitchen paper.

4 While the asparagus is cooking, half fill a frying pan with water and bring to the boil. Add the vinegar, then reduce the heat so the water is just simmering. Carefully crack 4 of the quail's eggs, one at a time, and slip into the water. Cook for 1 minute or until the yolks have just set. Remove the poached eggs from the water with a draining spoon and drain on kitchen paper. Keep warm while poaching the rest of the quail's eggs.

5 Pour the dressing over the salad and toss together. Spread out on a large serving platter. Arrange the asparagus on the salad and place the poached eggs on top. Scatter over the Parmesan shavings and grind a little pepper over the top. Serve immediately.

**Plus points**

● Though much smaller in size, quail's eggs have a very similar nutritional composition to hen's eggs. They therefore contain useful amounts of protein, plus vitamins A, E, B₂, B₁₂ and niacin.

● Asparagus is a good source of many of the B vitamins, including folate which is important during the early stages of pregnancy, to prevent birth defects such as spina bifida.

● Parmesan cheese has a higher content of vitamin B₁₂ than other cheeses. This vitamin is important for the formation of red blood cells and for helping to keep the nervous system healthy.

Soups and starters

## Some more ideas

- Use rocket instead of chicory.
- For quail's eggs with new potatoes and spinach, cook 500 g (1 lb 2 oz) scrubbed new potatoes in boiling water for about 15 minutes or until tender; drain and cut in half. While the potatoes are cooking, grill 4 rashers of lean back bacon until crisp, then drain on kitchen paper and crumble. Toss the warm potatoes and bacon with 300 g (10½ oz) baby spinach leaves and 1 small red onion, finely chopped. Keep warm. Poach 12 quail's eggs as in the main recipe. Set the eggs on top of the spinach and potato salad, season with a grinding of pepper and serve immediately.

# Quick bap pizzas

These are so simple and quick to prepare, yet they taste fantastic – almost as authentic as the real thing. The sweetness of the passata and yellow pepper contrasts deliciously with the savoury wholemeal baps, making this a tasty starter for healthy appetites.

**Makes 4 pizzas**

1 large courgette, thinly sliced
1 yellow pepper, seeded and thinly sliced
1 tbsp extra virgin olive oil
2 large wholemeal baps, split open in half
120 ml (4 fl oz) passata with onion and garlic
handful of fresh oregano leaves
200 g (7 oz) mozzarella cheese, sliced
salt and pepper

Preparation time: about 5 minutes
Cooking time: about 10 minutes

1 Preheat the grill to the hottest setting. Line the grill pan with a piece of foil. Put the courgette and pepper slices on the foil, sprinkle with the olive oil and toss together. Spread out the vegetables, then grill for about 5 minutes or until they begin to soften.

2 Add the baps, laying them on top of the vegetables, crust sides uppermost, and toast lightly on the crust side. Remove the baps. Turn the vegetables and continue grilling them while you add the topping to the baps.

3 Spread the untoasted cut side of each bap with passata, allowing it to soak into the bread. Add a few oregano leaves to each one, then arrange the grilled vegetables on top, sprinkling them with seasoning to taste. Lay the slices of mozzarella cheese over the vegetables.

4 Put the bap pizzas back in the grill pan. Cook under the hot grill for 3–5 minutes or until the cheese melts and begins to brown. Serve immediately, while piping hot.

**Plus points**

● Peppers – green, yellow, red or other colours – are excellent sources of vitamin C, and red peppers are in a league of their own as a source of vitamin A from the beta-carotene they contain, providing 685 mg per 100 g (3½ oz).

● Cheese is a good source of protein and calcium, as well as many of the B vitamins. Mozzarella contains less fat than many other cheeses – in 100 g (3½ oz) there are 21 g fat and 289 kcal, compared to 34 g fat and 412 kcal in the same weight of Cheddar.

**Some more ideas**

● Use 6 patty pan squashes instead of the courgettes, and green pepper instead of the yellow pepper.

● Tuck some other fresh herbs, such as basil or marjoram, under the vegetables.

● For mushroom pizzas, use 300 g (10½ oz) sliced button mushrooms instead of the courgette and yellow pepper.

**Each pizza provides**

kcal 325, **protein** 20 g, **fat** 15 g (of which saturated fat 7 g), **carbohydrate** 30 g (of which sugars 7 g), **fibre** 5 g

| | |
|---|---|
| ✓✓✓ | $B_{12}$, C |
| ✓✓ | A, $B_1$, $B_2$, E, folate, niacin, calcium, copper |
| ✓ | $B_6$, potassium, zinc |

Soups and starters

43

# Salads

In this selection of light side salads and hearty main dishes there is something to please everyone. With culinary influences from all over the world, this is a delicious way to boost your intake of garden-fresh vegetables. Try Rustic bread and cheese salad, Cajun-style ham and beans or Tabbouleh with goat's cheese. You can even indulge in Smoked salmon with pasta bows in the knowledge that it is a healthy, fast option.

# Feta and chickpea salad

Made from ewe's milk, Greek feta cheese has a tangy, salty flavour. Other countries produce cow's milk feta, which has a milder taste. Either type can be used in this classic Mediterranean salad, with tomatoes, olives, and chickpeas. Serve with warm pitta bread.

## Serves 4

2 Little Gem lettuces, separated into leaves

4 ripe tomatoes, chopped

1 green pepper, seeded and cut into 1 cm (½ in) squares

1 small red onion, thinly sliced

1 cucumber, cut into quarters lengthways and then into chunks

1 can chickpeas, about 410 g, drained and rinsed

60 g (2¼ oz) stoned black olives, preferably Greek Kalamata olives

150 g (5½ oz) feta cheese, cut into small cubes

### Parsley and mustard dressing

3 tbsp extra virgin olive oil

1½ tbsp lemon juice

1 tsp Dijon mustard

3 tbsp chopped fresh flat-leaf parsley

pepper

Preparation time: about 20 minutes

1 Put all the dressing ingredients into a large salad bowl, adding pepper to taste (there is no need to add salt as the cheese is salty). Whisk together.

2 Add the lettuce leaves, tomatoes, green pepper, onion, cucumber, chickpeas and olives, and toss gently to combine and coat everything with the dressing.

3 Scatter the cubes of feta cheese over the salad, toss again gently and serve immediately.

### Another idea

● Make a Middle Eastern-style goat's cheese and lentil salad. Cook 250 g (8½ oz) Puy lentils in boiling water for about 25 minutes, or according to the packet instructions, until tender. Drain thoroughly and leave to cool slightly, then add 6 tbsp of a basic vinaigrette flavoured with ½ tsp ground cumin and 2 tbsp chopped fresh coriander. Toss well. Add 1 sliced red onion, 4 chopped plum tomatoes and 1 large grated carrot, and toss again until well mixed. Spoon onto Little Gem lettuce leaves in a salad bowl, and crumble over 150 g (5½ oz) goat's cheese.

### Plus points

● Believing chickpeas to be a powerful aphrodisiac, the Romans fed them to their stallions to improve their performance. Although this reputation seems to be long forgotten, chickpeas do contribute valuable amounts of soluble fibre, iron, folate, vitamin E and manganese to the diet.

● The vitamin C from the lemon juice in the dressing will help to increase absorption of iron from the chickpeas.

● The strong taste of feta means that only a small amount of this cheese, high in saturated fat and salt, is needed.

### Each serving provides

Ⓥ

kcal 347, **protein** 16 g, **fat** 21 g (of which saturated fat 7 g), **carbohydrate** 24 g (of which sugars 8 g), **fibre** 8 g

| | |
|---|---|
| ✓✓✓ | A, B₁, B₆, C, E, niacin |
| ✓✓ | B₁₂, folate, calcium, iron, potassium |
| ✓ | copper, zinc |

# Chicken Caesar salad

A variation on the classic Caesar salad, this includes chunks of tender chicken, green beans and tasty anchovy croutons, all tossed in a light creamy dressing. Serve with warmed sesame-seed French bread.

**Serves 4**

200 g (7 oz) thin green beans

1–2 cos lettuces, about 450 g (1 lb) in total, torn into bite-sized pieces

1 small head chicory, sliced crossways

4 celery sticks, sliced

400 g (14 oz) cooked skinless boneless chicken breasts (fillets), cut into chunks

1 egg

1 can anchovy fillets, about 50 g

1 garlic clove, crushed

12 thin slices of French bread, about 100 g (3½ oz) in total

30 g (1 oz) Parmesan cheese, finely pared into shavings or grated

**Caesar dressing**

1 tsp Dijon mustard

3 tbsp extra virgin olive oil

2 tsp sherry vinegar or wine vinegar

2 tbsp plain low-fat yogurt

large pinch of caster sugar

½ tsp Worcestershire sauce

pepper

Preparation time: about 30 minutes

1 Preheat the oven to 200ºC (400ºF, gas mark 6). Cook the beans in a saucepan of boiling water for 3 minutes or until just tender. Drain and refresh under cold running water. Halve the beans and put into a large salad bowl. Add the lettuce, chicory, celery and chicken. Set aside in the fridge.

2 Put the egg in a saucepan, cover with cold water and bring to the boil. Reduce the heat and simmer for 10 minutes.

3 Meanwhile, tip the anchovies into a bowl with the oil from the can (about 1 tbsp). Add the garlic and mash with a fork to a paste. Spread thinly over one side of each slice of French bread. Arrange on a baking sheet and bake for about 10 minutes or until the croutons are crisp and golden. Cool slightly, then break into pieces.

4 While the croutons are baking, make the Caesar dressing. Whisk together the mustard, olive oil, vinegar, yogurt, sugar, Worcestershire sauce and pepper to taste. Cool the hard-boiled egg under cold running water, then peel and chop. Stir into the dressing.

5 Drizzle half of the dressing over the chilled salad and toss to coat everything evenly. Add the croutons and toss again. Drizzle over the remaining dressing and scatter the Parmesan shavings on top. Serve at once.

**Plus points**

• Caesar salad is usually very high in fat, partly due to the quantity of oil in the dressing. In this healthier version, some of the oil is replaced by yogurt, to make a dressing that is just as delicious.

• Although celery contains very little in the way of vitamins, it does provide useful amounts of potassium as well as a phytochemical called phthalide, which may help to lower high blood pressure.

**Each serving provides**

kcal 382, **protein** 37 g, **fat** 23 g (of which saturated fat 4 g), **carbohydrate** 20 g (of which sugars 5 g), **fibre** 4 g

| | |
|---|---|
| ✓✓✓ | B₁, B₆, B₁₂, E, niacin |
| ✓✓ | B₂, calcium, potassium, selenium, zinc |
| ✓ | iron |

Salads

## Some more ideas

- For a lower fat dressing, use only 1½ tbsp olive oil and increase the yogurt to 4 tbsp.
- For a more traditional Caesar salad, to serve as a starter or side salad, mix 1 torn cos lettuce and 1 Little Gem lettuce, separated into leaves, in a large salad bowl. Cut 140 g (5 oz) day-old crusty white bread into 2 cm (¾ in) cubes. Put on a baking sheet and drizzle with 2 tbsp extra virgin olive oil, then bake as in the main recipe. To make the dressing, heat 2 tbsp extra virgin olive oil in a small pan and gently cook 3 peeled garlic cloves for 3 minutes. Add 1 can anchovy fillets, about 50 g, drained, and cook for a further 2–3 minutes or until the garlic is soft. Lift out the anchovies and garlic, reserving the oil, and mash to a paste. Mix in 1 tbsp Dijon mustard, 2 tsp balsamic vinegar and pepper to taste. Gradually whisk in the reserved oil, then stir in 2 tbsp plain low-fat yogurt. Drizzle half the dressing over the salad leaves and toss well to coat, then add the croutons and toss again. Drizzle over the remaining dressing and top with the shavings of Parmesan.

# Smoked salmon with pasta bows

This colourful and nutritious salad is full of delicious textures and flavours. Little bows of pasta and peas are mixed with a creamy watercress and herb dressing, then garnished with more watercress and pieces of smoked salmon. It makes a feast for the eyes.

**Serves 4**

250 g (8½ oz) farfalle (pasta bows)
100 g (3½ oz) shelled fresh or frozen peas
150 g (5½ oz) watercress
1 garlic clove
4 sprigs of parsley
2 sprigs of fresh tarragon
5 spring onions, chopped
4 tbsp plain low-fat yogurt
2 tbsp mayonnaise
½ red onion, chopped
2 tbsp capers, rinsed
¼ cucumber, diced
1 tbsp sunflower oil
1 tbsp white wine vinegar, or to taste
125 g (4½ oz) smoked salmon, cut into thin strips
salt and pepper

Preparation time: about 30 minutes

**1** Cook the pasta in boiling water for 10–12 minutes, or according to the packet instructions, until al dente, adding the peas 2–3 minutes before the end of the cooking time. Drain in a sieve and rinse well with cold water, then drain again.

**2** While the pasta and peas are cooking, put 50 g (1¾ oz) of the watercress in a food processor or blender and process until finely chopped. Add the peeled garlic clove, parsley, tarragon and half of the spring onions, and process to a fine purée. Add the yogurt and mayonnaise, and process briefly to combine. Stir in the remaining spring onions, and season with salt and pepper to taste.

**3** Add the dressing to the cooked pasta and peas, and mix well together. Divide among 4 plates. Toss the remaining watercress with the red onion, capers, cucumber, oil and vinegar, and spoon over the pasta salad. Arrange the pieces of smoked salmon on top and serve.

**Another idea**

● Make a crab meat and rice noodle salad. Cut 85 g (3 oz) mange-tout and 1 small carrot into matchstick strips, and drop into a pan of boiling water with 1 thinly sliced courgette. Bring back to the boil, then remove from the heat. Add 250 g (8½ oz) thin rice noodles (ones that need no cooking) and leave to soak for 4 minutes. Drain, rinse with cold water and drain again. Toss the vegetables and noodles with 1 can crab meat, about 170 g, drained, 1 red pepper, seeded and thinly sliced, and 3 thinly sliced spring onions. Make a dressing with 2 tbsp toasted sesame oil, 1 tbsp rice vinegar, 1 tbsp dry sherry, 1 tbsp soy sauce, 1–2 chopped garlic cloves, 1 tbsp grated fresh root ginger and 1 tsp caster sugar. Serve on a bed of rocket, garnished with chopped fresh coriander.

**Plus points**

● Smoked salmon, like other oily fish, is a rich source of omega-3 fatty acids, which can help to protect against high blood pressure, heart disease and stroke. Omega-3 fatty acids also play a vital role in the development of eye and brain tissue, and studies suggest that there may be beneficial effects for the baby if mothers increase their intake of oily fish while they are pregnant and breast-feeding.

● Allicin, the compound that gives garlic its characteristic smell and taste, acts as an antibiotic and also has anti-fungal properties. Some allicin is destroyed in cooking, so for maximum benefit, eat garlic raw.

**Each serving provides**

kcal 379, **protein** 20 g, **fat** 12 g (of which saturated fat 2 g), **carbohydrate** 54 g (of which sugars 5 g), **fibre** 5 g

| | |
|---|---|
| ✓✓✓ | B$_1$, B$_6$, C, E, niacin |
| ✓✓ | A, folate, copper, selenium, zinc |
| ✓ | B$_2$, calcium, iron, potassium |

Salads

# Rustic bread and cheese salad

Inspired by the Italian salad called panzanella, this combines crisp, garlic-flavoured bread cubes with sweet, juicy tomatoes and crunchy salad vegetables. Gruyère and Parmesan cheeses add wonderful flavour as well as vital minerals.

### Serves 4

2 ciabatta rolls or 1 small baguette

2 garlic cloves, halved

1 egg, hard-boiled

1 tsp Dijon mustard

1 tbsp lemon juice

150 g (5½ oz) plain low-fat yogurt

75 g (2½ oz) Gruyère cheese

50 g (1¾ oz) Parmesan cheese

1 cos lettuce or 2 romaine lettuce hearts, cut into bite-sized chunks

2 beefsteak tomatoes or 4 plum tomatoes, skinned (optional) and cut into bite-sized chunks

1 bunch of spring onions, sliced

1 small bulb of fennel, thinly sliced

salt and pepper

Preparation time: about 20 minutes

1 Preheat the grill. Slice the rolls or bread horizontally in half and toast both sides lightly under the grill. Rub the cut sides of the garlic over the toasted sides of the bread. Reserve the garlic cloves. Cut the bread into bite-sized cubes and set aside.

2 Separate the yolk and white of the hard-boiled egg. Roughly chop the white and set it aside. Mash the yolk with the mustard in a small bowl, then gradually stir in the lemon juice and yogurt, with seasoning to taste, to form a smooth dressing.

3 Using a cheese plane or vegetable peeler, cut fine shavings or very thin slices from the Gruyère and Parmesan cheeses. Alternatively, coarsely grate the cheese.

4 Rub the inside of a salad bowl with the reserved garlic cloves, then discard the garlic. Place the lettuce in the bowl and add the tomatoes, spring onions and fennel.

5 Add the dressing to the salad and toss lightly. Scatter over the egg white, bread cubes and cheese. Mix gently and serve at once, before the bread begins to soften.

### Each serving provides ⓥ

kcal 265, **protein** 17 g, **fat** 13 g (of which saturated fat 7 g), **carbohydrate** 20 g (of which sugars 7 g), **fibre** 3 g

| | |
|---|---|
| ✓✓✓ | C, calcium |
| ✓✓ | A, B₁₂, E, folate, niacin |
| ✓ | B₁, B₂, B₆, copper, iron, potassium, selenium, zinc |

### Plus points

● The traditional combination of cheese and tomato offers a delicious source of protein, vitamins and minerals.

● In addition to calcium, Gruyère cheese is a good source of zinc, a mineral essential for the process of wound healing.

● Fennel is thought to aid digestion and relieve wind. It also provides phytoestrogen and it is a good source of potassium.

### Some more ideas

● Use 1 head of Chinese leaves, about 400–450 g (14–16 oz), and 200 g (7 oz) iceberg lettuce instead of cos or romaine lettuce. Shred and mix the Chinese leaves and iceberg.

● Try 170 g (6 oz) feta cheese, crumbled, instead of Gruyère and Parmesan and add a few black olives, stoned and chopped. Omit the dressing and instead serve lemon wedges and black pepper to sprinkle over the salad.

● Grilled haloumi cheese is excellent with a salad such as this. Cut the cheese into fairly thick slices and place them on a flameproof dish. Cook under a hot grill until golden on both sides, turning once. Lay the cheese on individual portions of the prepared salad (made without Gruyère and Parmesan) and serve straightaway.

# Bacon and broad bean salad

This delicious warm salad is packed with strong flavours and makes a fabulous supper or lunch served with chunks of crusty bread or a side dish of new potatoes. Use a mild smoked bacon, such as a maple cure, as it is slightly less salty than some of the other cures.

## Serves 4

1 tbsp sunflower oil

200 g (7 oz) lean smoked back bacon, rinded and snipped into large pieces

1 large red pepper, seeded and cut into strips

2 red onions, cut into wedges

2 slices of bread

400 g (14 oz) frozen broad beans, thawed

2 small firm heads of radicchio, cut into wedges

chopped fresh flat-leaf parsley to garnish (optional)

**Devilled dressing**

4 tbsp mayonnaise

2 tsp Worcestershire sauce

1 tbsp Dijon mustard

generous pinch of caster sugar

3–4 tbsp milk

salt and pepper

Preparation and cooking time: 30 minutes

1 Preheat the grill if not using a toaster for the bread. Make the dressing by mixing together the mayonnaise, Worcestershire sauce, Dijon mustard and sugar. Add enough milk to make a drizzling consistency. Season with salt and pepper to taste, and set aside.

2 Heat the sunflower oil in a large saucepan. Add the bacon, red pepper and onions, and fry over a high heat for 4 minutes, stirring, until the onions have softened.

3 Meanwhile, toast the bread in a toaster or under the grill. Cut it into cubes. Set aside.

4 Stir the broad beans into the bacon mixture and add 1 tbsp water. Heat until sizzling, then cover the pan and leave to cook for 4 minutes.

5 Arrange the wedges of radicchio on top of the bean and bacon mixture. Cover again and cook for 3 minutes or until the radicchio has wilted, but still holds its shape.

6 Spoon the salad into shallow bowls and drizzle over the dressing. Scatter the toasted bread cubes over the top, sprinkle with chopped flat-leaf parsley and serve.

**Some more ideas**

● If radicchio is unavailable, you can use 300 g (10½ oz) chicory or 2 crisp Little Gem lettuces.

● For a wilted chicory and bacon salad, make an orange and honey dressing by mixing the grated zest of ½ orange with 4 tbsp orange juice, 1 tbsp each lemon juice and honey, 2 tbsp extra virgin olive oil and 1 tsp balsamic vinegar. Season to taste. Cut the peel and pith from 2 oranges and slice between the membrane to release the segments. Cook the bacon, pepper and onion as in the main recipe, then add 340 g (12 oz) frozen peas instead of the broad beans. Cook for 4 minutes. Add 2 heads of chicory, cut into wedges, and cook for 2 more minutes. Toss with the orange segments, dressing and 45 g (1½ oz) watercress. Scatter over 45 g (1½ oz) toasted pecan nuts and serve warm.

## Each serving provides

kcal 350, **protein** 19 g, **fat** 20 g (of which saturated fat 4 g), **carbohydrate** 24 g (of which sugars 9 g), **fibre** 8 g

| | |
|---|---|
| ✓✓✓ | C, folate |
| ✓✓ | A, B$_1$, B$_2$, B$_6$, zinc |
| ✓ | copper, iron |

### Plus point

● Broad beans are a good source of soluble fibre, and one serving of this dish provides around one-third of the recommended daily amount. Broad beans also offer useful amounts of phosphorus, copper and the flavonoid quercetin, which can help to protect against heart disease.

Salads

# Gold on a bed of green leaves

This mixture of salad leaves and herbs, each with its own robust flavour, marries well with the sweetness and smooth texture of mango. The result is a colourful and refreshing salad, best enjoyed with warm mixed-grain bread or rolls.

**Serves 4**

1 large ripe mango

200 g (7 oz) mixed baby spinach leaves, watercress and rocket or frisée

about 12 fresh basil leaves, coarsely shredded or torn

about 6 sprigs of fresh coriander, stalks discarded, then coarsely chopped

30 g (1 oz) cashew nuts or peanuts, toasted and coarsely chopped

**Lime and ginger dressing**

grated zest of 1 lime

2 tbsp lime juice

2 tsp finely chopped or grated fresh root ginger

1 tbsp toasted sesame oil

1 tbsp sunflower oil

salt and pepper

Preparation time: 15 minutes

1 Peel the mango. Cut the flesh from both sides of the stone and slice it thinly lengthways.

2 Mix the salad leaves on a platter, adding the basil and coriander. Arrange the mango slices on and between the salad leaves.

3 Whisk the ingredients for the dressing together and spoon it over the salad. Sprinkle with the chopped cashew nuts or peanuts and serve.

**Some more ideas**

• Thin strips of peeled cooked beetroot and cooked or raw celeriac are delicious additions to this salad.

• Instead of mango, use seedless green grapes, halved if large, thinly sliced dessert apple, or diced avocado.

• Toasted pumpkin seeds, sesame seeds or pine nuts can be used instead of the cashew nuts or peanuts.

• Replace the nuts with spicy croûtons. Cut 2 slices of day-old bread into small pieces or neat cubes and place in a polythene bag. Add a pinch of chilli powder and 1 tbsp extra virgin olive oil, then hold the bag shut and shake well. Tip into a non-stick pan and stir-fry until crisp and golden brown. Add to the salad just before serving.

• For a completely fat-free dressing, mix 1 tbsp seasoned rice vinegar (the type sold for making Japanese sushi) with the ginger and lime zest and juice. Add 2 tbsp fresh orange juice.

Or mix 2 tbsp each of orange juice, dry sherry and soy sauce for a punchy dressing.

• A mixed green salad makes a versatile accompaniment for all meals or a useful base on which to serve ingredients such as fruit or smoked fish for a first course. Mix 225 g (8 oz) mixed salad leaves (cos, lamb's lettuce, Lollo Rosso, Little Gem, baby spinach or rocket) with about 45 g (1½ oz) mixed fresh herbs (basil, tarragon, chervil, flat-leaf parsley and mint), torn or coarsely chopped. Rub the inside of the salad bowl with a cut clove of garlic, if liked, then discard. Add the leaves and herbs to the bowl. For the dressing, whisk together 1 shallot, finely chopped, ½ tsp Dijon mustard, 2 tbsp white wine vinegar and 4 tbsp extra virgin olive oil with seasoning. Drizzle the dressing over the salad, then toss gently to coat the leaves.

**Plus points**

• Mango contains a wealth of carotenoids which protect against free radical attack and degenerative diseases. The fruit also supplies iron, potassium, magnesium, and vitamins E, C and B group.

• All the leaves provide minerals, such as potassium, calcium and iron. Raw spinach provides folate. All these minerals help to protect against cancer.

**Each serving provides** Ⓥ

kcal 125, **protein** 3 g, **fat** 10 g (of which saturated fat 2 g), **carbohydrate** 6 g (of which sugars 3 g), **fibre** 2 g

| | |
|---|---|
| ✓✓✓ | C |
| ✓✓ | A |
| ✓ | B₁, E, folate, calcium, copper, iron |

Salads

# Zesty tomato salad

Seek out the most delicious tomatoes available, preferably sun-ripened on the vine, and you will be rewarded with an incomparable flavour. Lemon, fresh coriander and mint add freshness and zest to the tomatoes in this tangy salad.

**Serves 4**

500 g (1 lb 2 oz) ripe tomatoes, sliced
pinch of caster sugar, or to taste
1 lemon
3 spring onions, thinly sliced
1 tbsp chopped fresh coriander
1 tbsp chopped fresh mint
sprigs of fresh mint to garnish

Preparation time: 10 minutes

**1** Place the tomatoes in a large shallow dish and sprinkle with the sugar. Cut the lemon in half lengthways. Set one half aside, then cut the other half lengthways into 4 wedges. Holding the wedges firmly together on a board, skin side up, thinly slice them across, including the peel. Discard the pips.

**2** Arrange the pieces of thinly sliced lemon over the top of the tomatoes, then sprinkle with the spring onions, coriander and mint. Squeeze the juice from the remaining lemon half and sprinkle it over the salad. Serve immediately or cover and chill until ready to serve. Garnish with sprigs of mint just before serving.

**Some more ideas**

● For a tomato salad with rosemary and basil, make a dressing by mixing together 1 tbsp each chopped fresh rosemary and basil, 1–2 garlic cloves, finely chopped, and 2 tsp raspberry vinegar or balsamic vinegar. Sprinkle the tomatoes with 3–4 pinches of sugar to emphasise their natural sweetness, and scatter over ½ red or white onion, thinly sliced. Sprinkle the dressing evenly over the tomatoes. Serve at once or cover and chill until ready to serve.

● A tomato salad makes a delicious filling for piping-hot baked potatoes, particularly baked sweet potatoes. Bake 4 large potatoes until crisp and golden outside and floury inside, then split and fill with the tomato salad. Top each potato with a spoonful of fromage frais or Greek-style yogurt and serve immediately.

● Tomato salads are good as omelette fillings. For each serving, make a plain omelette by lightly beating 2 eggs with 2 tbsp cold water and a little seasoning, then cooking in the minimum of olive oil in a very hot omelette pan until just set, lifting the edges to allow unset egg to run onto the hot pan. Spoon one-quarter of the tomato salad over half of the set omelette and fold the other half over. Slide the omelette onto a warmed plate. Serve with a mixed green salad and crusty bread.

**Plus points**

● Vitamin C, found in raw tomatoes, is an antioxidant that helps to protect against cancer. Tomatoes also contain lycopene, another valuable anti-cancer agent, believed to be particularly useful in protecting against prostate cancer. Lycopene is enhanced by cooking, so canned tomatoes, tomato purée or paste and tomato ketchup are better sources than fresh tomatoes.

**Each serving provides** Ⓥ

kcal 25, **protein** 1 g, **fat** 0.5 g (of which saturated fat 0.1 g), **carbohydrate** 4 g (of which sugars 3 g), **fibre** 1 g

| | |
|---|---|
| ✓✓✓ | C |
| ✓✓ | E |
| ✓ | A, folate |

Salads

# Cajun-style ham and beans

This tempting salad combines smoky ham, red onion, sweetcorn, black-eyed beans and fresh coriander in a spicy soured cream dressing. For generous, meaty chunks of ham, buy pieces from the deli counter. Serve with tomato wedges and crusty fresh bread.

### Serves 4

2 cans black-eyed beans, about 410 g each, drained and rinsed

350 g (12½ oz) frozen sweetcorn, cooked and drained

3 celery sticks, sliced

1 small red onion, chopped

1 green pepper, seeded and diced

200 g (7 oz) piece of smoked ham, cut into 1 cm (½ in) chunks

sprigs of fresh coriander to garnish

**Cajun dressing**

150 ml (5 fl oz) soured cream

1 tbsp tomato ketchup

15 g (½ oz) fresh coriander, finely chopped

1½ tsp Cajun seasoning

Tabasco sauce

salt and pepper

Preparation time: about 25 minutes

### Each serving provides

kcal 419, **protein** 33 g, **fat** 12 g (of which saturated fat 6 g), **carbohydrate** 48 g (of which sugars 9 g), **fibre** 10 g

| | |
|---|---|
| ✓✓✓ | $B_1$, $B_6$, C, E, folate, niacin, zinc |
| ✓✓ | A, $B_2$, iron, potassium |
| ✓ | calcium, selenium |

1 To make the dressing, put the soured cream, ketchup, coriander, Cajun seasoning, 2 shakes of Tabasco sauce, and salt and pepper to taste in a large bowl. Whisk together, then taste and add more Tabasco if liked.

2 Add the beans, sweetcorn, celery, red onion, green pepper and ham to the bowl, and stir until everything is well mixed. Garnish with sprigs of coriander and serve at once.

### Some more ideas

• If you cannot find Cajun seasoning, mix 1½ tsp paprika with ½ tsp cayenne pepper.

• Use a can of sweetcorn, about 340 g, drained and rinsed, instead of frozen sweetcorn.

• As an alternative to ham, try cooked gammon or roast chicken or turkey.

• Make a quick tandoori chicken and chickpea salad. For the dressing, mix 150 g (5½ oz) plain low-fat bio yogurt with 1 tbsp extra virgin olive oil, 15 g (½ oz) fresh coriander, finely chopped, 1 tsp toasted cumin seeds, the juice of 1 lemon, a shake of Tabasco sauce and seasoning to taste. Drain and rinse 1 can of chickpeas, about 410 g, and 1 can of red kidney beans, about 410 g, and add to the dressing together with 1 small red onion, finely chopped, ½ diced cucumber and 200 g (7 oz) shredded green spring cabbage. Cut 250 g (8½ oz) boneless tandoori chicken into cubes, and fold into the salad. Serve with naan bread.

### Plus points

• Black-eyed beans are a good low-fat source of protein and, in common with all other beans, they are a good source of dietary fibre, particularly soluble fibre. This can help to reduce high blood cholesterol levels, thereby lessening the risk of heart disease. Beans and other pulses also provide useful amounts of vitamin $B_1$.

• The canning process has little effect on the nutritional value of pulses, so canned beans are a nutritious ingredient to have on hand in the storecupboard. Rinsing the beans thoroughly will help to reduce some of the sugars that can cause flatulence.

• Sweetcorn offers vitamins A (from beta-carotene), C and folate as well as dietary fibre. Although the vitamins are lost in canned sweetcorn, they are retained in the frozen vegetable.

Salads

# Tabbouleh with goat's cheese

Tabbouleh is a classic Middle Eastern salad made with bulghur wheat. While the wheat is soaking, you have just enough time to chop the vegetables and herbs, and make the dressing. Serve with lavash or pitta bread.

### Serves 4

280 g (10 oz) bulghur wheat

1 yellow pepper, seeded and chopped

20 cherry tomatoes, quartered

1 small red onion, finely chopped

10 cm (4 in) piece of cucumber, seeded and chopped

1 large carrot, grated

5 tbsp chopped parsley

2 tbsp chopped fresh coriander

2 tbsp chopped fresh mint

1 small fresh red chilli, seeded and finely chopped (optional)

200 g (7 oz) rindless soft goat's cheese, crumbled

salt and pepper

### Lemon and cumin dressing

¼ tsp ground cumin

1 small garlic clove, very finely chopped

1 tbsp lemon juice

3 tbsp extra virgin olive oil

### To serve

lettuce leaves

12 radishes, sliced

Preparation time: about 30 minutes

**1** Put the bulghur wheat in a mixing bowl, pour over enough boiling water to cover and stir well. Leave to soak for 15–20 minutes.

**2** Meanwhile, make the dressing. Whisk together the cumin, garlic and lemon juice in a small bowl, then whisk in the olive oil.

**3** Drain the bulghur wheat in a sieve, pressing out excess water, then return it to the bowl. Add the pepper, tomatoes, onion, cucumber, carrot, parsley, coriander and mint, plus the chilli, if using. Pour the dressing over the top and season with salt and pepper to taste. Fold gently to mix well.

**4** Arrange the lettuce leaves on 4 plates or a serving platter. Pile the bulghur salad on the leaves and sprinkle the goat's cheese over the top. Garnish with the radishes and serve.

### Plus points

• Bulghur wheat is a good, low-fat source of starchy (complex) carbohydrate. Because it retains the nutritious outer layers of the wheat grain, it contains useful amounts of B vitamins, particularly B$_1$.

• Goat's cheese is a tasty source of protein and calcium and lower in fat than cheeses such as Cheddar and Parmesan.

### Some more ideas

• Use feta cheese instead of goat's cheese.

• For an apricot tabbouleh side salad, mix the soaked bulghur wheat with the yellow pepper and red onion, plus 4 chopped celery sticks and 115 g (4 oz) snipped, ready-to-eat dried apricots (omit the other vegetables and the herbs, as well as the goat's cheese). Add ½ tsp ground cinnamon to the dressing.

• For a spicy tabbouleh with chicken to serve 6, replace the goat's cheese with 2 cooked skinless boneless chicken breasts, about 280 g (10 oz) in total, cut into cubes. Mix the soaked bulghur wheat with the chicken, pepper, onion, carrot and parsley (omit the other vegetables and herbs). For the dressing, gently warm 3 tbsp extra virgin olive oil in a small frying pan with 1 finely chopped garlic clove. Add ½–1 tsp each of ground cumin, ground coriander, dry mustard and curry powder, and continue cooking for 1 minute. Stir in 2 tbsp lemon juice and seasoning to taste. Pour the dressing over the salad and stir gently to combine. Garnish with sliced cucumber rounds.

### Each serving provides

kcal 473, **protein** 16 g, **fat** 18 g (of which saturated fat 7 g), **carbohydrate** 64 g (of which sugars 10 g), **fibre** 3 g

| | |
|---|---|
| ✓✓✓ | B$_1$, B$_6$, B$_{12}$, E, niacin |
| ✓✓ | A, B$_2$, C, folate, calcium, copper, iron |
| ✓ | potassium |

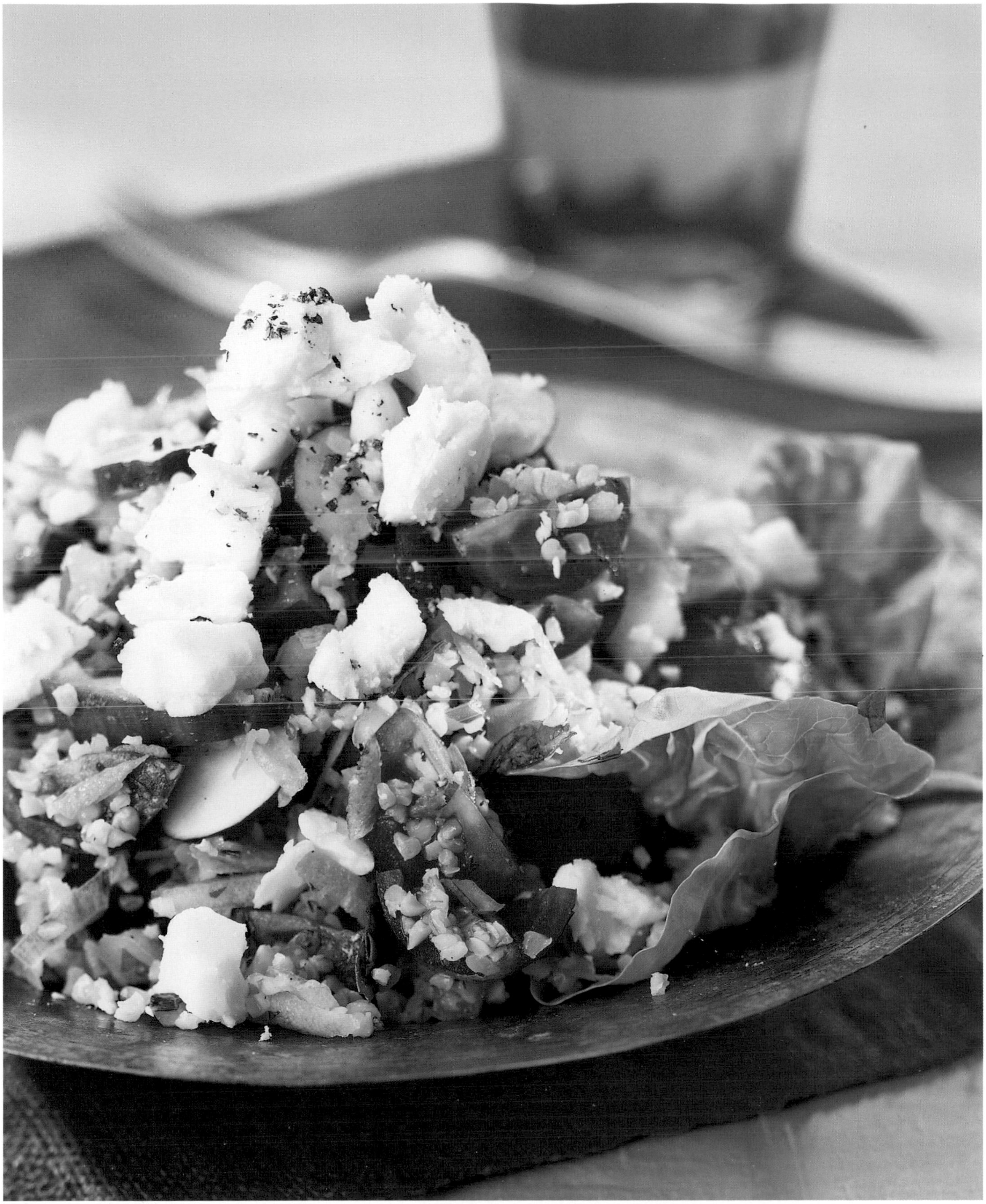

# Apple and fennel with blue cheese dressing

This tasty salad is perfect for the winter months when salad leaves and tomatoes are not at their best. Bulb fennel has a sweet aniseed flavour that works well with bitter chicory and refreshing apple. A creamy blue cheese dressing is the perfect partner.

**Serves 4**

30 g (1 oz) shelled hazelnuts

1 large bulb of fennel, thinly sliced

1 large head of chicory, cut across into shreds

2 red-skinned dessert apples

100 g (3½ oz) radicchio leaves

2 tbsp snipped fresh chives

**Blue cheese dressing**

55 g (2 oz) blue cheese, such as Danish Blue, crumbled

2 tbsp tepid water

6 tbsp plain low-fat bio yogurt

pepper

Preparation time: about 20 minutes

1 To make the dressing, put the blue cheese in a bowl with the water and mash to a smooth paste using the back of a spoon. Stir in the yogurt to make a thick, fairly smooth dressing. Season to taste with pepper. Set aside.

2 Heat a small non-stick frying pan over a high heat. Add the hazelnuts and toast for about 2 minutes or until they smell nutty, stirring frequently. Immediately tip onto a clean tea-towel and rub to remove the papery outer skins. Coarsely chop the nuts.

3 Add the fennel and chicory to the dressing and stir to combine. Core the apples and cut into very thin slices, then add to the salad. Toss gently, making sure the apples are coated in dressing. Fold in the hazelnuts.

4 Arrange the radicchio leaves on 4 plates. Top with the salad and sprinkle with the chives. Serve at once.

**Another idea**

● For a Cheddar cheese and apple salad, make the dressing by mixing 100 g (3½ oz) finely grated mature Cheddar cheese with 6 tbsp plain low-fat bio yogurt or reduced-fat crème fraîche (it will not be completely smooth). Core and chop 2 red apples and 2 green apples, and stir them into the dressing together with 2 thinly sliced celery sticks and 2 tbsp chopped parsley. Season to taste. Arrange 150 g (5½ oz) mixed salad leaves and 85 g (3 oz) watercress on 4 plates, and top with the cheese and apple salad. Serve immediately, as a light main dish.

**Plus points**

● Chicory is native to India but was known to the Greeks and Romans. It is a useful source of vitamin C, beta-carotene and potassium. It is widely used in herbal medicine – as an appetite stimulant, to stimulate the liver and gall bladder, and to treat urinary tract infections.

● Apples provide good amounts of potassium and soluble fibre in the form of pectin. Eating apples can benefit the teeth too, by helping to prevent gum disease.

**Each serving provides** Ⓥ

kcal 141, **protein** 5 g, **fat** 10 g (of which saturated fat 3 g), **carbohydrate** 10 g (of which sugars 8 g), **fibre** 4 g

| | |
|---|---|
| ✓✓✓ | B₁, B₆, E, niacin |
| ✓✓ | C, folate |
| ✓ | A, calcium, copper |

Salads

**65**

# Poultry

Poultry is extremely versatile, and with the recipe ideas in this chapter you can be sure of creating wonderfully tasty dishes each and every time with the minimum amount of effort. From Spicy drumsticks with Creole rice to Turkey escalopes with chestnut mushrooms and Madeira to Chicken jamboree, these are quick dishes suitable for any occasion and all appetites.

# Spicy drumsticks with Creole rice

These succulent chicken drumsticks, coated in a mixture of dried herbs and delicious spices, can be cooked under the grill in next to no time. They are served with crunchy and colourful Creole-style red beans and rice.

**Serves 4**

1 tbsp plain flour

1 tsp paprika

1 tsp ground black pepper

1 tsp garlic granules

½ tsp crushed dried chillies

1 tsp dried thyme

8 chicken drumsticks, about 675 g (1½ lb) in total, skinned

1 tbsp extra virgin olive oil

salt and pepper

sprigs of fresh parsley to garnish

**Creole rice**

1 tbsp extra virgin olive oil

1 onion, chopped

1 red pepper, seeded and diced

2 celery sticks, diced

170 g (6 oz) long-grain rice

600 ml (1 pint) vegetable stock

1 can red kidney beans, about 410 g, drained and rinsed

2 tbsp chopped parsley

Preparation and cooking time: 30 minutes

**Each serving provides**

kcal 480, **protein** 41 g, **fat** 11 g (of which saturated fat 2 g), **carbohydrate** 58 g (of which sugars 5 g), **fibre** 6 g

✓✓ B₁, B₆, niacin, iron, selenium, zinc

✓ folate, calcium, copper, potassium

**1** Preheat the grill to moderate. Put the flour, paprika, pepper, garlic granules, chillies, thyme and a pinch of salt in a polythene bag and shake to mix. Make 2 slashes in each chicken drumstick and rub with the olive oil. Toss them one at a time in the bag to coat with the spice mixture. Shake off any excess mixture and place the chicken on the grill rack. Grill for 20–25 minutes or until golden and cooked through, turning often.

**2** Meanwhile, make the Creole rice. Heat the oil in a large saucepan, add the onion, pepper and celery, and cook for 2 minutes or until softened. Stir in the rice, then add the stock and kidney beans. Bring to the boil. Cover and simmer gently for 15–20 minutes or until all the stock has been absorbed and the rice is tender.

**3** Stir the chopped parsley into the rice and season with salt and pepper to taste. Spoon the rice onto 4 plates and place 2 drumsticks on top of each portion. Serve hot, garnished with sprigs of parsley.

**Another idea**

● For sticky chilli drumsticks, mix 2 tbsp tomato ketchup with 1 tbsp soy sauce and 2 tbsp sweet chilli sauce or paste. Rub onto the chicken drumsticks and grill as in the main recipe. Meanwhile, put 125 g (4½ oz) bulghur wheat in a heatproof bowl, pour over enough boiling water to cover and soak for 15–20 minutes. Squeeze out any excess water, then mix with 1 can borlotti beans, about 410 g, drained, ¼ diced cucumber, 2 chopped tomatoes, 2 tbsp chopped fresh mint and 2 tbsp chopped parsley. Add 1 tbsp lemon juice and 2 tbsp extra virgin olive oil and season to taste. Toss to mix. Serve with the sticky chilli drumsticks.

**Plus points**

● Chicken is an excellent source of protein and provides many B vitamins, in particular niacin. The dark meat contains twice as much iron and zinc as the light meat. Eaten without the skin, chicken is low in fat and what fat it does contain is mostly unsaturated.

● Celery helps the kidneys to function efficiently, at the same time as helping to maintain healthy blood pressure.

Poultry

# Stir-fried chicken and avocado salad with hot balsamic dressing

This is an excellent, easily prepared salad, combining stir-fried strips of chicken and smoked turkey rashers in a hot piquant dressing with creamy avocado and sweet cherry tomatoes. Smoked turkey rashers are a great low-fat alternative to bacon.

**Serves 4**

3 tbsp extra virgin olive oil

2 garlic cloves, cut into slivers

300 g (10½ oz) skinless boneless chicken breasts (fillets), cut into strips

2 tbsp clear honey

1 tbsp balsamic vinegar

1 tbsp wholegrain mustard

150 g (5½ oz) smoked turkey rashers, diced

salt and pepper

**Tomato and avocado salad**

2 Little Gem lettuces, separated into leaves

55 g (2 oz) watercress sprigs

2 ripe avocados

juice of ½ lemon

250 g (9 oz) cherry tomatoes, halved

1 small red onion, thinly sliced

Preparation time: 15 minutes

Cooking time: 10 minutes

---

**Each serving provides**

kcal 385, protein 29 g, fat 24 g (of which saturated fat 4.5 g), carbohydrate 14 g (of which sugars 13 g), fibre 4 g

| | |
|---|---|
| ✓✓✓ | B$_6$ |
| ✓✓ | C, E, niacin, potassium |
| ✓ | A, B$_1$, B$_2$, B$_{12}$, folate, copper, iron, selenium, zinc |

---

1 First prepare the salad. Put the lettuce and watercress in a large wide salad bowl. Peel and thickly slice the avocados and toss with the lemon juice to prevent discoloration. Scatter the avocados, tomatoes and red onion on top of the lettuce and watercress. Set the salad aside.

2 Heat the oil in a large frying pan, add the garlic and stir round the pan for just 30 seconds or so until softened. Toss in the strips of chicken and stir-fry for 2–3 minutes or until they change colour.

3 Add the honey, vinegar and mustard, and stir to mix well. Add the diced turkey rashers and stir-fry for 1 more minute or until they are cooked, but still tender and moist (take care not to overcook or they will be dry). Season to taste.

4 Spoon the chicken mixture over the salad. Toss together, then serve immediately with crusty bread.

**Some more ideas**

• For a turkey and artichoke salad with a lemon dressing, replace the chicken with 2 small skinless turkey breast steaks, about 300 g (10½ oz) in total, and use 2 lean rashers of smoked back bacon instead of the smoked turkey rashers. Stir-fry the turkey with the bacon and garlic for 5–6 minutes or until lightly golden, then add the grated zest and juice of 1 lemon to the pan with the honey and balsamic vinegar (omit the mustard). Instead of the tomato and avocado salad, serve the turkey stir-fry spooned over an artichoke salad made with 100 g (3½ oz) baby spinach leaves, 55 g (2 oz) rocket and a 285 g jar of well-drained antipasto artichokes.

• For a milder flavour, 2 shallots can be used instead of the small red onion.

**Plus points**

• Turkey rashers, which are widely available in large supermarkets, contain a fraction of the fat of bacon and are lower in calories: 100 g (3½ oz) contains just 1.6 g fat and 99 kcal, compared with 21 g fat and 249 kcal in the same weight of back bacon.

• Avocados supply vitamin C, riboflavin, vital for the release of energy from food, and manganese, essential for activating many enzyme systems.

# Chicken and sweet potato hash

This hash is a great dish to make with leftover roast chicken or turkey. Sweet potatoes are a colourful addition to the potatoes traditionally used, and sweetcorn adds a delightful texture. The hash needs only a crisp salad and crusty bread to make a delicious meal.

**Serves 4**

300 g (10½ oz) potatoes, peeled

500 g (1 lb 2 oz) orange-fleshed sweet potatoes, peeled

225 g (8 oz) leeks, sliced

2 tbsp sunflower oil

225 g (8 oz) cooked chicken meat, without skin, diced

170 g (6 oz) frozen sweetcorn, thawed with boiling water and drained

8 sun-dried tomatoes packed in oil, drained and chopped

1 tsp paprika

salt

**Yogurt-garlic sauce**

150 g (5½ oz) plain low-fat yogurt

1 small garlic clove, crushed

½ tsp paprika

Preparation time: 10–15 minutes

Cooking time: 10–12 minutes

**1** Cut the potatoes and sweet potatoes into small bite-sized chunks. Drop into a pan of boiling water, bring back to the boil and boil for 2 minutes. Add the leeks and cook for a further 1 minute. Drain well.

**2** Heat the oil in a large non-stick frying pan and add the leeks and potatoes. Cook over a moderate heat, stirring frequently, for 3–4 minutes or until beginning to brown.

**3** Add the chicken, sweetcorn, sun-dried tomatoes, paprika and salt to taste, and mix thoroughly. Continue cooking for 3–5 minutes, pressing down well to make a cake in the pan, and turning it over in chunks, until brown and crispy on both sides.

**4** For the sauce, put the yogurt, garlic and paprika in a bowl and stir to mix. Serve portions of hash topped with the yogurt sauce.

**Some more ideas**

● Use 1 can sweetcorn, packed without sugar, about 200 g, well drained, instead of the frozen sweetcorn.

● To make a fruity, spicy chicken or turkey hash, chop 1 onion, 1 red pepper and 1 red-skinned dessert apple, and sauté together in the oil for 2 minutes. Then stir in 1 tbsp of your favourite curry spice blend and 2 tbsp sultanas or raisins. Add 550 g (1¼ lb) cooked potatoes and/or cooked sweet potatoes, cut into small bite-sized chunks, and cook over a moderate heat until beginning to brown. Mix in the cooked chicken or turkey together with 1 tbsp mango chutney, and finish cooking for 3–5 minutes, pressing into a cake and turning in chunks. Serve topped with tzatziki.

**Plus points**

● Sweet potatoes are an excellent source of beta-carotene, an antioxidant that helps to protect against heart disease and cancer. Sweet potatoes also provide good amounts of vitamin C and potassium, and contain more vitamin E than any other vegetable.

● Both potatoes and sweet potatoes are starchy carbohydrate foods, as are pasta, rice, bread and other grains. Starchy carbohydrates should make up almost half of the daily calorie intake in a healthy diet.

**Each serving provides**

kcal 460, **protein** 23 g, **fat** 18 g (of which saturated fat 3 g), **carbohydrate** 56 g (of which sugars 16 g), **fibre** 6 g

| | |
|---|---|
| ✓✓✓ | A, B$_6$, C, E |
| ✓✓ | B$_1$, folate, copper, iron, potassium |
| ✓ | B$_2$, niacin, calcium, selenium, zinc |

Poultry

# Chicken jamboree

This healthy chicken and vegetable casserole makes an easy mid-week meal. To make it even quicker, you could use supermarket washed-and-cut carrots and broccoli, ready to go from packet to pan. Mixed wild and long-grain rice goes well with the casserole.

**Serves 4**

2 tbsp extra virgin olive oil

350 g (12½ oz) skinless boneless chicken breasts (fillets), cut into small cubes

1 small onion, chopped

225 g (8 oz) button mushrooms

1 bay leaf

2 large sprigs of fresh thyme or ½ tsp dried thyme

3 large sprigs of fresh tarragon or ½ tsp dried tarragon (optional)

grated zest of 1 small lemon or ½ large lemon

150 ml (5 fl oz) dry sherry

300 ml (10 fl oz) boiling water

225 g (8 oz) baby carrots

225 g (8 oz) broccoli florets

1 tbsp cornflour

3 tbsp chopped parsley

salt and pepper

Preparation time: 10 minutes

Cooking time: about 20 minutes

1 Heat the oil in a large sauté pan with a lid or fairly deep frying pan. Add the chicken and brown the pieces over a high heat for 3 minutes, stirring constantly. Reduce the heat to moderate. Stir in the onion, mushrooms, bay leaf, thyme, tarragon if used and lemon zest. Cook for 4 minutes or until the onion and mushrooms are beginning to soften.

2 Pour in the sherry and water. Add the carrots and seasoning to taste, and stir to mix all the ingredients. Bring to the boil, then reduce the heat and cover the pan. Simmer for 5 minutes.

3 Stir in the broccoli florets. Increase the heat to bring the liquid back to a steady simmer. Cover the pan and cook for 5 minutes or until the pieces of chicken are tender and the vegetables are just cooked. Remove and discard the bay leaf, and the sprigs of thyme and tarragon, if used.

4 Blend the cornflour to a smooth paste with 2 tbsp cold water. Stir the cornflour paste into the casserole and simmer for 2 minutes, stirring constantly, until thickened and smooth. Check the seasoning, then stir in the parsley and serve.

**Plus points**

● Broccoli and related cruciferous vegetables (such as cabbage and cauliflower) contain several potent phytochemicals that help to protect against cancer. Broccoli is also an excellent source of the antioxidant vitamins C and E and beta-carotene. It provides good amounts of the B vitamins $B_6$ and niacin, and useful amounts of folate.

● This recipe uses vegetables to extend a modest amount of chicken. Served with a starchy (complex) carbohydrate, such as rice, it makes a well-balanced meal, especially if followed by fresh fruit for a vitamin boost.

---

**Each serving provides**

kcal 260, **protein** 23 g, **fat** 10 g (of which saturated fat 2 g), **carbohydrate** 11 g (of which sugars 6 g), **fibre** 4 g

| | |
|---|---|
| ✓✓ | $B_6$, C |
| ✓ | folate, niacin, selenium |

Poultry

### Some more ideas

• Semolina or fine oatmeal can be used to thicken the casserole instead of cornflour. Use 1 tbsp of either ingredient. Blend the oatmeal to a smooth paste with cold water and add as for the cornflour; sprinkle the semolina into the casserole, stirring, and continue stirring until the sauce boils and thickens.

• Small patty pan squash are good in this casserole. Trim off and discard the stalk ends from 225 g (8 oz) squash and slice them horizontally in half. Add them to the pan with the broccoli. When cooked, the patty pan should be tender but still slightly crunchy.

• For a creamy chicken and mushroom casserole, increase the quantity of button mushrooms to 340 g (12 oz) and leave out the broccoli. Simmer for 5 minutes longer in step 2. Stir in 4 tbsp single cream after thickening the casserole with the cornflour, then heat for a few more seconds.

• Ready-prepared stir-fry strips of turkey, pork or chicken are ideal for this casserole. They reduce preparation time and cook quickly.

# Sweet roasted chicken bap

Sandwiches – as a snack or light meal – are wonderfully versatile, convenient and as healthy as you want them to be. Try this sweet and spicy combination of lean chicken roasted with a honey and mustard dressing, juicy mango slices and crisp lettuce leaves.

**Serves 4**

6 tbsp wholegrain mustard

4 tsp clear honey

4 skinless boneless chicken thighs, about 85 g (3 oz) each

4 large baps, plain or wholemeal

8 small cos lettuce leaves

2 small ripe mangoes, sliced

2 spring onions, thinly sliced (optional)

salt and pepper

Preparation time: 10 minutes
Cooking time: 12–15 minutes

**Each serving provides**

kcal 365, **protein** 25 g, **fat** 9 g (of which saturated fat 2 g), **carbohydrate** 49 g (of which sugars 19 g), **fibre** 7 g

✓✓✓ C

✓✓ A, B₆, B₁₂, niacin, copper, iron, selenium, zinc

✓ B₁, B₂, E, folate, calcium, potassium

1 Preheat the oven to 180°C (350°F, gas mark 4). Mix the mustard and honey together and season to taste.

2 Enlarge the hollow left by the bone in each chicken thigh, cutting to open them out. Press to flatten them a little. Place the thighs, smooth side up, in a lightly oiled ovenproof dish or small roasting tin. Set aside about 2 tbsp of the honey and mustard mixture, and spread the remainder over the top of the chicken thighs. Roast for 12–15 minutes or until the juices run clear when a thigh is pierced with a knife.

3 Meanwhile, split open the baps and toast them. Place a lettuce leaf on the bottom half of each bap, top with the mango slices and sprinkle with the spring onions, if using. Spread the reserved honey and mustard mixture over the underside of the top halves.

4 Put the roasted chicken thighs on top of the mango and spring onions, then top with the remaining lettuce. Put the tops of the baps on and press the sandwiches gently together. Serve immediately.

**Some more ideas**

● You can roast the chicken in advance and serve it chilled, rather than hot.

● To make an open-face sandwich, place the lettuce, mango slices and chicken thighs on toasted thick slices of country-style bread.

● Use turkey breast fillets instead of chicken thighs. Because they are a denser meat they cook more quickly – roast for 10–12 minutes.

● Ring the changes with the fruit you use – try slices of fresh pineapple, peach or kiwi. If you use canned fruits, select ones canned in fruit juice rather than syrup, to keep the calorie count low.

● For a chicken and vegetable sandwich, top the roasted mustard-glazed chicken with the grated courgette, carrot and sweet onion salad, or serve with a carrot and white cabbage coleslaw.

● Wholegrain mustard adds texture to the sandwich, but if you prefer you can substitute a smooth German-style mustard.

**Plus point**

● Wholegrain mustard, which includes oil, has 10.2 g fat and 140 kcal per 100 g (3½ oz), but this is significantly less than mayonnaise, which contains a whopping 75.6 g fat and 691 kcal for the same amount.

Poultry

# Moroccan chicken with couscous

Aromatic cumin, coriander and cinnamon give these chicken breasts a Middle Eastern flavour, and serving them with chickpeas further enhances this theme. Quick-cooking couscous makes the perfect accompaniment to this colourful dish.

**Serves 4**

400 g (14 oz) skinless boneless chicken breasts (fillets)

2 tbsp extra virgin olive oil

1 large onion, finely chopped

2 garlic cloves, finely chopped

1 tsp ground cumin

1 tsp ground coriander

1 cinnamon stick

325 g (11½ oz) courgettes, halved lengthways and sliced

1 can chopped tomatoes, about 400 g

200 ml (7 fl oz) vegetable stock

250 g (8½ oz) couscous

400 ml (14 fl oz) boiling water

200 g (7 oz) sugarsnap peas

1 can chickpeas, about 410 g, drained and rinsed

10 g (¼ oz) butter

salt and pepper

chopped fresh coriander to garnish

Preparation and cooking time: 30 minutes

**Each serving provides**

kcal 500, **protein** 35 g, **fat** 15 g (of which saturated fat 4 g), **carbohydrate** 55 g (of which sugars 8 g), **fibre** 7 g

| | |
|---|---|
| ✓✓✓ | B$_6$, C |
| ✓✓ | A, B$_1$, E, niacin, copper, iron |
| ✓ | B$_2$, folate, calcium, potassium, zinc |

1 Cut the chicken on the diagonal into strips about 1 cm (½ in) thick. Heat half the oil in a wok or heavy-based frying pan. Add the chicken, onion and garlic, and cook over a moderately high heat, stirring constantly, for 2 minutes or until the chicken turns white with golden brown flecks.

2 Reduce the heat to low and add the cumin, coriander and cinnamon stick. Cook, stirring constantly, for 1 minute. Add the courgettes and stir well, then add the tomatoes with their juice and the stock. Cook for 5 minutes, stirring occasionally.

3 Meanwhile, put the couscous in a saucepan and pour over the boiling water. Add the remaining 1 tbsp oil. Stir well, cover and leave to soak, off the heat, for 5 minutes.

4 Add the sugarsnap peas and chickpeas to the chicken mixture. Cook for a further 5 minutes, stirring frequently.

5 Stir the butter into the couscous and cook over a moderate heat for 3 minutes, fluffing up with a fork to separate the grains. Pile the couscous onto a serving platter. Spoon the chicken on top and garnish with chopped coriander. Serve hot.

**Another idea**

● For a Middle Eastern prawn and bean couscous, use 400 g (14 oz) cooked peeled prawns (thawed if frozen), and replace the chickpeas with canned black-eyed beans. In step 1, cook the onion and garlic in the oil for 2 minutes. In step 2, omit the courgettes. In step 4, add the prawns and black-eyed beans, and instead of sugarsnap peas add 250 g (8½ oz) frozen peas, thawed, and 200 g (7 oz) green beans.

**Plus points**

● Couscous is low in fat and high in starchy carbohydrate. It scores low on the Glycaemic Index, which means that it breaks down slowly in the body, releasing energy gradually into the bloodstream.

● Courgettes, a type of small marrow, are naturally low in calories. They have tender, edible skins and this is where the majority of the nutrients are found. They are a good source of beta carotene, which the body converts to vitamin A, and a useful source of vitamin C and folate. Even the orangey-yellow flowers can be eaten, raw or cooked.

# Chicken and pinto bean tacos

Here, chicken in a spicy mixture is quickly cooked to make a succulent filling for crisp taco shells. Peppers and pinto or borlotti beans add to the mix, as does lettuce, spring onions and avocado. A dash of Tabasco sauce or other bottled hot sauce gives a piquant kick.

**Serves 4**

350 g (12½ oz) skinless boneless chicken breasts (fillets), cut into strips

3 garlic cloves, chopped

juice of 1 lime

¾–1 tsp Mexican seasoning mix

1 tbsp extra virgin olive oil

2 red, green or yellow peppers, seeded and thinly sliced

1 can pinto or borlotti beans, about 400 g, drained and rinsed

8 taco shells (crisp corn tortilla shells)

1 avocado

85 g (3 oz) crisp lettuce leaves, torn or shredded

3 spring onions, thinly sliced

3 tbsp fresh coriander leaves

1 tomato, diced or sliced

Tabasco or other hot sauce to taste

4 tbsp fromage frais

salt and pepper

Preparation and cooking time: 25 minutes

1 Preheat the oven to 180°C (350°F, gas mark 4). Put the chicken, garlic, lime juice and Mexican seasoning mix in a bowl and season to taste with salt and pepper. Mix well.

2 Heat the oil in a heavy non-stick frying pan or wok. Add the chicken mixture and cook for 1 minute without stirring. Add the peppers and stir-fry over a high heat for 3–5 minutes or until the chicken is lightly browned. Add the beans and heat them through, stirring occasionally.

3 Meanwhile, arrange the taco shells, open end down, on a baking tray and warm in the oven for 2–3 minutes. Peel and dice the avocado.

4 Spoon the chicken and pepper mixture into the taco shells, dividing it equally among them. Add the avocado, lettuce, spring onions, tomato, coriander and Tabasco or other hot sauce to taste. Serve at once, with the fromage frais to be spooned on top of the tacos.

**Some more ideas**

● Use 1 red or green pepper and replace the other pepper with 150 g (5½ oz) baby corn or sweetcorn kernels (frozen or canned). Add to the pan with the chicken mixture.

● For lamb and hummus wraps, trim any fat from 250 g (8½ oz) lean boneless lamb, such as leg, and slice thinly. Heat 1 tbsp extra virgin olive oil in a frying pan, add the lamb with 1 red pepper, seeded and cut into thin strips, 3 chopped garlic cloves, the juice of 1 lemon, ½ tsp ground cumin, and salt and pepper to taste, and fry for 7–10 minutes. Meanwhile, heat 4 large plain or tomato-flavoured flour tortillas in the oven or microwave, according to the packet instructions. Spread each tortilla with about 45 g (1½ oz) hummus, top with a portion of the lamb mixture and add some sliced or diced cucumber, sliced or diced tomatoes and chopped fresh mint and coriander. Sprinkle with 2–3 chopped spring onions and a little Tabasco or other hot sauce, if desired, then roll up. Serve hot.

**Each serving provides**

kcal 490, **protein** 32 g, **fat** 21 g (of which saturated fat 3 g), **carbohydrate** 45 g (of which sugars 4 g), **fibre** 3 g

| | |
|---|---|
| ✓✓✓ | B₆, C |
| ✓✓ | B₁, E, folate, niacin, copper, iron, zinc |
| ✓ | A, B₂, selenium |

**Plus points**

● Avocados are a rich source of monounsaturated fat and vitamin $B_6$ – one small avocado provides over half the daily requirement for $B_6$. They also contribute useful amounts of vitamin E and several important phytochemicals.

● Herbs, spices and mixtures such as the Mexican seasoning used in this recipe are a good way of adding flavour to food rather than using lots of salt.

Poultry

**81**

# Chicken and artichoke sauté

Chicken with artichokes is a classic flavour combination, here given a Mediterranean touch with thin slices of red pepper, black olives, thyme and a hint of lemon. Boiled rice or new potatoes are ideal accompaniments for this quick, tasty dish.

**Serves 4**

4 tbsp plain flour

1 tbsp dried thyme

8 skinless boneless chicken thighs, about 450 g (1 lb) in total

3 tbsp sunflower oil

1 garlic clove, crushed

1 can artichokes (canned in water), about 400 g, drained and halved

2 red peppers, seeded and thinly sliced

85 g (3 oz) stoned black olives, halved

4 tbsp dry white wine

125 ml (4½ fl oz) chicken stock, preferably home-made

finely grated zest of 1 lemon

salt and pepper

**To garnish**

sprigs of fresh thyme

lemon wedges

Preparation time: about 5 minutes
Cooking time: 20 minutes

**Each serving provides**

kcal 350, protein 25 g, fat 17 g (of which saturated fat 3.5 g), carbohydrate 21.5 g (of which sugars 6 g), fibre 2.5 g

| | |
|---|---|
| ✓✓✓ | A, B$_6$, B$_{12}$, C |
| ✓✓ | E, niacin, copper, iron |
| ✓ | B$_1$, B$_2$, potassium, selenium, zinc |

**1** Place the flour and dried thyme in a large polythene bag and season with salt and pepper. Add the chicken thighs to the bag, a few at a time, and shake until they are lightly and evenly coated. Remove the chicken to a plate, shaking off any excess coating. Preheat the oven to its lowest setting.

**2** Heat a large, heavy-based frying pan, preferably non-stick, over a high heat. Reduce the heat to moderate and add the oil. When the oil is hot, add the thighs, smooth side down, and sauté for about 3 minutes, moving them around occasionally to prevent them from sticking, until they are golden brown. (If the pan is not large enough to hold the thighs in a single layer, fry them in batches.)

**3** Turn the thighs over and cook for a further 8 minutes or until the juices run clear when they are pierced with a knife. Transfer the thighs to a heatproof platter lined with a double thickness of kitchen paper, then place in the oven to keep warm.

**4** Pour off any excess oil from the pan, leaving just a thin film, then add the garlic and cook for 10 seconds, stirring. Add the halved artichokes and sliced red peppers, and sauté for 3–5 minutes, stirring frequently, until the peppers are tender. Stir in the black olives halves.

**5** Add the wine and allow to bubble, stirring, until it has evaporated. Stir in the stock and lemon zest, bring to the boil and cook until reduced by about half. Season to taste.

**6** Transfer the chicken thighs to serving plates and spoon the artichoke and pepper mixture alongside. Garnish with thyme sprigs and lemon wedges, and serve.

**Plus points**

● As well as being low in calories and fat, globe artichokes provide calcium and vitamins A and C.

● Although olives have a high fat content, most of this fat is unsaturated, the type of fat believed to be the most healthy to consume.

● Investing in a good-quality non-stick frying pan makes sense if you want to keep fat consumption low. But whatever pan you use, if you heat it before you add the oil, you will not need as much because the food is less likely to stick to a hot pan.

Poultry

## Some more ideas

- You can prepare 4 skinless turkey breast fillets in the same way.
- For a colourful variation, replace the red peppers with yellow or orange peppers, the olives with 200 g (7 oz) sliced courgettes and the artichokes with 100 g (3½ oz) sliced meaty mushrooms, such as shiitake. Sauté the mushrooms with the garlic until they give off their juices, then add the peppers and courgettes and sauté for 3–5 minutes or until the courgettes are just tender but not too soft.
- Use 225 g (8 oz) asparagus tips, or chopped large asparagus spears, instead of the artichokes. Add with the red peppers.

# Chicken livers sautéed with sage

Chicken livers can be found in most supermarkets and are an extremely economical ingredient to have in the freezer. The addition of a few well-chosen flavours, like the sage and balsamic vinegar used here, can transform the livers into something rather special.

## Serves 4

8 rounds French bread
2 tbsp extra virgin olive oil
15 g (½ oz) butter
1 small red onion, finely chopped
2 garlic cloves, chopped
400 g (14 oz) chicken livers
225 g (8 oz) small chestnut or button
    mushrooms, quartered
3 tbsp balsamic vinegar
2 tbsp shredded fresh sage
salt and pepper
small sprigs of fresh sage to garnish

Preparation time: 5 minutes
Cooking time: 12–15 minutes

**1** Preheat the oven to 180°C (350°F, gas mark 4). Arrange the French bread on a baking tray. Using 1 tbsp of the oil, lightly brush the slices of bread on the top side, then bake for 10 minutes or until golden brown.

**2** Meanwhile, heat the remaining 1 tbsp of oil with the butter in a heavy-based frying pan. Add the onion and garlic, and sauté over a moderately high heat for 2–3 minutes or until softened.

**3** Add the chicken livers and mushrooms, and cook, stirring constantly, to brown on all sides. As they cook, break up any large livers into bite-sized pieces, using the side of the spatula.

**4** Add the balsamic vinegar, shredded sage and seasoning to taste. Reduce the heat a little and continue cooking for 5–10 minutes or until the livers are just cooked through.

**5** Serve the chicken livers on top of the baked French bread rounds, garnished with sprigs of fresh sage.

### Plus points

• Like all liver, chicken livers are a rich source of iron, necessary to help prevent anaemia.
• Garlic (along with leeks, onions and chives) contains allicin, which has anti-fungal and antibiotic properties. Garlic also contains other compounds which in animal studies have been shown to inactivate carcinogens and suppress the growth of tumours.

### Some more ideas

• Serve on thick slices of toast rather than French bread, or with a celeriac and potato purée.
• For a Provençal version, replace the balsamic vinegar with 4 tbsp red wine and use 1 tsp dried herbes de Provence instead of the fresh sage. Serve with rice.
• The chicken livers can be baked instead of sautéed. Put all the ingredients in an ovenproof dish (melting the butter first) and mix together. (If preparing in advance, cover and refrigerate until ready to cook.) Place in the oven preheated to 220°C (425°F, gas mark 7) and bake for 12–15 minutes.

### Each serving provides

kcal 315, **protein** 24 g, **fat** 12.5 g (of which saturated fat 4 g), **carbohydrate** 29 g (of which sugars 2 g), **fibre** 1.5 g

| | |
|---|---|
| ✓✓✓ | A, B₂, B₆, B₁₂, folate, copper, iron |
| ✓✓ | B₁, C, niacin, selenium, zinc |
| ✓ | E |

Poultry

**85**

# Greek chicken pittas

These chicken pittas are packed with tasty salad leaves and the Greek cucumber and yogurt sauce called tzatziki. They are incredibly quick and easy to prepare, so when you are next short of time, why not put together these delicious, healthy pittas.

**Serves 4**

550 g (1¼ lb) skinless boneless chicken
    breasts (fillets)

4 tbsp instant polenta

½ tsp dried onion granules

1 tsp paprika

1 tsp cumin seeds

1 tsp coarsely ground black pepper

½ tsp salt

2 tbsp extra virgin olive oil

4 pitta breads

115 g (4 oz) mixed herb salad leaves

**Tzatziki**

7.5 cm (3 in) piece cucumber, grated

100 g (3½ oz) Greek-style yogurt

100 g (3½ oz) plain low-fat yogurt

1 large garlic clove, crushed

1 tsp mint sauce

1 tbsp chopped fresh mint

Preparation time: 15 minutes

Cooking time: about 8 minutes

**Each serving provides**

kcal 555, **protein** 44 g, **fat** 13 g (of which saturated fat 3 g), **carbohydrate** 69 g (of which sugars 5 g), **fibre** 3 g

✓✓    B₁, B₂, B₆, niacin, calcium, iron,
       potassium, selenium, zinc

✓    folate, copper

1 Cut the chicken breasts into thin strips. Mix together the polenta, onion granules, paprika, cumin seeds, pepper and salt in a polythene bag. Add the chicken strips, a few at a time, and toss well to coat all over. Remove, shaking off the excess, and set aside on a plate while making the tzatziki.

2 Squeeze the grated cucumber, in handfuls, to remove excess moisture, then put into a bowl. Add the remaining ingredients and stir to mix. Set aside.

3 Preheat the grill. Heat a griddle or heavy-based frying pan and add half the oil, swirling it round the pan until lightly coated. Add half the chicken strips and cook over a high heat for 2–3 minutes or until golden brown all over and cooked through, turning once. Keep hot while cooking the remaining chicken strips, using the rest of the oil.

4 Meanwhile, warm the pitta breads under the grill for 1 minute on each side. Split down the side of each pitta to make a pocket.

5 Fill the pitta pockets with the salad leaves. Pile in the chicken strips, spoon over the tzatziki and serve.

**Plus points**

● Yogurt is a good source of calcium and, generally, low in fat. Traditional Greek-style yogurt is higher in fat than plain low-fat yogurt (1.35 g fat per level tbsp as compared to 0.12 g), but mixing the two together means you reduce the total amount of fat while retaining the creaminess that Greek yogurt gives. Look out for 'lite' Greek-style yogurt, which still has all the properties of traditional Greek yogurt with only 0.75 g fat per tbsp.

● Always serve snack foods with plenty of fresh salads and vegetables. Even a spoonful of chopped parsley will increase the iron and vitamin C content of the meal.

### Some more ideas

• Use wholemeal pitta for extra fibre.

• If you cannot find dried onion granules, use onion salt and omit the ½ tsp salt.

• For a hot Middle Eastern-style sandwich, put the whole chicken breasts between sheets of cling film and bat out with a rolling pin to a thickness of about 1 cm (½ in) all over. Lightly beat 1 egg and pour onto a plate. Put 100 g (3½ oz) fine fresh white breadcrumbs on another plate. Season each chicken escalope, then dip into the egg and coat both sides in breadcrumbs, patting them on lightly. Heat half the oil in a griddle or frying pan and add 2 of the chicken breasts. Cook for 6 minutes, turning once, until golden. Keep hot while cooking the other 2 chicken breasts. Meanwhile, finely shred 100 g (3½ oz) each white and red cabbage, and thinly slice 75 g (2½ oz) sweet white onion such as Vidalia. Toss with 2 tbsp chopped parsley and 2 tbsp lemon juice. Spoon 1 tbsp hummus into each warmed pitta pocket, add some cabbage salad and fill with the hot chicken escalopes.

# Turkey escalopes with chestnut mushrooms and Madeira

Lean and tender turkey escalopes – breast steaks pounded until thin – only need brief cooking. Simmered with chestnut mushrooms and a creamy Madeira sauce, they make a dish that is perfect for easy entertaining. Serve with basmati rice and a leafy salad.

## Serves 4

4 small skinless turkey breast steaks, about 115 g (4 oz) each

2 tbsp plain flour

1 tbsp sunflower oil

25 g (scant 1 oz) butter

1 small onion, finely chopped

250 g (8½ oz) chestnut mushrooms, sliced

4 tbsp Madeira

2 tsp wholegrain mustard

1 tbsp chopped fresh oregano or 1 tsp dried oregano

150 ml (5 fl oz) chicken or turkey stock

2 tbsp crème fraîche

salt and pepper

2 tbsp chopped parsley to garnish

Preparation time: 15 minutes
Cooking time: 15 minutes

## Each serving provides

kcal 355, **protein** 43 g, **fat** 13 g (of which saturated fat 6 g), **carbohydrate** 13 g (of which sugars 2 g), **fibre** 1.5 g

| | |
|---|---|
| ✓✓✓ | copper |
| ✓✓ | B$_6$, B$_{12}$, C, niacin, iron |
| ✓ | B$_2$, E, folate, potassium, zinc |

1 Put the turkey steaks between sheets of cling film and pound them to flatten to about 5 mm (¼ in) thickness. Mix the flour with some salt and pepper, and use to coat the escalopes, shaking off the excess.

2 Heat the oil and butter in a large frying pan. Add the turkey escalopes, in one layer, and fry for 2–3 minutes on each side. Transfer the turkey to a plate and keep warm.

3 Add the onion to the pan and soften gently for 2–3 minutes. Add the mushrooms and cook for a further 1 minute or until softened.

4 Stir in the Madeira and allow to bubble for about 2 minutes, then stir in the mustard, oregano and stock. Return the escalopes to the pan and simmer gently for 3–4 minutes.

5 Using a draining spoon, spoon the turkey and mushrooms onto a warm serving platter. Stir the crème fraîche into the sauce and warm through, then check the seasoning. Pour the sauce over the turkey, sprinkle with parsley and serve.

## Some more ideas

● Use veal escalopes or slices of pork fillet (tenderloin) in place of the turkey.

● Replace the mushrooms with 2 sliced courgettes, and use sherry instead of the Madeira.

● For a smart-occasion version, use a mixture of mushrooms, such as smoky-flavoured shiitake, subtle oyster mushrooms and whole baby button mushrooms.

## Plus points

● Turkey has even less fat than chicken. Their nutritional profiles are similar, although turkey contains slightly more vitamin B$_{12}$, niacin and zinc.

● There are 2500 varieties of mushrooms that grow around the world, though not all of them are edible. Mushrooms are low in fat and calories, with 0.5 g fat and 13 kcal in 100 g (3½ oz).

Poultry

89

# Chinese-style omelette

This is a dish you will find wherever Chinese culture flourishes. Combining fresh vegetables with bits of turkey or chicken is a great way to stretch a small amount of protein. Use a non-stick pan or a heavy, well-seasoned frying pan so that you need only a little oil.

**Serves 4**

100 g (3½ oz) minced turkey

2 tsp soy sauce

2 tbsp sunflower oil

200 g (7 oz) Chinese leaves, cut into shreds

100 g (3½ oz) bean sprouts

30 g (1 oz) frozen peas, thawed with boiling water and drained

125 g (4½ oz) smoked turkey or chicken, cut into thin slices

100 g (3½ oz) canned water chestnuts, sliced or quartered

2 spring onions, thinly sliced

2 tbsp chopped fresh coriander

6 eggs

2 garlic cloves, finely chopped

2 tsp finely chopped fresh root ginger

2 tbsp dry sherry

**To finish**

½ tsp toasted sesame oil

1½ tbsp Chinese bean sauce

1 tbsp balsamic vinegar

few drops of Chinese chilli sauce

fresh coriander leaves to garnish

Preparation time: 20 minutes

Cooking time: about 10 minutes

1 Preheat the grill to high. Mix the minced turkey with 1 tsp of the soy sauce, rubbing together with your fingers. Heat the oil in a heavy frying pan, about 26 cm (10½ in) in diameter, add the turkey and cook, breaking it up with a spoon, for 3–5 minutes or until it is lightly browned and crumbly. Add the Chinese leaves, bean sprouts, peas, smoked turkey or chicken, water chestnuts, spring onions and coriander, and stir-fry for 2–3 minutes.

2 Lightly beat the eggs with the garlic, ginger, sherry and remaining 1 tsp of soy sauce. Add to the pan, pouring the egg mixture evenly over the vegetables and turkey. Cook, stirring gently with a wooden spatula and lifting the sides of the omelette to let the uncooked egg mixture run onto the pan, until the omelette is set on the base. Slide the pan under the grill (keeping the handle away from the heat if it isn't ovenproof) and cook briefly to set the egg on top.

3 Meanwhile, mix together the sesame oil, bean sauce, balsamic vinegar and chilli sauce.

4 Cut the omelette into wedges and serve drizzled with the bean sauce mixture and garnished with coriander.

**Plus points**

● Eggs contain useful amounts of protein, which is essential for good health and well-being, plus vitamins A, $B_2$, $B_{12}$, E and niacin.

● Frozen vegetables often contain more vitamin C than fresh vegetables. For example, frozen peas retain 60–70% of their vitamin C content after freezing and maintain this level throughout storage.

● Chinese leaves are a good source of B vitamins, particularly folate, and of vitamin C.

**Each serving provides**

kcal 300, **protein** 28 g, **fat** 18 g (of which saturated fat 4 g), **carbohydrate** 5 g (of which sugars 3 g), **fibre** 1.5 g

| | |
|---|---|
| ✓✓✓ | $B_{12}$, folate |
| ✓✓ | A, $B_2$, $B_6$, C, E, iron, zinc |
| ✓ | $B_1$, niacin, calcium, copper, potassium, selenium |

## Another idea

● For rolled Chinese omelettes filled with turkey meatballs, use 150 g (5½ oz) minced turkey mixed with 1½ tsp soy sauce; roll into 20 tiny meatballs. Brown lightly for 5–6 minutes, then remove from the pan with a draining spoon.

Stir-fry all the vegetables in the frying pan (omit the smoked turkey or chicken). Heat 1 tsp sunflower oil in an 18 cm (7 in) omelette pan and pour in one-quarter of the egg mixture. Sprinkle one-quarter of the turkey meatballs and stir-fried vegetables over the top, then roll

up as the egg mixture cooks and sets. The egg will tend to fall apart as the filling is heavy and the egg delicate, but just turn it, with the help of a palette knife. Make 4 omelettes in all. Serve with the dipping sauce, garnished with a sprinkling of chopped fresh coriander.

Poultry

# Polenta with turkey and wild mushroom sauce

This flavoursome dish combines leftover turkey or chicken, with lots of tasty mushrooms and a herby soft polenta. The sauce is very quick to make and can be served in many other ways, such as over plain boiled or steamed rice or to stuff baked potatoes.

**Serves 4**

15 g (½ oz) butter

1 tbsp extra virgin olive oil

115 g (4 oz) shallots or onion, finely chopped

1 garlic clove, crushed (optional)

300 g (10½ oz) chestnut mushrooms, sliced

170 g (6 oz) mixed wild mushrooms, pulled into pieces or sliced

3 tbsp dry sherry

1 tbsp tomato purée

200 g (7 oz) cooked turkey meat, without skin, cut into chunks

4 tbsp single cream

salt and pepper

sprigs of fresh flat-leaf parsley to garnish

**Herby polenta**

1 litre (1¾ pints) chicken stock, preferably home-made, or vegetable stock

200 g (7 oz) instant polenta

3 tbsp finely chopped fresh flat-leaf parsley

Preparation time: 10 minutes
Cooking time: 15 minutes

1 Heat the butter and oil in a large frying pan, add the shallots or onion and garlic, if used, and cook over a moderate heat for 2 minutes or until softened but not brown.

2 Add all the mushrooms to the pan and cook, stirring frequently, for 3–4 minutes or until just softening and the juices are beginning to run.

3 Add the sherry, tomato purée and chunks of turkey, and stir to mix well. Reduce the heat to low and leave to heat through.

4 Meanwhile, prepare the polenta. Bring the stock to the boil in a saucepan, then gradually pour in the polenta, stirring constantly. When all the polenta has been added, stir in the parsley. Reduce the heat to moderate and cook for 2 minutes, stirring, until the polenta is thick. Season to taste.

5 Add the cream to the turkey and mushroom sauce and stir to mix, then remove from the heat. Taste and add seasoning, if required.

6 Spoon the polenta to one side of 4 warmed plates and serve the sauce alongside. Garnish with parsley sprigs.

**Some more ideas**

● Enrich the sauce with Greek-style yogurt instead of cream.

● Make a simpler, everyday version of the sauce using 450 g (1 lb) button mushrooms. Omit the sherry and flavour instead with 2 tsp Worcestershire sauce. This is particularly good with baked potatoes.

● For a very special flavour, replace the sherry and tomato purée with a few drops of truffle oil or truffle paste. Serve with rice – wild rice or red Carmargue rice are ideal.

**Plus points**

● Mushrooms are low in fat and calories – 0.5 g fat and 13 kcal in 100 g (3½ oz).

● Polenta is a good gluten-free source of starchy carbohydrate.

**Each serving provides**

kcal 380, **protein** 23 g, **fat** 12.5 g (of which saturated fat 5 g), **carbohydrate** 41 g (of which sugars 3 g), **fibre** 3 g

| | |
|---|---|
| ✓✓✓ | B$_{12}$, copper |
| ✓✓ | B$_2$, B$_6$, C, folate, niacin, iron |
| ✓ | A, B$_1$, potassium, selenium, zinc |

Poultry

# Braised duck with crunchy Oriental salad

Braising duck breasts in red wine with garlic and ginger, plus a little redcurrant jelly for sweetness, produces moist, delicious meat. The duck is cut into strips and served on a colourful bed of raw vegetables and fruit. Rice cakes make an interesting accompaniment.

## Serves 4

3 boneless duck breasts, about 525 g
 (1 lb 3 oz) in total
120 ml (4 fl oz) red wine
1 tbsp redcurrant jelly
1 tsp bottled chopped garlic in oil, drained
1 tsp bottled chopped root ginger in oil,
 drained
2 tbsp extra virgin olive oil
2 tsp balsamic or sherry vinegar
2 oranges
225 g (8 oz) red cabbage, finely shredded
¼ head of Chinese leaves, shredded
150 g (5½ oz) beansprouts
85 g (3 oz) watercress
1 can water chestnuts, about 220 g, drained
 and sliced
salt and pepper

Preparation and cooking time: 30 minutes

### Each serving provides

kcal 334, **protein** 31 g, **fat** 12 g (of which saturated fat 3 g), **carbohydrate** 20 g (of which sugars 16 g), **fibre** 4 g

| | |
|---|---|
| ✓✓✓ | B₆, B₁₂, C |
| ✓✓ | B₁, B₂, folate, niacin, copper, iron, potassium, zinc |
| ✓ | A, calcium |

$\checkmark\checkmark\checkmark$ B$_6$, B$_{12}$, C

$\checkmark\checkmark$ B$_1$, B$_2$, folate, niacin, copper, iron, potassium, zinc

$\checkmark$ A, calcium

**1** Preheat the oven to 220ºC (425ºF, gas mark 7). Remove all the skin and fat from the duck breasts. Place them in an ovenproof dish, pour over the wine and add the redcurrant jelly, garlic and ginger. Place the dish in the oven and cook the duck for 20–25 minutes or until tender.

**2** Meanwhile, mix together the oil, vinegar and salt and pepper to taste in a large salad bowl. Cut the peel and pith from the oranges with a sharp knife and, holding each orange over the bowl to catch the juice, cut between the membrane to release the segments. Add them to the bowl. Add the red cabbage, Chinese leaves, beansprouts, watercress (reserving a few sprigs for garnishing) and water chestnuts. Toss well to coat everything with the dressing.

**3** Remove the duck from the oven and transfer it to a warm plate. Pour the cooking liquid into a saucepan. Boil the liquid rapidly for 1–2 minutes to reduce slightly, while cutting the duck diagonally across the grain into neat slices. Pour the wine sauce over the salad and toss together. Pile the slices of duck on top, garnish with the reserved sprigs of watercress and serve.

### Plus points

• All types of cabbage are rich in a range of vitamins, minerals and cancer-fighting phytochemicals.

• Duck is higher in fat than other poultry; however, removing the skin and all visible fat reduces the fat content considerably. The meat is rich in minerals, providing iron and zinc, as well as B vitamins.

• This salad contains a wide selection of different vegetables served raw, which preserves their vitamin value.

• Red wine is a rich source of flavonols, which are powerful antioxidants.

Poultry

## Some more ideas

• If fresh redcurrants are available, add a handful to the salad for extra vitamins and flavour.

• For a sesame roast pork salad, use 450 g (1 lb) pork fillet (tenderloin). Mix together 1 tbsp groundnut oil, 2 tbsp hoisin sauce and 1 tsp five-spice powder, and spoon the mixture over the pork. Sprinkle with 1 tsp sesame seeds. Roast in a preheated 180ºC (350ºF, gas mark 4) oven for 20–25 minutes. Make the salad using 1 cos lettuce, shredded, 1 orange pepper, seeded and chopped, 125 g (4½ oz) sliced mushrooms, 125 g (4½ oz) mange-tout, and the sliced water chestnuts. Toss the salad with 1 tbsp each olive oil and toasted sesame oil. Serve with the sliced pork on top.

• Other vegetables that could be added to the salad are lightly cooked baby corn, sliced raw courgettes or steamed asparagus spears.

• Sprinkle the salad with toasted cashew nuts.

# Meat

The succulent textures and tastes of pork, beef, and lamb lend themselves well to all sorts of flavours and seasonings. There are really no limits to the fast and tasty dishes you can create. Take your pick from tempting dishes such as Seared pork with kumquats, Aromatic beef curry, Hot harissa lamb in pitta pouches, and so much more.

# Hoisin beef stir-fry

For a quick supper, try this colourful stir-fry of strips of tender steak with fresh ginger, mushrooms, red peppers and crisp mange-tout, served on egg noodles. Hoisin sauce, a sweet Chinese sauce made from soya and red beans, gives the stir-fry a rich flavour.

### Serves 2

2 sheets medium Chinese egg noodles, about 170 g (6 oz) in total

1 tbsp sunflower oil

2 large garlic cloves, cut into shreds

1 tsp grated fresh root ginger

1 large red pepper, seeded and thinly sliced

125 g (4½ oz) baby button mushrooms, halved

1 sirloin steak, about 200 g (7 oz), trimmed of fat and cut into thin strips

85 g (3 oz) mange-tout, halved lengthways

4 spring onions, cut into chunky lengths

3 tbsp hoisin sauce

1 tbsp light soy sauce

1 tsp toasted sesame oil (optional)

shredded spring onion to garnish

Preparation time: 15 minutes
Cooking time: 6 minutes

1 Put the noodles in a bowl, cover with boiling water and leave to soak for 5 minutes, or according to the packet instructions.

2 Meanwhile, heat the sunflower oil in a wok or large frying pan, add the garlic and ginger, and cook very briefly to release their flavour. Toss in the red pepper and mushrooms, then stir-fry over a high heat for 2–3 minutes or until starting to soften.

3 Add the strips of steak, mange-tout and spring onions, and stir-fry for a further 1–2 minutes or until the meat just turns from pink to brown.

4 Mix in the hoisin and soy sauces and stir well until bubbling, then drizzle in the sesame oil, if using. Drain the noodles. Serve the stir-fry on the noodles, garnished with shredded spring onion.

### Some more ideas

● Use skinless boneless chicken breasts (fillets) or pork fillet (tenderloin) instead of steak.

● To make turkey pan-fry with fresh basil and chilli, use 200 g (7 oz) skinless turkey breast steaks, cut into thin strips. Mix together 2 tbsp fish sauce, 2 tbsp light soy sauce, 1 tsp cornflour and 2 tsp light soft brown sugar. Instead of ginger, stir-fry a fresh red chilli, seeded and sliced, with the garlic. Add the turkey with the mange-tout and spring onions and stir-fry for about 4 minutes. Add 1 tsp ground coriander and stir well, then pour in the fish sauce mixture and stir until lightly thickened. Toss in 2 tbsp shredded fresh basil, then serve, with the noodles or jasmine rice.

### Plus points

● Beef has received a great deal of bad press in recent years. However, it has nutritional benefits that should not be overlooked: in common with other red meats, beef is an excellent source of zinc and a good source of iron. The iron in meat is much more easily absorbed by the body than iron from vegetable sources.

● As a result of modern breeding techniques beef is now much leaner than it used to be – the leanest cuts contain less than 3% fat.

● Red peppers offer an impressive arsenal of disease-fighting chemicals. In addition to vitamin C and beta-carotene, they also contain two other important phytochemicals, lutein and zeaxanthin. Studies suggest that these can help to protect against the eye disease, age-related macular degeneration (AMD), which affects 20% of people over the age of 65 and is the leading cause of blindness in the Western world.

### Each serving provides

kcal 620, protein 38 g, fat 20 g (of which saturated fat 5 g), carbohydrate 76 g (of which sugars 11 g), fibre 6 g

| | |
|---|---|
| ✓✓✓ | A, B$_6$, B$_{12}$, C, copper, iron, zinc |
| ✓✓ | B$_1$, B$_2$, E, folate, niacin, potassium |
| ✓ | calcium, selenium |

Meat

# Steak sandwich

This bumper sandwich is made with half-size ciabatta loaves baked until crusty, then split and packed with quick-fried steak and healthy salad. If you just need a fast dish for one, scale the recipe down and use one half-size ciabatta loaf and 85 g (3 oz) steak.

**Serves 4**

4 ready-to-bake half ciabatta loaves, about 150 g (5½ oz) each
12 thin slices flash-fry or sandwich steak, about 340 g (12 oz) in total
2 tsp extra virgin olive oil
3 tbsp black olive paste (tapenade)
4 tomatoes, about 340 g (12 oz) in total, sliced
45 g (1½ oz) rocket leaves
juice of ½ lemon
salt and pepper

Preparation and cooking time: about 20 minutes

**Each serving provides**
kcal 500, **protein** 31 g, **fat** 13 g (of which saturated fat 4 g), **carbohydrate** 66 g (of which sugars 4 g), **fibre** 4 g

| | |
|---|---|
| ✓✓✓ | B₁, B₆, B₁₂, E, niacin |
| ✓✓ | C, iron, zinc |
| ✓ | A, B₂, folate |

Meat

1 Preheat the oven to 200°C (400°F, gas mark 6). Bake the ciabatta for 8–10 minutes or according to the packet instructions. Remove the bread from the oven and keep warm.

2 Heat a ridged cast-iron grill pan or non-stick frying pan until hot. Season the steak with salt and pepper to taste. Brush the pan with the oil, then add the steak slices, in batches if necessary, and cook for 30 seconds on each side for rare, 1 minute on each side for medium to well-done.

3 Quickly split each loaf in half lengthways. Spread the bottom halves with the olive paste. Cover with sliced tomatoes and top with the steak.

4 Toss the rocket leaves with the lemon juice. Pile on top of the steak, then drizzle the pan juices over and top with the remaining bread halves. Serve immediately, with more rocket and sliced tomatoes.

**Some more ideas**
• For a slightly different toasted sandwich, fry 2 thinly sliced red onions in 1 tbsp extra virgin olive oil for 5 minutes or until softened and just browned. Lift out of the pan with a draining spoon and set aside. Fry the steak. Split and toast 4 baguettines (short French sticks). Mix 2 tsp sun-dried tomato paste with 2 tbsp mayonnaise and spread over the bottom halves. Top with 55 g (2 oz) mixed salad leaves or watercress tossed with lemon juice and salt and pepper to taste, then add the steak. Drizzle with the pan juices and top with the remaining toasted bread halves.
• Sliced and toasted focaccia, walnut bread or multigrain bread also make delicious sandwiches, as does toasted pitta bread or warmed flat Arab bread or flour tortillas (which are ideal to wrap around a filling).
• Well-trimmed lean sirloin steaks can be used instead of thin steak slices. The steaks can be left whole or sliced diagonally.
• Add extra flavour by frying the steak in a herb-flavoured oil or by mixing herbs with the rocket. Try torn fresh basil leaves or chopped fresh marjoram.

**Plus points**
• Rocket, with its peppery flavour, is rich in iron, crucial for the formation of haemoglobin to transport oxygen around the body. It also supplies some carotenoids, which can help to neutralise free radicals.
• Beef is now far leaner than it used to be, and a well-trimmed lean cut such as rump steak contains only 4.1% fat.

# Bolognese beef pot

Lemon and fennel bring wonderfully fresh flavours to familiar braised minced beef in this simple, Italian-inspired dish. Serve with a crispy leafy salad plus plenty of bread or rolls to mop up the deliciously tangy tomato sauce.

## Serves 4

340 g (12 oz) extra lean minced beef

1 onion, chopped

2 garlic cloves, crushed

600 g (1 lb 5 oz) potatoes, scrubbed and finely diced

2 cans chopped tomatoes, about 400 g each

150 ml (5 fl oz) chicken stock, bought chilled or made from a cube

finely shredded zest and juice of 1 lemon

1 tbsp soft light brown sugar

1 bulb of fennel, thinly sliced

100 g (3½ oz) frozen green beans

salt and pepper

**To garnish**

chopped leaves reserved from the fennel bulb

chopped fresh flat-leaf parsley

Preparation time: 10 minutes

Cooking time: 20 minutes

**1** Place the minced beef, onion and garlic in a large saucepan and cook over a moderate heat for 5 minutes, stirring frequently, until the mince is broken up and evenly browned.

**2** Stir in the potatoes, tomatoes with their juice, stock, half the lemon zest, the sugar and a little seasoning. Bring to the boil, then reduce the heat and cover the pan. Simmer the mince and vegetable mixture for 10 minutes, stirring once or twice to ensure that the potatoes cook evenly.

**3** Stir in the fennel, frozen beans and lemon juice. Cover the pan again and simmer for a further 5 minutes or until the potatoes are tender and the fennel and beans are lightly cooked, but still crisp.

**4** Taste and adjust the seasoning, if necessary, then spoon the mixture into serving bowls. Garnish with the remaining lemon zest, the chopped fennel leaves and flat-leaf parsley.

### Some more ideas

• Use minced turkey, chicken, pork or lamb instead of beef.

• Carrots and canned beans can be used instead of potatoes. Add 1 can cannellini or black-eyed beans, about 400 g, drained and rinsed, and 250 g (8½ oz) finely diced carrots.

• If serving this dish to young children, do not add the lemon juice. Instead, serve with lemon wedges so the juice can be added to taste.

• A green salad tossed with thinly sliced red onion, a handful of fresh basil, a few black olives and a lemon and olive oil dressing tastes excellent with this dish, providing contrasting texture as well as flavour.

### Plus points

• Extra lean minced beef contains 9.6 g fat per 100 g (3½ oz). Provided you use a heavy-based or good-quality non-stick pan, there is no need to add any fat when browning minced meat.

• Tomatoes are a rich source of vitamin C – fresh raw tomatoes contain 17 mg per 100 g (3½ oz) and canned tomatoes about 12 mg.

• Scrubbing potatoes rather than peeling them retains vitamins and minerals found just beneath the skin. The skin also provides valuable fibre.

• Frozen green beans are convenient and versatile for everyday dishes. They are a useful source of fibre and a good source of folate, which is essential for a healthy pregnancy. Folate may also contribute to protection against heart disease.

### Each serving provides

kcal 300, **protein** 26 g, **fat** 5 g (of which saturated fat 2 g), **carbohydrate** 40 g (of which sugars 14 g), **fibre** 5 g

| | |
|---|---|
| ✓✓✓ | B₆, B₁₂, C |
| ✓✓ | folate, iron |
| ✓ | B₁, niacin, potassium, selenium |

Meat

# Aromatic beef curry

This will satisfy even the most demanding curry addict. Tender sirloin steak is quickly cooked with lots of spices, tomatoes, mushrooms and spinach, with yogurt added to give a luxurious feel. Served with cardamom-spiced rice, it makes a healthy and nutritious meal.

## Serves 4

1 tbsp sunflower oil

1 large onion, thinly sliced

150 g (5½ oz) button mushrooms, sliced

400 g (14 oz) sirloin steak, trimmed of fat and cut into thin strips

1½ tsp bottled chopped root ginger in oil, drained

2 garlic cloves, crushed

½ tsp crushed dried chillies

2 tsp ground coriander

¼ tsp ground cardamom

½ tsp turmeric

¼ tsp grated nutmeg

1 can chopped tomatoes, about 400 g

1 tsp cornflour mixed with 1 tbsp water

300 g (10½ oz) plain whole-milk yogurt

1 tbsp clear honey

125 g (4½ oz) young spinach leaves

juice of ½ lime

2 tbsp chopped fresh coriander, plus extra leaves to garnish

### Cardamom rice

340 g (12 oz) basmati rice, well rinsed

1 cinnamon stick

8 whole green cardamom pods, cracked

juice of ½ lemon

salt

Preparation time: 10 minutes

Cooking time: 20 minutes

1 Heat the oil in a large saucepan and add the onion and mushrooms. Cook over a high heat for 2 minutes or until the onion slices begin to colour.

2 Add the beef together with the ginger, garlic, chillies, ground coriander, cardamom, turmeric and nutmeg. Cook for 2 minutes, stirring well, then add the tomatoes with their juice and the cornflour mixture. Bring to the boil, stirring. Stir in the yogurt and honey. Bring back to the boil, then reduce the heat, cover and simmer gently for 20 minutes.

3 Meanwhile, prepare the cardamom rice. Put 450 ml (15 fl oz) cold water in a saucepan and bring to the boil. Add the rice, cinnamon stick and cardamom pods. Bring back to the boil, then cover tightly and cook for 10 minutes or until the rice is tender. Drain off any excess water and return the rice to the saucepan. Stir in the lemon juice and keep covered until the curry is ready to serve.

4 Stir the spinach, lime juice and chopped coriander into the curry and allow the leaves to wilt down into the sauce. To serve, spoon the curry over the rice and garnish with fresh coriander leaves.

## Plus points

- Cardamom is believed to be helpful for digestive problems, such as indigestion, flatulence and stomach cramps.
- Mushrooms are low in fat and calories and provide useful amounts of the B vitamins niacin, $B_6$ and folate. They are also a good source of copper.
- Along with its many other nutritional benefits, beef provides vitamins from the B group and is a useful source of vitamin D, which is found in relatively few foods.

### Each serving provides

kcal 590, protein 36 g, fat 11 g (of which saturated fat 4 g), carbohydrate 86 g (of which sugars 16 g), fibre 2 g

| | |
|---|---|
| ✓✓✓ | iron, zinc |
| ✓✓ | A, $B_6$, $B_{12}$, C, calcium, copper, potassium |
| ✓ | $B_1$, $B_2$, E, folate, selenium |

Meat

## Some more ideas

- If you like a hot curry, add a halved fresh red chilli to the sauce towards the end of the cooking time. The chilli can be left in the sauce or discarded before serving.
- Make a Thai-style pork and potato curry. Soften the onion and garlic in the oil with 200 g (7 oz) new potatoes, scrubbed and cut into small cubes, for 5 minutes. Stir in 300 g (10½ oz) pork fillet (tenderloin), thinly sliced, and 2 tbsp Thai red curry paste. Cook for 2 minutes or until browned. Add the canned chopped tomatoes, 150 ml (5 fl oz) vegetable stock and 100 g (3½ oz) ready-to-eat dried apricots, chopped. Bring to the boil, then cover and simmer for 20 minutes or until the pork is tender. Mix ½ tsp cornflour with 1 tbsp cold water and stir into the curry with 150 g (5½ oz) plain whole-milk yogurt, 1 tsp caster sugar and the spinach. Cook until the leaves wilt down into the sauce, then serve on plain rice.

Meat

# Japanese beef with soba noodles

Here strips of steak are coated in an intensely flavoured mixture, then stir-fried with vegetables and noodles to make an all-in-one dish. The Japanese ingredients are available from large supermarkets, health food shops and Oriental food stores.

**Serves 4**

5 tbsp dark soy sauce

2 garlic cloves, crushed

1 tbsp cornflour

1 tsp wasabi paste (Japanese horseradish)

450 g (1 lb) lean sirloin steak, trimmed of fat and cut into strips

300 g (10½ oz) soba (Japanese buckwheat noodles)

2 tbsp sunflower oil

1 large red pepper, seeded and thinly sliced

1 bunch of spring onions, sliced diagonally into 5 cm (2 in) lengths

125 g (4½ oz) shiitake mushrooms, sliced

750 ml (1¼ pints) dashi stock, made with dashi powder

1 sheet nori (Japanese seaweed), cut into thin strips

15 g (½ oz) fresh coriander, chopped

Preparation and cooking time: 30 minutes

**Each serving provides**

kcal 534, **protein** 36 g, **fat** 11 g (of which saturated fat 3 g), **carbohydrate** 70 g (of which sugars 4 g), **fibre** 5 g

| | |
|---|---|
| ✓✓✓ | B₁, B₂, B₆, B₁₂, C, E, niacin, zinc |
| ✓✓ | folate, copper, potassium |
| ✓ | iron, magnesium, selenium |

1 Mix together 3 tbsp of the soy sauce, the garlic, cornflour and wasabi in a medium-sized bowl. Add the beef and stir until well coated. Set aside.

2 Bring a saucepan of water to the boil, add the noodles and cook for 5 minutes or according to the packet instructions.

3 Meanwhile, heat a wok or heavy-based frying pan until really hot, then add half of the oil and swirl to coat the wok. Toss in the red pepper, spring onions and mushrooms and stir-fry for 4 minutes or until softened. Remove from the wok with a draining spoon. Drain the noodles well and set aside.

4 Heat the remaining oil in the wok, then add the beef and stir-fry for about 4 minutes or until just tender. Remove with the draining spoon.

5 Pour the stock and remaining 2 tbsp soy sauce into the wok and add the noodles and vegetables with the nori and coriander. Toss well, then add the beef and toss again. Pile the noodles, vegetables and beef into bowls and spoon over the broth. Serve immediately.

**Some more ideas**

● Beef stock, preferably home-made, can be used instead of dashi stock.

● For a teriyaki pan-fry, omit the wasabi and replace with 1 tsp finely grated fresh root ginger and 1 tbsp dry sherry.

● For a spicier flavour, stir-fry 1 seeded and finely chopped fresh red chilli with the vegetables.

● In place of the mushrooms, use 100 g (3½ oz) each baby leaf spinach and bean sprouts, adding them at the end of cooking.

**Plus points**

● Nori is a good source of iodine, essential for the healthy function of the thyroid gland. It is also a good source of vitamin B₁₂, being one of the few plant sources of this vitamin.

● Garlic and spring onions can help to lower high blood pressure and reduce cholesterol levels by increasing levels of high-density lipoproteins, which carry cholesterol away from body tissues and artery walls. These points in turn help to prevent coronary heart disease, heart attacks and strokes.

Meat

# Calf's liver with sherry sauce

Calf's liver is more expensive than other livers, but has the most delicate flavour. It only needs to be lightly cooked – overcooking will make it tough. Adding cranberry sauce and fresh thyme to the sauce gives a fresh flavour to the classic combination of liver and sherry.

**Serves 4**

400 g (14 oz) sliced calf's liver

2 tbsp plain flour

400 g (14 oz) pappardelle or other wide flat noodles

1 tbsp sunflower oil

15 g (½ oz) butter

6 tbsp dry sherry

300 ml (10 fl oz) beef stock

2 tbsp cranberry sauce

2 tbsp tomato purée

½ tbsp chopped fresh thyme

75 g (2½ oz) watercress, roughly chopped

salt and pepper

Preparation and cooking time: about 20 minutes

1 Place the liver on a plate, pat dry with kitchen paper and snip off any gristly pieces with scissors. Mix the flour with some salt and pepper on another plate. Dip the liver in the seasoned flour until coated on both sides. Shake off the excess flour.

2 Cook the pasta in boiling water for 10–12 minutes, or according to the packet instructions, until al dente.

3 Meanwhile, heat the oil and butter in a non-stick frying pan and gently fry the liver over a moderate heat for 3–4 minutes, turning once. Transfer the liver to a plate and keep warm.

4 Add the sherry to the pan and allow to bubble for 1 minute or until reduced to half the quantity. Stir in the stock, cranberry sauce, tomato purée and thyme, and add salt and pepper to taste. Reduce the heat and cook for 4–5 minutes. Return the liver to the pan and heat through gently for 1–2 minutes.

5 Drain the pasta and mix with the watercress. Serve with the liver.

**Some more ideas**

• Use thinly sliced lamb's liver, and redcurrant jelly in place of the cranberry sauce. This is delicious with garlicky beans: drain and rinse a can of haricot beans, about 410 g, and warm through gently with 1 tbsp extra virgin olive oil, 1 crushed garlic clove and lots of chopped parsley.

• Instead of pasta, serve the liver with mashed potatoes, stirring the chopped watercress into the potatoes after mashing.

**Plus points**

• Liver is an excellent source of iron, zinc, copper, vitamin A and several of the B vitamins. It also offers useful amounts of vitamin D.

• Being a starchy carbohydrate, pasta provides energy and is a very satisfying food. It scores healthily low on the Glycaemic Index, which means that it breaks down slowly into glucose and glycogen in the body, so helping to prevent between-meal hunger pangs.

**Each serving provides**

kcal 625, **protein** 34 g, **fat** 15 g (of which saturated fat 5 g), **carbohydrate** 88 g (of which sugars 6 g), **fibre** 4 g

| | |
|---|---|
| ✓✓✓ | A, $B_2$, $B_6$, $B_{12}$, niacin, copper, iron, zinc |
| ✓✓ | C, folate, selenium |
| ✓ | $B_1$, calcium |

Meat

**109**

# Greek lamb kebabs

Cubes of lamb flavoured with a mixture of garlic, lemon and fresh oregano are cooked on skewers and served with a Greek-style tomato and cabbage salad and pitta bread for a deliciously aromatic main dish.

**Serves 4**

1 tbsp extra virgin olive oil

2 large garlic cloves, crushed

juice of ½ lemon

1 tbsp chopped fresh oregano

450 g (1 lb) boneless leg of lamb, trimmed of all fat and cut into 2.5 cm (1 in) cubes

salt and pepper

**Greek-style salad**

6 tomatoes, thickly sliced

1 red onion, finely chopped

1 baby white cabbage, about 225 g (8 oz), core removed and thinly shredded

4 tbsp chopped fresh mint

¼ cucumber, halved and thinly sliced

juice of ½ lemon

1 tbsp extra virgin olive oil

**To serve**

4 pitta breads, cut into triangles

Greek-style yogurt (optional)

Preparation and cooking time: 30 minutes

---

**Each serving provides**

kcal 470, **protein** 32 g, **fat** 16 g (of which saturated fat 5 g), **carbohydrate** 52 g (of which sugars 10 g), **fibre** 5 g

| | |
|---|---|
| ✓✓✓ | B₁₂, C |
| ✓✓ | A, B₆, E, iron, zinc |
| ✓ | B₁, folate, niacin, potassium |

**Meat**

**110**

1 Preheat the grill or heat a ridged cast-iron grill pan. Put the olive oil, garlic, lemon juice and chopped oregano in a bowl and stir to mix together. Add the cubes of lamb and turn until very well coated. Thread the cubes onto 4 skewers.

2 Cook the lamb under the grill or on the grill pan for 7–8 minutes or until tender, turning frequently. Towards the end of cooking, warm the pitta bread under the grill or on the grill pan.

3 Meanwhile, make the salad. Put all the ingredients in a salad bowl and season with salt and pepper to taste. Toss together gently.

4 Serve the kebabs with the salad, pitta bread and, if required, yogurt.

**Another idea**

• To make chilli beef kebabs, use 4 beef fillet or sirloin steaks, about 400 g (14 oz) in total, cut into 2.5 cm (1 in) cubes. Mix together 1 tsp chilli powder, ¼ tsp ground cumin, 1 tbsp extra virgin olive oil, 2 large garlic cloves, crushed, the juice of ½ lime and seasoning to taste. Coat the steak cubes on all sides with the spice mixture, then thread onto 4 skewers. Cook with 1 large sliced onion under the grill or on the ridged grill pan for 4–6 minutes or until tender, turning frequently. Take the skewers from the pan and continue cooking the onion until tender. Meanwhile, to make the salad, mix 1 can red kidney beans, about 410 g, drained and rinsed, with 1 large diced avocado, the juice of 1 lime, 1½ tbsp extra virgin olive oil, ½ red onion, very finely chopped, 1 fresh green chilli, seeded and finely chopped, 300 g (10½ oz) cherry tomatoes, halved, and 15 g (½ oz) chopped fresh coriander. Season to taste and add a pinch of caster sugar. Remove the steak from the skewers and divide with the onion among 8 warmed flour tortillas. Add 1 tbsp bottled Caesar salad dressing and some of the salad to each tortilla, and roll up into wraps. Serve with the rest of the salad.

**Plus points**

• Lamb is a rich source of B vitamins, needed for a healthy nervous system. It is also a good source of zinc and iron.

• Cabbage belongs to a family of vegetables that contain a number of different phytochemicals that may help to protect against breast cancer. They are also a good source of vitamin C and among the richest vegetable sources of folate.

• Onions, along with chicory, leeks, garlic, Jerusalem artichokes, asparagus, barley and bananas, contain a type of dietary fibre called fructoligosaccharides (FOS). This is believed to stimulate the growth of friendly bacteria in the gut while inhibiting the growth of bad bacteria.

# Aromatic spiced lamb cutlets

This dish is very quick and easy to make, and the results are delicious. In addition, the ingredients in this Middle Eastern recipe offer a good range of nutrients, including lots of vitamins and minerals.

**Serves 4**

8 lamb best end of neck cutlets, about
   400 g (14 oz) in total, trimmed of fat

1 tsp cumin seeds

1 tsp coriander seeds

juice of ½ lemon

2 garlic cloves, crushed

2 tbsp extra virgin olive oil

salt and pepper

sprigs of fresh mint to garnish

**Minted yogurt sauce**

¼ cucumber

150 g (5½ oz) plain low-fat yogurt

1 garlic clove, crushed

1 tsp bottled mint sauce

1 tbsp chopped fresh mint

**Apricot and almond couscous**

280 g (10 oz) couscous

100 g (3½ oz) dried apricots, chopped

500 ml (17 fl oz) boiling vegetable stock

50 g (1¾ oz) whole blanched almonds,
   toasted

2 tbsp chopped fresh mint

2 tbsp chopped fresh coriander

juice of ½ lemon

2 tbsp extra virgin olive oil

Preparation time: 15 minutes
Cooking time: 12–14 minutes

1 Preheat the grill to high. Place the lamb cutlets in a shallow dish. Grind the cumin and coriander seeds briefly in a pestle and mortar to crack them, then mix with the lemon juice, garlic and oil, and season with salt and pepper to taste. Pour the mixture over the lamb cutlets, turn them over to coat both sides and set aside to marinate while you make the sauce.

2 Cut the cucumber in half lengthways and scoop out the seeds with a teaspoon. Grate the cucumber coarsely and drain off any excess water. Mix with the yogurt, garlic, mint sauce and fresh mint. Set aside.

3 Place the lamb cutlets on the rack in the grill pan and grill for 10–12 minutes, turning once. The cutlets will be medium-rare; if you prefer them medium to well-done, cook for 12–14 minutes.

4 Meanwhile, put the couscous and apricots in a large bowl and pour over the boiling stock. Stir well, then cover with a plate and set aside to soak for 5 minutes.

5 Stir the almonds, chopped mint and coriander, lemon juice and oil into the couscous. Spoon the couscous onto plates, top each serving with 2 lamb cutlets and put a spoonful of the sauce on the side. Garnish with sprigs of fresh mint and serve immediately.

**Plus points**

● Almonds are a source of fibre, vitamin E and several minerals. They are also high in fat, although most of it is unsaturated.

● People in Hunza, a region in northern Kashmir, are famous for their long lives – and some have put this down to eating dried apricots. Whether true or not, dried apricots are a good source of fibre and iron and a useful source of vitamin A.

● Coriander seeds help to stimulate the digestive system. In addition, both the seeds and the leaves of the fresh plant help to strengthen the urinary tract and clear up infections that occur there.

● There are over 30 varieties of mint, all containing oils that have antiseptic properties. Mint is also believed to relieve indigestion – peppermint tea made from fresh mint leaves is drunk throughout the Middle East as an aid to digestion.

**Each serving provides**

kcal 615, **protein** 39 g, **fat** 30 g (of which saturated fat 8 g), **carbohydrate** 51 g (of which sugars 15 g), **fibre** 3 g

| | |
|---|---|
| ✓✓✓ | $B_1$, $B_6$, $B_{12}$, E, niacin, iron, zinc |
| ✓✓ | $B_2$ |
| ✓ | C, folate, selenium |

## Another idea

● Trim the fat from 400 g (14 oz) lean lamb neck fillet, cut the meat across the grain into strips and toss in the marinade. Heat a ridged cast-iron grill pan or non-stick frying pan over a moderate heat until hot. Brush with a little olive oil, then cook the lamb strips in batches for 2–3 minutes or until tender, turning them often. Finely shred 170 g (6 oz) cos lettuce and mix with 1 thinly sliced red onion, 1 coarsely grated carrot and the juice of ½ lemon. Spoon into warmed pitta breads and add the lamb strips. Top with some of the yogurt and cucumber sauce, add a drizzle of hot chilli sauce if you like, and serve immediately.

Meat

# Hot harissa lamb in pitta pouches

Warm pitta bread stuffed with spicy lamb and crisp salad makes a quick and tasty light lunch. In this North African-style recipe, lean lamb is stir-fried with garlic, ginger, harissa and mint for an exciting authentic flavour.

### Serves 4

4 wholemeal pitta breads

2 tbsp extra virgin olive oil

400 g (14 oz) boneless leg of lamb or neck fillet, trimmed of fat and thinly sliced

1 large garlic clove, crushed

1 tbsp finely chopped fresh root ginger

2 tsp harissa (hot chilli sauce)

4 tbsp roughly chopped fresh mint or coriander, or to taste

4 tbsp plain low-fat yogurt

**Cucumber salad**

100 g (3½ oz) crisp green salad leaves, shredded

½ red onion, thinly sliced

7.5 cm (3 in) piece cucumber, diced

juice of ½ lemon

salt and pepper

Preparation and cooking time: 25–30 minutes

### Each serving provides

kcal 480, **protein** 28 g, **fat** 21 g (of which saturated fat 7 g), **carbohydrate** 48 g (of which sugars 6 g), **fibre** 5 g

| | |
|---|---|
| ✓✓✓ | B₁, B₆, B₁₂, E, niacin, zinc |
| ✓✓ | C, folate, iron |
| ✓ | B₂, calcium, potassium |

**Meat**

1 First prepare the salad and pitta. Combine the salad leaves, red onion and cucumber in a bowl. Sprinkle over the lemon juice, season with salt and pepper to taste and toss together. Using a sharp knife, split the pitta breads open down one side to make pouches. Set the salad and pitta aside.

2 Preheat the grill to high. Heat a wok or heavy-based frying pan until really hot, then add the oil and swirl to coat the wok. Add the lamb, garlic and ginger, and stir-fry for 4–5 minutes or until lightly browned. Add the harissa and stir-fry for a further 2 minutes. Reduce the heat to very low and keep the lamb warm.

3 Place the pitta on the rack of the grill pan and grill for 1 minute on each side or until warm. Meanwhile, increase the heat under the lamb, add the mint or coriander and toss together.

4 Divide the lamb and salad among the warmed pitta pouches, top each serving with 1 tbsp yogurt and serve immediately.

### Some more ideas

● If you can't get North African harissa, use another chilli sauce, or a few drops of Tabasco sauce. Or, if you think these may be too spicy, use 2 tsp sun-dried tomato paste instead.

● Chickpeas are a great addition to these pouches. Use only 250 g (8½ oz) lamb and add a can of chickpeas, about 400 g, drained and rinsed, with the harissa in step 2. Alternatively, for a vegetarian version, omit the lamb altogether and stir-fry the garlic and ginger with the chickpeas, then add the harissa and mint. Spread the insides of the pittas with hummus before putting in the filling.

● In place of pitta bread, wrap the lamb and salad in warmed flour tortillas or Californian flat bread. To warm these, wrap them, stacked together, in foil and heat in a 180°C (350°F, gas mark 4) oven for 4–5 minutes, or according to the packet instructions.

### Plus points

● Each 100 g (3½ oz) serving of lamb provides over 50% of the adult RNI for zinc, a mineral that is vital for normal growth, reproduction and immunity. Zinc is also involved in the release of insulin from the pancreas, which controls blood sugar levels.

● Weight for weight, wholemeal pitta bread contains more than twice as much fibre as white pitta, and also provides higher levels of B vitamins.

● Sprinkling the salad with lemon juice not only adds a fresh, zingy flavour but also boosts the vitamin C content of this dish. With the natural fat in the lamb, there is no need to use an oily dressing.

# Lamb steaks with rosemary

Quick-cooking lamb steaks are coated with a rich-flavoured sauce made with red onions, rosemary and black olives, and served with a garlicky flageolet bean mash. Serve with crusty bread and a green vegetable such as grilled courgettes or pan-wilted fresh spinach.

**Serves 4**

2 tbsp extra virgin olive oil

2 large red onions, thinly sliced

3 large garlic cloves, thinly shredded

6 sprigs of fresh rosemary, each about 2.5 cm (1 in) long, plus extra sprigs to garnish

4 lean lamb steaks, about 130 g (4¾ oz) each

1 tbsp balsamic vinegar

4 tbsp red wine

30 g (1 oz) stoned black olives, sliced

1 tsp sugar

200 ml (7 fl oz) vegetable stock

**Flageolet bean and garlic mash**

1 tbsp extra virgin olive oil

3 garlic cloves

2 cans flageolet beans, about 400 g each, drained and rinsed

5 tbsp vegetable stock

3 tbsp chopped parsley

salt and pepper

Preparation and cooking time: 30 minutes

**Each serving provides**

kcal 500, **protein** 40 g, **fat** 21 g (of which saturated fat 6 g), **carbohydrate** 38 g (of which sugars 12 g), **fibre** 12 g

| | |
|---|---|
| ✓✓✓ | B₁₂, iron, zinc |
| ✓✓ | B₁, C, niacin, calcium |
| ✓ | A, B₂, E, copper, potassium, selenium |

1 Heat the olive oil in a large frying pan, add the onions, garlic and rosemary, and cook over a moderate heat for about 10 minutes, stirring frequently, until the onions have softened and are starting to turn golden.

2 Meanwhile, make the flageolet bean and garlic mash. Heat the olive oil in a saucepan, add the peeled garlic cloves and cook over a very low heat for 4–5 minutes or until tender. Add the flageolet beans and vegetable stock, cover the pan and cook gently for 4–5 minutes to heat through. Mash until smooth, season to taste and stir in the parsley. Keep warm.

3 Push the onions to the side of the frying pan, and add the lamb steaks. Fry for 3–4 minutes on each side, depending on how well done you like your meat.

4 Lift the lamb steaks from the pan and place on warmed serving plates. Add the balsamic vinegar, wine, olives and sugar to the frying pan and cook over a high heat until the liquid has evaporated. Stir in the stock and bubble for 1 more minute, then pour the sauce over the lamb. Garnish with fresh sprigs of rosemary and serve with the flageolet bean mash.

**Some more ideas**

• This is delicious with grilled courgettes. Halve the courgettes lengthways, then brush the cut side with extra virgin olive oil and season to taste (flavour the oil with a little garlic, if liked). Grill, cut side up, for 10 minutes or until the courgettes are tender and golden.

• Use 2 tbsp shredded fresh basil instead of parsley in the mash.

• To make Italian-style pork chops with olives, sear 4 boneless pork loin chops with 2 sliced garlic cloves in 1 tbsp extra virgin olive oil for 3–4 minutes on each side. Lift the meat from the pan and keep warm. Add 4 large tomatoes, chopped, to the pan with 6 anchovy fillets, chopped, 2 tbsp extra dry white vermouth, 100 ml (3½ fl oz) vegetable stock, 30 g (1 oz) sliced black olives and ½ vegetable stock cube. Bring to the boil, stirring, and simmer for 5 minutes to make a sauce for the chops.

**Plus points**

• Red onions have been shown to contain higher levels of flavonoids (compounds that can help to protect against heart disease) than white onions.

• Parsley is a good source of vitamin C, and is rich in beta-carotene and potassium.

Meat

**117**

# Seared pork with kumquats

Here, thinly sliced pork fillet is quickly browned in a sizzling hot, ridged cast-iron grill pan, then simmered with tangy kumquats, honey, mustard, white wine and stock. It is served on a bed of puréed potato, accompanied by crisp green beans.

**Serves 4**

675 g (1½ lb) floury potatoes, peeled and cut into chunks

340 g (12 oz) green beans

1 tbsp extra virgin olive oil

400 g (14 oz) pork fillet (tenderloin), thinly sliced

1 small onion, thinly sliced

115 g (4 oz) kumquats

1 tbsp clear honey

1 tbsp Dijon mustard

150 ml (5 fl oz) dry white wine

150 ml (5 fl oz) vegetable stock

3 tbsp semi-skimmed milk

freshly grated nutmeg

salt and pepper

snipped fresh chives to garnish (optional)

Preparation and cooking time: 30 minutes

**Each serving provides**

kcal 380, **protein** 26 g, **fat** 11 g (of which saturated fat 3 g), **carbohydrate** 38 g (of which sugars 12 g), **fibre** 5 g

| | |
|---|---|
| ✓✓✓ | B$_1$, B$_6$, B$_{12}$, C |
| ✓✓ | niacin, copper, iron, potassium, zinc |
| ✓ | B$_2$, folate, calcium, selenium |

1 Cook the potatoes in a saucepan of boiling water for 15 minutes or until tender. Steam the green beans in a steamer basket or colander over the potato pan for the last 5 minutes of the cooking time.

2 Meanwhile, heat the oil in a large ridged cast-iron grill pan. Add the slices of pork in batches and fry over a very high heat for 1 minute on each side or until browned. Lift the slices out of the pan and set aside.

3 Add the onion to the pan and fry over a high heat for 3 minutes, stirring. Reduce the heat slightly, then return the pork to the pan and fry for a further 5 minutes.

4 Thinly slice the kumquats, skin and all. Add to the pan together with the honey and cook for 1 minute. Mix the mustard, wine and stock together, and pour the mixture into the pan. Season with salt and pepper to taste and simmer for 3 minutes.

5 Drain the potatoes and mash them with the milk. Season with salt, pepper and nutmeg. Spoon the mashed potato into the centre of 4 serving plates. Arrange the pork slices on top of the mash and pour over a little of the sauce. Add the kumquats and beans and pour over the remaining sauce. Garnish with chives, if using.

**Some more ideas**

● Make a potato and celeriac mash by cooking 400 g (14 oz) celeriac, cut into 2 cm (¾ in) chunks, with 450 g (1 lb) potatoes.

● Use 4 duck breasts, about 1 kg (2¼ lb) in total, instead of the pork. Remove the skin and fat from the breasts. Halve each breast crossways, then cut through the thickness of each piece to make 4 thin slices. Fry as for the pork. In step 4, add a 2.5 cm (1 in) piece fresh root ginger, finely chopped, in place of the mustard. Serve with mash – either potato and celeriac or potato and carrot or swede – and green beans or steamed pak choy.

**Plus points**

● Pork, in common with all meat, is an excellent source of zinc. It also provides useful amounts of iron and the B vitamins, particularly B$_1$, B$_6$, B$_{12}$ and niacin. Most cuts are now so lean that they have the same amount of fat as cottage cheese.

● Like all citrus fruit, kumquats are an excellent source of vitamin C. Because they are eaten with their skin they are also a useful source of fibre – weight for weight kumquats provide twice as much fibre as oranges.

Meat

# Oriental pork and cabbage rolls

Here, crunchy water chestnuts, minced pork, soy sauce, fresh ginger and five-spice powder make a flavoursome, Oriental-style filling for green cabbage leaves. Serve with steamed white rice and a simple red pepper, chicory and onion salad for a quick-and-easy meal.

**Serves 4**

500 g (1 lb 2 oz) extra-lean minced pork
1 can water chestnuts, about 220 g, drained and finely chopped
2 tsp five-spice powder
1 tbsp finely grated fresh root ginger
2 spring onions, finely chopped
2 tbsp dark soy sauce
2 garlic cloves, crushed
1 egg, beaten
8 large green cabbage leaves
450 ml (15 fl oz) hot chicken stock
2 tsp cornflour
1 tsp sweet chilli sauce, or to taste
curled strips of spring onion garnish

Preparation time: 10 minutes
Cooking time: 15 minutes

**Each serving provides**
kcal 234, **protein** 32 g, **fat** 7 g (of which saturated fat 2 g), **carbohydrate** 12 g (of which sugars 5 g), **fibre** 2 g

| ✓✓✓ | $B_1$, $B_2$, $B_6$, $B_{12}$, C, niacin |
| ✓✓ | folate, selenium, zinc |
| ✓ | A, copper, iron |

Meat

120

1 Place the pork in a bowl and add the water chestnuts, five-spice powder, ginger, spring onions, soy sauce, garlic and egg. Mix thoroughly with your hands or a fork until the ingredients are well blended, then divide into 8 equal portions.

2 Cut the tough stalk from the base of each cabbage leaf with a sharp knife. Place a portion of the pork mixture in the centre of each cabbage leaf, then wrap the leaf around the filling to enclose it.

3 Pour the stock into the bottom section of a large steamer. Arrange the cabbage rolls, join side down, in one layer in the top section. Cover and steam for 15 minutes or until the cabbage is tender and the rolls are firm when pressed. Remove the top section from the steamer and keep the cabbage rolls hot.

4 Mix the cornflour with 2 tbsp water, then stir this mixture into the stock in the bottom of the steamer. Bring to the boil and simmer, stirring constantly, until slightly thickened. Add the chilli sauce.

5 Serve the cabbage rolls with the sauce spooned over and sprinkled with curls of spring onion.

**Some more ideas**
• Instead of flavouring the pork filling with soy sauce, use 2 tbsp hoisin sauce.
• For Chinese pork balls with wilted greens and oyster sauce, shape the pork mixture into 16 balls. Place in the steamer over the pan of stock and steam for 12 minutes. Meanwhile, heat 1 tbsp sunflower oil in a wok and stir-fry 1 sliced bunch of spring onions with 200 g (7 oz) small broccoli florets and 200 g (7 oz) sugarsnap peas for 4 minutes. Add 4 tbsp water and 200 g (7 oz) pak choy separated into leaves, and stir-fry for a further 3 minutes or until all the vegetables are tender. Finally, add 4 tbsp oyster sauce, or to taste. Serve the vegetables topped with the pork balls.

**Plus points**
• Extra-lean minced pork is lower in fat than minced beef or lamb and only slightly fattier than skinless chicken breast.
• Water chestnuts provide small amounts of potassium, iron and fibre, but their big advantage is that they contain no fat and very few calories.
• Cabbage, like broccoli and cauliflower, contains flavonoids, which research has shown help to suppress cancer-causing cells. It also contains the beneficial anti-cancer antioxidants, vitamins C and E.

# Pork chops in barbecue sauce

A sweet and sour barbecue sauce is the perfect partner for simply cooked pork chops. With a fruit and pine nut pilaf and a mixed leaf salad, this makes a tempting and substantial supper.

**Serves 4**

1 tbsp sunflower oil

4 boneless pork loin chops, about 140 g (5 oz) each, trimmed of fat

100 ml (3½ fl oz) orange juice

4 tbsp clear honey

2 tbsp soy sauce

2 tbsp dry sherry

2 tbsp red wine vinegar

2 tbsp French mustard

2 tbsp tomato purée

salt and pepper

**Pine nut and raisin pilaf**

250 g (8½ oz) basmati rice

1 tbsp sunflower oil

1 onion, sliced

1 garlic clove, finely chopped

50 g (1¾ oz) pine nuts

50 g (1¾ oz) raisins

600 ml (1 pint) vegetable stock

Preparation and cooking time: 30 minutes

---

**Each serving provides**

kcal 671, **protein** 40 g, **fat** 19 g (of which saturated fat 2 g), **carbohydrate** 85 g (of which sugars 33 g), **fibre** 1 g

✓✓✓  $B_1$, $B_6$, $B_{12}$, E, zinc

✓✓  $B_2$, C, iron, magnesium, potassium, selenium

---

1 Heat the oil in a frying pan and add the chops. Fry for 5 minutes or until browned on both sides, turning them over once.

2 In a small bowl, blend together the orange juice, honey, soy sauce, sherry, vinegar, mustard and tomato purée. Pour over the chops, then leave to simmer for 15 minutes or until the chops are cooked through and tender, turning them once or twice.

3 Meanwhile, make the pilaf. Put the rice in a sieve and rinse under cold running water until the water is clear. Drain well. Heat the oil in a saucepan, add the onion and garlic and cook for 5 minutes or until softened and beginning to brown. Sprinkle in the pine nuts and raisins and cook, stirring, for 2–3 minutes or until the nuts turn golden brown.

4 Add the rice and stir well to mix. Pour in the stock and bring to the boil. Reduce the heat, cover and simmer for 10 minutes or until the rice is tender and all the stock has been absorbed. Season to taste.

5 To serve, spoon the pilaf onto warmed plates and arrange the chops in barbecue sauce alongside.

**Some more ideas**

• For a fruity sauce, omit the honey, soy sauce, vinegar and mustard and increase the orange juice to 250 ml (8½ fl oz).

• Replace the pork chops with medallions of pork fillet (tenderloin) or skinless boneless chicken breasts (fillets). The cooking time for these will be 15–20 minutes.

• Use different nuts, such as pistachios or cashews.

**Plus points**

• Rice is one of the most important staple crops, the very basis of life for millions of people worldwide. Polishing the grains to produce the familiar white varieties partially removes B vitamins; however, in this recipe, the pork more than makes up for this loss as it is an excellent source of vitamin $B_{12}$ and a good source of vitamins $B_1$ and $B_6$.

• Pine nuts are a good source of vitamin E and potassium, and they also contribute useful amounts of vitamin $B_1$, magnesium, zinc and iron.

Meat

# Spicy sausage paprikash

Here, pork sausages are cooked in a tasty sauce with lots of colourful vegetables – red onions, carrots and green peppers. The dish is finished with paprika and soured cream before serving on a bed of ribbon noodles. A fresh green salad goes well with this.

**Serves 4**

1 tbsp sunflower oil

400 g (14 oz) high-meat-content premium pork sausages

2 red onions, thinly sliced

2 garlic cloves, crushed

4 baby carrots, halved

2 green peppers, seeded and cut into 2.5 cm (1 in) dice

4 celery sticks, thinly sliced

2 tsp plain flour

325 ml (10½ fl oz) vegetable stock

¼–½ tsp crushed dried chillies

good pinch of dried marjoram

400 g (14 oz) pappardelle or other wide flat noodles

salt and pepper

**To finish**

1 tbsp paprika

2 tbsp soured cream

Preparation and cooking time: 30 minutes

**Each serving provides**

kcal 655, **protein** 27 g, **fat** 22 g (of which saturated fat 7 g), **carbohydrate** 92 g (of which sugars 11 g), **fibre** 7 g

| | |
|---|---|
| ✓✓✓ | A, C |
| ✓✓ | $B_6$, $B_{12}$, copper, iron, zinc |
| ✓ | $B_1$, $B_2$, E, folate, niacin, calcium, potassium |

**1** Heat the sunflower oil in a large, deep frying pan that has a lid, or in a flameproof casserole. Add the sausages and quickly brown on all sides over a moderately high heat. Remove the sausages from the pan with kitchen tongs and leave to cool slightly on a board. Pour off all but 1 tbsp of the fat remaining in the pan.

**2** Add the onions and garlic to the pan and stir well, then cover, reduce the heat and cook gently for 5 minutes. Add the carrots, peppers and celery and stir well to mix. Stir in the flour, then gradually mix in the stock. Bring to the boil, stirring.

**3** Cut the sausages into thick slices and return them to the pan. Stir in the crushed chillies and marjoram, and season with salt and pepper to taste. Cover and simmer gently for 15 minutes, stirring occasionally.

**4** Meanwhile, cook the pappardelle in boiling water for 10–12 minutes, or according to the packet instructions, until al dente. Drain and keep warm.

**5** Sprinkle the paprika over the sausage mixture and stir in. Taste and add more crushed chillies or seasoning, if liked. Drizzle the soured cream over the top of the sausage mixture and serve, with the noodles.

**Some more ideas**

• Replace the carrots with 200 g (7 oz) small button mushrooms.

• For chicken paprikash, use 8 skinless boneless chicken thighs, about 675 g (1½ lb) in total. Cut each thigh in half before browning, and cook for 20–25 minutes. Serve with boiled or steamed new potatoes.

• For a traditional veal paprikash, use 400 g (14 oz) diced lean boneless veal, and cook for 20–25 minutes in the sauce.

**Plus points**

• Sausages with a high lean meat content are the best healthy choice. They are a good source of protein and iron.

• Carrots are rich in beta-carotene. Cooking makes them more nutritious as the body is able to convert more of their beta-carotene into vitamin A.

• Pasta is an excellent source of starchy carbohydrate and it is low in fat. It also contains valuable vitamins, in particular the water-soluble B vitamins that we need to take in regularly.

Meat

# Five-spice pork

The simple Oriental technique of stir-frying is perfect for preparing meals in a hurry. It is also a great healthy cooking method because it uses just a small amount of oil and cooks vegetables quickly so that most of their beneficial vitamins and minerals are preserved.

### Serves 4

400 g (14 oz) pork fillet (tenderloin), trimmed of fat

250 g (8½ oz) medium Chinese egg noodles

1 tbsp sunflower oil

1 large onion, finely chopped

1 large garlic clove, crushed

1 tbsp five-spice powder

300 g (10½ oz) mange-tout or sugarsnap peas

2 large red peppers (or 1 red and 1 yellow or orange), seeded and thinly sliced

120 ml (4 fl oz) hot vegetable stock

salt and pepper

fresh coriander leaves to garnish

Preparation and cooking time: 30 minutes

1 Cut the pork fillet across into 5 mm (¼ in) slices, then cut each slice into 5 mm (¼ in) strips. Cover the meat and set aside.

2 Cook the noodles in a saucepan of boiling water for 4 minutes, or cook or soak them according to the packet instructions. Drain the noodles well and set aside.

3 While the noodles are cooking, heat a wok or a large heavy based frying pan until hot. Add the oil and swirl to coat the wok, then add the onion and garlic and stir-fry for 1 minute. Add the five-spice powder and stir-fry for another minute.

4 Add the pork strips to the wok and stir-fry for 3 minutes. Add the mange-tout or sugarsnap peas and the peppers and stir-fry for a further 2 minutes. Pour in the stock, stir well and bring to the boil.

5 Add the noodles to the wok and stir and toss for 2–3 minutes or until all the ingredients are well combined. Season to taste and serve immediately, sprinkled with coriander leaves.

### Some more ideas

● To reduce the fat content of this dish even further, use just 250 g (8½ oz) pork and add 250 g (8½ oz) firm tofu. Drain the tofu well and cut it into 2.5 cm (1 in) cubes, then add in step 5 with the mange-tout and peppers. Add 2 tbsp light soy sauce with the stock.

● For a vegetarian dish, replace the pork with 450 g (1 lb) drained and diced firm tofu and add 140 g (5 oz) broccoli florets. Add the tofu and broccoli with the mange-tout and peppers in step 5, and add 75 g (2½ oz) bean sprouts with the noodles in step 6.

### Each serving provides

kcal 467, **protein** 34 g, **fat** 13 g (of which saturated fat 3 g), **carbohydrate** 58 g (of which sugars 12 g), **fibre** 6 g

| | |
|---|---|
| ✓✓✓ | A, B$_1$, B$_6$, B$_{12}$, C, E, niacin, zinc |
| ✓✓ | B$_2$, folate, potassium |
| ✓ | calcium, iron, selenium |

### Plus points

● Peppers have a naturally waxy skin that helps to protect them against oxidisation and prevents loss of vitamin C during storage. As a result, their vitamin C content remains high even several weeks after harvesting.

● Heating the pan until hot before adding any oil not only helps to prevent ingredients sticking, it also means less oil is needed.

● Chinese egg noodles are a low-fat source of starchy carbohydrate and also offer some protein. When they are eaten with ingredients high in vitamin C, such as the peppers in this recipe, the body is able to absorb the iron they contain.

Meat

# Sausage and bean hotpot

For this supper dish, grilled sausages in a spicy tomato and bean sauce are topped with a fluffy potato and parsnip mash. Use meaty pork sausages – there are many varieties available, with different flavours. Serve with a green vegetable such as steamed broccoli.

**Serves 4**

4 good-quality, high-meat-content pork
    sausages, about 280 g (10 oz) in total

1 can chopped tomatoes, about 400 g

2 cans red kidney or borlotti beans, about
    410 g each, drained and rinsed

2 tbsp tomato chutney

2 tsp paprika

**Potato and parsnip topping**

750 g (1 lb 10 oz) potatoes, peeled and cut
    into cubes

1 large parsnip, about 170 g (6 oz), chopped

2 tbsp semi-skimmed milk

1 tbsp extra virgin olive oil

salt and pepper

Preparation and cooking time: 30 minutes

**1** Preheat the grill to moderate. Place the sausages under the grill and cook for about 15 minutes, turning regularly, until evenly browned all over and cooked through.

**2** Meanwhile, cook the potatoes and parsnip in a saucepan of boiling water for 15 minutes or until tender.

**3** At the same time, put the tomatoes with their juice, the kidney or borlotti beans, chutney and paprika in a saucepan and heat gently until bubbling.

**4** Remove the sausages from the grill (leave the grill on). Allow to cool slightly, then cut each one diagonally into 4 thick slices. Add them to the tomato and bean mixture. Pour into a flameproof dish.

**5** Drain the potatoes and parsnip, and mash with the milk and olive oil. Season with salt and pepper to taste.

**6** Spoon the mash evenly over the top of the sausage and bean mixture. Brown under the grill for 5 minutes or until golden and crisp. Serve hot.

### Another idea

● For sausage and lentil stew with couscous, grill 4 garlicky Italian pork sausages or Toulouse sausages (choose those with a high meat content). Meanwhile, pour 250 ml (8½ fl oz) boiling vegetable stock over 250 g (8½ oz) couscous and stir, then cover and leave for 5 minutes so the couscous can absorb the stock. Fluff up with a fork, then stir in the grated zest and juice of 1 lemon, 2 tbsp capers and 3 tbsp chopped fresh flat-leaf parsley. Cover and keep warm. Heat 1 can chopped tomatoes, about 400 g, with 1 can green lentils, about 410 g, drained and rinsed. Add 2 tbsp chopped fresh mint and seasoning to taste. Thickly slice each sausage into 4 and add to the tomato and lentil mixture. Spoon the sausages and sauce over the couscous. Garnish with sprigs of flat-leaf parsley and serve hot.

### Each serving provides

kcal 525, **protein** 24 g, **fat** 18 g (of which saturated fat 5.5 g), **carbohydrate** 72 g (of which sugars 17 g), **fibre** 13 g

| | |
|---|---|
| ✓✓✓ | B₁, B₆, C |
| ✓✓ | E, folate, niacin, calcium, copper, iron, potassium, zinc |
| ✓ | A, B₂, B₁₂, selenium |

**Plus points**

● Including pulses in a dish such as this allows the quantity of meat to be reduced, while maintaining a good protein content. Using a mixture of pulses and meat also reduces the amount of fat in the dish.

● Canned tomatoes are an ideal item to keep in the storecupboard, not only because they are convenient, but also because they are very nutritious. Lycopene, a valuable antioxidant contained in tomatoes, is enhanced by cooking, so canned tomatoes are a better source than fresh tomatoes.

Meat

# Three-bean and ham stir-fry

If you've never thought of using pulses in a stir-fry, here's a satisfying recipe to try. It combines 2 kinds of canned beans with fresh green beans, plus strips of ham, onions and a creamy mustard sauce. Tossed with pasta, this is a great meal produced in a single pot.

**Serves 4**

250 g (8½ oz) short-cut macaroni

170 g (6 oz) fine green beans, cut in half

2 tsp extra virgin olive oil

15 g (½ oz) unsalted butter

1 bunch large spring onions, about 300 g (10½ oz) in total, sliced

2 tbsp crème fraîche

2 tsp wholegrain mustard

grated zest of 1 lemon

225 g (8 oz) thickly sliced cooked ham or smoked pork loin, trimmed of all fat and cut into fine strips

1 can red kidney beans, about 410 g, drained and rinsed

1 can cannellini beans, about 410 g, drained and rinsed

3 tbsp chopped parsley

salt and pepper

Preparation and cooking time: 30 minutes

1 Cook the pasta in a large pan of boiling water for 10–12 minutes, or according to the packet instructions, until al dente. Add the green beans for the last 3 minutes of the cooking time. Drain well.

2 While the pasta is cooking, heat the oil and butter in a large non-stick frying pan or wok until the butter starts to sizzle. Add the spring onions and cook for 3–4 minutes over a moderate heat, turning frequently, until softened.

3 Blend together the crème fraîche, mustard and lemon zest, and add to the pan or wok. Stir in the ham or pork and the canned kidney and cannellini beans. Cook gently for 2–3 minutes, stirring frequently, until piping hot.

4 Season with salt and pepper to taste. Add the pasta and green beans, and stir to mix. Sprinkle over the parsley and serve.

**Some more ideas**

● For a vegetarian version, replace the ham or pork with a 225 g (8 oz) packet of smoked tofu, cut into 2.5 cm (1 in) cubes.

● Make a smoked turkey, apple and bean sauté. Core and thickly slice 2 dessert apples. Cook in 15 g (½ oz) butter in a non-stick frying pan over a moderate heat for 3–4 minutes, turning once, until golden on both sides and just tender. Remove and set aside. Put 1 can borlotti beans, about 410 g, and 1 can flageolet beans, about 410 g, both drained and rinsed, in the pan. Add 225 g (8 oz) thickly sliced smoked turkey, cut into fine strips, 3 tbsp apple juice and 2 tsp maple syrup. Heat through gently for 2 minutes, stirring occasionally, then return the apples to the pan together with 1 tbsp chopped fresh sage. Season to taste. Heat for a further minute. Serve with crusty French bread.

**Each serving provides**

kcal 575, **protein** 30 g, **fat** 20 g (of which saturated fat 8 g), **carbohydrate** 73 g (of which sugars 10 g), **fibre** 12 g

✓✓  A, B₁,C, folate, niacin, copper, iron, potassium, selenium, zinc

✓  B₂, B₆, calcium

**Plus points**

● Pulses such as red kidney and cannellini beans have a low GI (Glycaemic Index) factor, which means they release energy slowly into the bloodstream and so can help to control hunger and appetite.

● Like all onions, spring onions contain some vitamin C and B vitamins.

● Green beans are a good source of dietary fibre and contain valuable amounts of folate.

Meat

# Bacon and mushroom kebabs

In this dish, three favourite breakfast ingredients – bacon, mushrooms and tomatoes – are cooked on skewers with new potatoes and patty pan squash. The kebabs are served on toasted ciabatta with a refreshing citrus salad.

**Serves 4**

1–2 tbsp extra virgin olive oil

grated zest of ½ orange

4 lean back bacon rashers, rinded

12 button mushrooms, about 125 g (4½ oz) in total

2 limes, quartered

12 cherry tomatoes

6 patty pan squash, halved, or 3 small courgettes, quartered

20 small new potatoes, about 500 g (1 lb 2 oz) in total, cooked

12 slices ciabatta or baguette

**Citrus salad**

1 pink grapefruit

1 bunch of watercress, thick stalks discarded

1 head of chicory, sliced

4 Agen prunes, pitted and sliced, or ready-to-eat dried apricots

2 tbsp chopped fresh mint

Preparation time: 15 minutes

Cooking time: 7–10 minutes

**Each serving provides**

kcal 580, **protein** 24 g, **fat** 13 g (of which saturated fat 3 g), **carbohydrate** 98 g (of which sugars 15 g), **fibre** 7 g

| | |
|---|---|
| ✓✓✓ | $B_1$, $B_6$, C, folate, niacin |
| ✓✓ | calcium, copper, iron, potassium, selenium, zinc |
| ✓ | A, $B_2$, E |

1 Place the oil in a small bowl and add the orange zest. Set aside to infuse while you make the salad.

2 Peel the grapefruit, removing all the pith. Holding the grapefruit over a large bowl to catch the juice, cut the segments from between the membranes that separate them, and drop them into the bowl. Squeeze the juice from the membrane before discarding it. Add the watercress, chicory, prunes and mint, and mix well. Set the salad aside.

3 Cut each bacon rasher into thirds by cutting off the thin end, then cutting the remaining piece in half lengthways. Wrap a piece of bacon around each mushroom.

4 Thread the lime quarters, bacon-wrapped mushrooms, tomatoes, squash or courgettes and cooked potatoes onto 8 metal skewers, dividing the ingredients equally between servings (2 skewers to each serving).

5 Preheat the grill to high. Brush the kebabs lightly with the orange-flavoured oil and cook under the grill for 7–10 minutes, turning once, until the bacon is golden brown and crisp.

6 Toast the slices of ciabatta or baguette on one side. Brush the untoasted sides lightly with the remaining orange-flavoured oil, then toast until lightly browned. Place on warmed serving plates. Add a pair of kebabs to each plate, laying them across the bread slices, and spoon the salad alongside. Serve immediately.

**Some more ideas**

● Replace the toasted ciabatta with couscous or rice tossed with finely chopped parsley.

● To make a meat-free version, omit the bacon. To add a vegetarian source of protein, use cubes of tofu instead of the mushrooms, and replace the tomatoes with 1 red pepper, seeded and cut into cubes. Make a basting sauce with the juice of 1 lime, 1 tsp honey, 1 tbsp light soy sauce, a pinch of cayenne pepper or chilli powder and a pinch of garlic salt. Serve with warm pitta bread and the citrus salad.

**Plus points**

● Bacon, like other meat, provides iron. Another bonus of both pork and bacon is that they have a high vitamin $B_1$ content. This vitamin is essential for maintaining a healthy nervous system.

● These kebabs provide excellent quantities of vitamin C from the grapefruit, tomatoes and potatoes.

Meat

# Fish

Fish is, without doubt, one of the healthiest foods available, and with this great selection of fast and easy recipes you need never worry about not making the most of it. Sample tastes from around the world with Malay-style braised fish and Pan-fried swordfish steaks with Mexican salad, or experience new combinations such as Sautéed tiger prawns with feta and Anchovy and sesame-topped tuna.

# Pan-fried swordfish steaks with Mexican salad

The lively flavours of Mexico combine in this dish of spicy swordfish steaks paired with a salsa-style kidney bean salad based on the famous avocado dip, guacamole. Serve with boiled brown or white rice or, to carry through the Mexican theme, warm flour tortillas.

## Serves 4

2 tbsp extra virgin olive oil

1 garlic clove, crushed

½ tsp ground coriander

4 swordfish steaks, about 450 g (1 lb) in total

2 avocados

6 ripe plum tomatoes, chopped

1 red onion, finely chopped

1 fresh red chilli, seeded and chopped

6 tbsp chopped fresh coriander

juice of 2 limes

1 can red kidney beans, about 400 g, drained

salt and pepper

85 g (3 oz) mixed salad leaves to garnish

Preparation time: 15 minutes

Cooking time: 6–10 minutes

**1** Mix the oil with the garlic and ground coriander, and season with salt and pepper to taste. Brush this mixture over both sides of the swordfish steaks.

**2** Heat a ridged cast-iron grill pan or non-stick frying pan until hot. Fry the fish steaks for 3–5 minutes on each side or until just cooked – they should still be very slightly translucent in the centre, as swordfish becomes dry if overcooked.

**3** Meanwhile, make the salad. Peel, stone and chop the avocados, and mix with the tomatoes, onion, chilli, coriander and lime juice. Stir in the red kidney beans and season to taste.

**4** Serve the spicy swordfish steaks with the salad and a garnish of mixed salad leaves.

### Some more ideas

● To make spicy swordfish wraps, after cooking the fish, flake it into bite-sized pieces. While still hot, toss with 1 red pepper, seeded and finely shredded, and the salad, made without the beans. Add some fresh salad leaves tossed with sprigs of watercress and wrap the mixture in 8 warmed flour tortillas.

● As an alternative to swordfish, try shark steaks which are similar in appearance. They have a surprisingly soft flesh when cooked.

● Canned chickpeas make a nutty-textured alternative to red kidney beans.

### Plus points

● Swordfish is an excellent source of niacin. This B vitamin is involved in the release of energy in cells.

● Avocados are rich in vitamin E, which has important antioxidant properties.

● Red kidney beans are a good source of soluble fibre. They also contain good amounts of the B vitamins $B_1$, $B_6$ and niacin.

● Fresh coriander is prescribed by herbalists as a tonic for the stomach, and both the seeds and leaves are recommended for urinary tract problems.

### Each serving provides

kcal 460, **protein** 31 g, **fat** 26 g (of which saturated fat 5 g), **carbohydrate** 27 g (of which sugars 10 g), **fibre** 11 g

| | |
|---|---|
| ✓✓✓ | $B_1$, $B_6$, $B_{12}$, niacin, selenium |
| ✓✓ | C, E, iron, potassium |
| ✓ | A, $B_2$, folate, calcium, copper, zinc |

Fish

# Anchovy and sesame-topped tuna

Peppers, tomatoes and a touch of chilli make a zesty topping for quickly prepared tuna steaks, which are baked with a crisp topping. Tagliatelle is a good accompaniment, along with a crisp mixed salad or lightly steamed broccoli.

**Serves 4**

1½ tbsp extra virgin olive oil
1 large onion, thinly sliced
1 large red pepper, seeded and thinly sliced
1 large yellow pepper, seeded and thinly sliced
2 garlic cloves, finely chopped
1 can chopped tomatoes, about 400 g
1 tbsp tomato purée
1 bay leaf
½ tsp chilli purée
2 large tuna steaks, 2 cm (¾ in) thick, about 550 g (1¼ lb) in total

**Anchovy and sesame topping**

55 g (2 oz) fresh wholemeal breadcrumbs
1 garlic clove
4 anchovy fillets, drained
10 g (¼ oz) parsley
2 tbsp sesame seeds
2 tsp extra virgin olive oil
salt and pepper

Preparation time: 20 minutes
Cooking time: 10 minutes

---

**Each serving provides**

kcal 384, **protein** 39 g, **fat** 17 g (of which saturated fat 3 g), **carbohydrate** 21 g (of which sugars 13 g), **fibre** 5 g

| | |
|---|---|
| ✓✓✓ | A, B₁, B₆, B₁₂, C, niacin, selenium |
| ✓✓ | E, copper, iron, potassium |
| ✓ | folate, calcium, zinc |

1 Preheat the oven to 200°C (400°F, gas mark 6). Heat the oil in a frying pan or wide saucepan over a moderate heat and add the onion, peppers and garlic. Cover and cook, stirring frequently, for 3–4 minutes or until the onion has softened. Stir in the tomatoes and their juice, the tomato purée, bay leaf and chilli purée. Cover again and cook, stirring frequently, for about 7 minutes or until the peppers are just tender.

2 Meanwhile, make the topping. Combine all the ingredients in a blender or food processor and process until finely chopped. Alternatively, chop together the breadcrumbs, garlic, anchovies and parsley, put in a bowl and mix in the sesame seeds and oil with a fork until well combined.

3 Turn the pepper mixture into an ovenproof dish large enough to hold the fish in one layer. Season the tuna steaks and cut each one in half. Lay the 4 pieces in the dish and spoon over the topping to cover them evenly. Bake for 10 minutes or until the fish is just cooked. It will still be a little pink in the centre. If you prefer tuna more well done, cook for 1–2 minutes longer. Serve immediately.

**Some more ideas**

● Bake the anchovy and sesame-topped tuna on a bed of leeks and cabbage. Heat 1 tbsp extra virgin olive oil in a frying pan and add 2 large leeks, thinly sliced, and 400 g (14 oz) finely shredded young green cabbage. Sauté together until wilted, then spoon into the ovenproof dish and set the tuna on top.

● Instead of baking the tuna, griddle it and serve with 400 g (14 oz) tagliatelle, tossed with the pepper and tomato mixture. Lightly oil a ridged cast-iron grill pan and heat over a high heat. Brush the tuna lightly with olive oil and season to taste, then cook for about 3 minutes on each side. Serve immediately.

● If you're not fond of anchovies, simply omit them – the recipe will still be delicious.

**Plus points**

● Extra virgin olive oil is made from the first pressing of top grade olives from which the stones have been removed. It is green in colour, has a rich flavour and is high in monounsaturated fatty acids. These are the kinds of fat that can help to lower cholesterol levels in the blood.

● Anchovies contain calcium and phosphorus, both essential minerals for the maintenance of healthy bones and teeth. These minerals are retained in canned anchovy fillets.

Fish

# Sole goujons with tartare dip

These strips of lemon sole in breadcrumbs are baked until crisp on the outside and tender in the middle. They're served with a tangy tartare dip – perfect for any simply cooked fish dish. New potatoes and a baby plum tomato and basil salad are ideal side dishes.

**Serves 4**

450 g (1 lb) lemon sole or plaice fillets, skinned
3 tbsp plain flour
1 large egg, beaten
75 g (2½ oz) fine fresh white breadcrumbs
2 tbsp sesame seeds
1 tbsp extra virgin olive oil
salt and pepper

**Tartare dip**

3 tbsp crème fraîche
3 tbsp mayonnaise
1 tsp Dijon mustard
4 midget gherkins, finely chopped
1 tbsp bottled capers, drained and chopped
2 tbsp chopped parsley
1 tbsp lemon juice

Preparation time: 20 minutes
Cooking time: 10 minutes

1 Preheat the oven to 220°C (425°F, gas mark 7). Using scissors or a sharp knife, cut the fish fillets across into strips about 6 x 2 cm (2½ x ¾ in).

2 Season the flour and spread on a plate. Put the egg on another plate, and mix the breadcrumbs with the sesame seeds on a third plate. Toss the fish strips in the seasoned flour, shaking off any excess, then dip each strip into the egg and, finally, coat all over with the crumbs.

3 Brush a large non-stick baking sheet with the olive oil and lay the fish strips on the sheet in one layer. Bake for 5 minutes. Turn the strips over and bake for a further 5 minutes or until the goujons are crisp and pale golden.

4 Meanwhile, make the tartare dip. Stir all the ingredients together and spoon into 4 small bowls. Serve the goujons with the tartare dip.

**Some more ideas**

● For home-made fish fingers, cut 550 g (1¼ lb ) thick cod loin (skinless, boneless cod) into 12 strips that are 2.5 cm (1 in) thick and about 7.5 cm (3 in) long. Coat the strips with the seasoned flour, egg and crumbs and arrange on an oiled baking sheet in one layer. Drizzle a little olive oil over each strip and bake for 10–15 minutes or until golden and the fish flakes easily. Serve with the tartare dip.

● Make a watercress dip. Blend together 150 g (5½ oz) Greek-style yogurt, 2 tbsp mayonnaise, 45 g (1½ oz) chopped watercress, a large pinch of cayenne pepper and 1 tbsp lemon juice.

**Each serving provides**

kcal 398, **protein** 26 g, **fat** 23.5 g (of which saturated fat 6 g), **carbohydrate** 22 g (of which sugars 1.5 g), **fibre** 1.5 g

| | |
|---|---|
| ✓✓✓ | B₁, B₁₂, niacin, selenium |
| ✓✓ | E, iron |
| ✓ | B₆, calcium, copper, potassium, zinc |

**Plus points**

● Sole is a useful source of potassium, essential for the regulation of body fluids. Potassium cannot be stored in the body, so daily losses must be replaced by eating foods that provide this mineral.
● Bread is a good source of starchy carbohydrate. At least half the calories in a healthy diet should come from starchy foods.

Fish

# Seafood jambalaya

Mixed with rice and plenty of vegetables, a small amount of succulent salmon and prawns goes a long way, making this temptingly spicy, Louisiana-style dish. As an added bonus for the busy cook, it is cooked in just one pan.

**Serves 4**

1½ tbsp extra virgin olive oil

1 onion, chopped

2 celery sticks, sliced

1 green or red pepper, seeded and cut into strips

2 garlic cloves, crushed

½ tsp ground ginger

½ tsp cayenne pepper

1 tsp mild chilli powder

340 g (12 oz) long-grain white rice

900 ml (1½ pints) hot vegetable stock

1 can chopped tomatoes, about 225 g

3 tbsp coarsely chopped parsley

100 g (3½ oz) peeled large raw prawns

200 g (7 oz) skinned salmon fillet, cut into 2.5 cm (1 in) cubes

dash of Tabasco sauce (optional)

salt and pepper

Preparation and cooking time: 30 minutes

**Each serving provides**

kcal 483, **protein** 22 g, **fat** 11 g (of which saturated fat 2 g), **carbohydrate** 80 g (of which sugars 5 g), **fibre** 2 g

| | |
|---|---|
| ✓✓✓ | B₁₂, C |
| ✓✓ | B₆, E, niacin, copper, selenium, zinc |
| ✓ | B₁, folate, iron, potassium |

**1** Heat the oil in a large, wide pan over a moderately high heat. Add the onion and cook, stirring, for about 3 minutes. Add the celery, green or red pepper, garlic, ginger, cayenne, chilli powder and rice, and cook, stirring, for 2 minutes.

**2** Pour in the hot stock and stir well, then reduce the heat so that the stock is simmering gently. Cover the pan with a tight-fitting lid and simmer for 15 minutes.

**3** Stir in the chopped tomatoes with their juice and 2 tbsp of the parsley, then add the prawns and salmon. Cover again and simmer for 3–4 minutes or until the seafood is just cooked and the rice has absorbed most of the liquid and is tender.

**4** Add the Tabasco sauce, if using, and salt and pepper to taste. Sprinkle with the remaining 1 tbsp parsley and serve hot.

**Some more ideas**

● Use brown rice instead of white. It will take 30–40 minutes to cook and will need about 150 ml (5 fl oz) more stock.

● For a pork and smoked sausage jambalaya, cut 200 g (7 oz) pork fillet (tenderloin) into thin strips and brown in 1 tbsp extra virgin olive oil, then remove from the pan and set aside. Add 1 chopped red onion to the pan and cook for 5 minutes or until almost soft. Stir in the rice and cook for 2–3 minutes, then pour in 750 ml (1¼ pints) vegetable stock. Cover and simmer for 10 minutes. Stir in 1 can tomatoes with added peppers and basil, about 400 g, with the juice, and 200 g (7 oz) sliced courgettes. Cover and cook for a further 5 minutes. Return the pork to the pan together with 115 g (4 oz) sliced smoked sausage and cook, covered, for 5 more minutes or until all the liquid has been absorbed and the rice is tender. Serve sprinkled with 2 tbsp chopped parsley.

**Plus points**

● Prawns are low in fat and high in protein. They are also a good source of the antioxidant mineral selenium, which helps to protect the cardiovascular system.

● Salmon provides vitamins B₆ and B₁₂ and the minerals selenium and potassium.

● Rice requires more water for growing than any other cereal crop. However, the main purpose of the standing water in paddy fields is to drown the 'weed' competition that the rice seedlings face.

# Chinese-style steamed plaice rolls

Here rolled up plaice fillets, flavoured with oyster sauce, ginger and spring onions, are set on a bed of the sea vegetable samphire and then steamed. They're served with a mixture of long-grain and wild rice.

## Serves 4

340 g (12 oz) mixed long-grain and wild rice

4 plaice fillets, about 600 g (1 lb 5 oz) in total, skinned

2 tbsp oyster sauce

½ tsp caster sugar

3 garlic cloves, finely chopped

1 tsp finely chopped fresh root ginger

3 spring onions, thinly sliced

100 g (3½ oz) fresh samphire

1 carrot, shaved into strips using a vegetable peeler

1 tsp toasted sesame oil

1 tbsp chopped fresh coriander

sprigs of fresh coriander to garnish

Preparation and cooking time: 25 minutes

## Each serving provides

kcal 455, **protein** 32 g, **fat** 4 g (of which saturated fat 0.5 g), **carbohydrate** 78 g (of which sugars 3 g), **fibre** 1 g

| | |
|---|---|
| ✓✓✓ | $B_1$,$B_6$, $B_{12}$, niacin, selenium |
| ✓✓ | A |
| ✓ | $B_2$, C, folate, calcium, copper, iron, potassium, zinc |

1 Add the rice to a large saucepan of cold water and bring to the boil. Reduce the heat and simmer for about 15 minutes, or cook according to the packet instructions, until tender. Drain well.

2 While the rice is cooking, cut the fish fillets in half lengthways. Arrange the strips, skinned side uppermost, on a plate and spread over the oyster sauce. Sprinkle with the sugar, half of the garlic, half of the ginger and half of the spring onions. Roll up the strips.

3 Place the samphire in a steamer and arrange the fish rolls on top. Sprinkle with the remaining chopped garlic and ginger, and add the carrot shavings. Cover and steam over a high heat for 5–6 minutes or until the fish will flake easily and the samphire is just tender.

4 Arrange the samphire and plaice rolls on plates with the carrot shavings. Drizzle with the sesame oil and sprinkle with the remaining spring onions and the chopped coriander. Garnish the rice with coriander sprigs, and serve.

### Plus points

• Wild rice is not a true rice but the seeds of a North American grass. It contains more protein than ordinary rice and is rich in the essential amino acid, lysine, which is usually in short supply in most grains. Amino acids are the building blocks of protein.

• Using the green leaves of spring onions increases the beta-carotene content of the onions.

### Some more ideas

• Use mixed Chinese greens, thinly sliced, or 225 g (8 oz) broccoli, cut into small florets, instead of the samphire.

• Serve the fish with fried rice. Cook 280 g (10 oz) long-grain rice in boiling water for 10–12 minutes, or according to the packet instructions, until tender. Drain. Stir-fry 1 onion, chopped, ½ red pepper, seeded and chopped, 1 stalk celery, diced, 3 garlic cloves, chopped, and 1 tsp chopped fresh root ginger in 1 tbsp groundnut oil for 2–3 minutes. Remove from the wok and set aside. Heat another 1 tbsp oil in the wok and add the rice, spreading it out in a thin layer. Cook over a moderate heat until lightly browned on one side. Turn over, add the stir-fried vegetables and stir-fry for 2 minutes. Add 2 tsp soy sauce and 55 g (2 oz) frozen peas and stir-fry for another 2 minutes. Sprinkle with chopped fresh coriander and serve.

Fish

# Linguine with pan-fried salmon

All the ingredients for this dish are quickly assembled and cooked, and the result is truly delicious as well as visually impressive. With the addition of bread and salad, it makes a hearty and well-balanced meal.

### Serves 4

400 g (14 oz) salmon fillet, skinned

grated zest and juice of 1 lemon

2 tbsp chopped fresh dill

340 g (12 oz) linguine

225 g (8 oz) carrots, cut into matchstick strips

225 g (8 oz) courgettes, cut into matchstick strips

1 tsp sunflower oil

100 g (3½ oz) reduced-fat crème fraîche

salt and pepper

### To garnish

sprigs of fresh dill (optional)

1 lemon, cut into wedges

Preparation time: 10 minutes, plus optional marinating

Cooking time: 15 minutes

1 Cut the salmon into chunks and place in a dish. Add the lemon zest and juice, and the dill. Turn the chunks of salmon to coat them evenly. If time permits, cover and marinate in the fridge for at least 10 minutes.

2 Cook the linguine in boiling water for 10 minutes, or according to the packet instructions, until al dente. Add the carrots to the pasta after 8 minutes cooking, then add the courgettes 1 minute later.

3 Meanwhile, brush a non-stick or heavy-based frying pan with the oil and heat thoroughly. Drain the salmon, reserving the lemon juice marinade. Add the salmon to the hot pan and cook, turning the pieces occasionally, for 3–4 minutes, or until the fish is firm and just cooked.

4 Add the reserved marinade and the crème fraîche to the salmon, and cook for a few seconds. Remove from the heat and stir in seasoning to taste.

5 Drain the pasta and vegetables, and transfer them to a serving dish or to individual plates. Add the salmon mixture, garnish with fresh dill, if liked, and serve with lemon wedges.

### Plus points

- Salmon is an oily fish rich in omega-3 fatty acids, which can help to reduce the risk of heart disease.
- Cutting the courgettes and carrots into thin, pasta-like strips and mixing them with pasta is a good way of presenting them to children who are reluctant to eat vegetables.

### Some more ideas

- Trout fillets, asparagus tips and broad beans are an excellent alternative combination to the salmon, carrot and courgette. Cook the asparagus tips and beans with the pasta for the last 4–5 minutes.
- Use the recipe as a basis for a quick, healthy storecupboard supper dish, adding frozen green beans and sweetcorn to the pasta, and using well-drained canned salmon instead of the fresh fish. There is no need to marinate or cook the canned salmon: the heat of the pasta will bring out its flavour beautifully.

### Each serving provides

kcal 560, protein 33 g, fat 18 g (of which saturated fat 5 g), carbohydrate 70 g (of which sugars 6 g), fibre 4.5 g

| | |
|---|---|
| ✓✓✓ | A, B$_{12}$, niacin |
| ✓✓ | B$_1$, B$_6$, C, copper, selenium |
| ✓ | E, folate, potassium |

Fish

# Classic grilled Dover sole

Few classy meals could be quicker and simpler. Dover sole – usually sold skinned and cleaned – is a real treat and its superb taste can be fully appreciated in this dish. New potatoes with fresh mint and spinach complement this elegant fish dish.

**Serves 4**

4 small Dover sole, about 225 g (8 oz) each, cleaned and skinned

750 g (1 lb 10 oz) baby new potatoes, scrubbed

1 large sprig of fresh mint

40 g (1¼ oz) unsalted butter

finely grated zest and juice of 1 large lemon

450 g (1 lb) baby leaf spinach

freshly grated nutmeg (optional)

salt and pepper

sprigs of fresh mint to garnish

lemon wedges to serve

Preparation and cooking time: 30 minutes

**Each serving provides**

kcal 412, **protein** 43 g, **fat** 13 g (of which saturated fat 6 g), **carbohydrate** 32 g (of which sugars 4 g), **fibre** 4 g

| | |
|---|---|
| ✓✓✓ | A, B₁, B₆, C, folate, niacin, iron, potassium, selenium |
| ✓✓ | calcium |
| ✓ | B₂, E, copper, zinc |

1 Preheat the grill to high. Cut a piece of foil to fit the grill pan and lay the fish on top (depending on the size of the grill, you may have to cook the sole in 2 batches).

2 Put the potatoes in a saucepan, cover with boiling water and add the sprig of mint. Cook for about 15 minutes or until the potatoes are just tender.

3 Meanwhile, melt the butter in a small saucepan and mix in the lemon zest and juice. Season with salt and pepper. Brush the lemon butter over the fish and grill for 5–6 minutes or until the flesh close to the bone flakes easily when pierced with a knife. Carefully turn the fish over, brush again with the lemon butter and grill for a further 5–6 minutes.

4 While the fish is cooking, steam the spinach for 2–3 minutes or until just wilted. Season with salt, pepper and nutmeg to taste.

5 Drain the potatoes and put into a warmed serving dish. Add plenty of black pepper, toss gently and garnish with mint sprigs. Transfer the sole to warmed dinner plates and spoon over any cooking juices from the grill pan. Add lemon wedges and serve, with the potatoes and spinach.

**Some more ideas**

● Other, less expensive flat fish such as lemon sole, Torbay sole or small whole plaice are also delicious grilled with lemon butter. Allow 4–5 minutes cooking each side. Instead of spinach, serve with broccoli florets steamed for 2–3 minutes or until barely tender.

● Smooth, creamy mashed potatoes flavoured with herbs are another good accompaniment for grilled sole. Peel and cut up 900 g (2 lb) floury potatoes and cook in boiling water for 15–20 minutes or until tender. Drain thoroughly, then mash until smooth. Beat in 100 ml (3½ fl oz) hot semi-skimmed milk and 15 g (½ oz) unsalted butter. Season to taste, then mix in 3 tbsp chopped fresh herbs – a combination of parsley, chives and lovage is particularly good.

**Plus points**

● Sole is a useful source of vitamin B₁₂, which plays a critical role in the production of DNA and RNA, the genetic material in cells.

● New potatoes cooked in their skins have one-third more fibre than peeled potatoes, and the nutrients found just under the skin are preserved.

Fish

# Stir-fried scallops and prawns

For a fast and delicious treat, this Oriental seafood stir-fry is hard to beat. It requires very little oil and the seaweed and vegetables add lots of flavour and texture. Pickled ginger can be found in larger supermarkets.

## Serves 4

juice of 1 lemon or 1 lime

2 tsp clear honey

2 tbsp light soy sauce

4 medium-sized scallops, about 200 g (7 oz) in total, quartered

24 peeled raw tiger prawns, about 170 g (6 oz) in total

10 g (¼ oz) dried wakame seaweed

340 g (12 oz) fine Chinese egg noodles

1 tbsp stir-fry oil, or 2 tsp sunflower oil mixed with 1 tsp toasted sesame oil

300 g (10½ oz) bean sprouts

150 g (5½ oz) pak choy, shredded

1½ tbsp pickled ginger

Preparation time: 10 minutes, plus 5 minutes marinating

Cooking time: 5–7 minutes

### Each serving provides

kcal 492, **protein** 33 g, **fat** 11 g (of which saturated fat 3 g), **carbohydrate** 70 g (of which sugars 7 g), **fibre** 5 g

| | |
|---|---|
| ✓✓✓ | B₁, B₁₂, niacin, iron |
| ✓✓ | folate, copper, selenium, zinc |
| ✓ | B₆, C, E, calcium, potassium |

1 Mix together the lemon or lime juice, honey and 1 tbsp of the soy sauce. Pour this marinade over the scallops and prawns and set aside to marinate for about 5 minutes.

2 Meanwhile, place the wakame in a bowl, cover with 300 ml (10 fl oz) cold water and leave for 8–10 minutes to rehydrate. Place the noodles in a large mixing bowl and pour in enough boiling water to cover them generously. Leave to soak for 4 minutes, or according to packet instructions, until tender. Drain when they are ready.

3 Drain the scallops and prawns, reserving the marinade, and pat dry with kitchen paper. Heat a wok or heavy-based frying pan until very hot, then add the oil and swirl to coat the wok or pan. Add the scallops and prawns and stir-fry for 2–3 minutes or until the prawns have turned pink and the scallops are opaque. Remove the scallops and prawns from the wok and set aside.

4 Add the bean sprouts, pak choy, reserved marinade, remaining 1 tbsp soy sauce and the pickled ginger to the wok and stir-fry for 1–2 minutes.

5 Return the scallops and prawns to the wok with the well-drained wakame and stir-fry for 1 minute or until just heated through. Serve the stir-fry with the egg noodles.

### Some more ideas

● Use 200 g (7 oz) queen scallops and 170 g (6 oz) cooked peeled prawns. It will take only 1–2 minutes of stir-frying to cook the scallops and reheat the prawns.

● For a delicious vegetable-rich version of this dish, instead of bean sprouts and pak choy, use 200 g (7 oz) mixed Chinese vegetables, such as choy sam and Chinese cabbage, shredded, 4 spring onions, thinly sliced, 150 g (5½ oz) mange-tout or sugarsnap peas, 100 g (3½ oz) mushrooms, thinly sliced, and 1 can water chestnuts, about 220 g, drained and sliced. Omit the seaweed and pickled ginger. Serve the scallop and prawn stir-fry with boiled rice instead of noodles.

### Plus points

● The sprouted seed has been used in Asia since ancient times but is a fairly new arrival in the West, made popular by Chinese and Japanese restaurants. Nutritionally the most significant change when a seed is sprouted is the increase in water content. Twice as much sprouted seed as dry seed must be eaten to provide the same amount of protein, carbohydrate and other nutrients.

● Wakame seaweed is usually sold dried and is then rehydrated with water. It contains some of the essential minerals – calcium, phosphorus, magnesium and iodine.

Fish

# Malay-style braised fish

Gentle braising is an excellent cooking method for fish, keeping it moist and succulent. Spiced and simmered in coconut milk, the fish here is delicious with plain noodles or rice. For a livelier flavour, leave the seeds in the chilli or use a tiny, very hot Thai chilli.

**Serves 4**

1 tbsp sunflower oil

4 spring onions, chopped

1 red chilli, seeded and thinly sliced

2 celery sticks, thinly sliced

1 red pepper, seeded and thinly sliced

1 garlic clove, crushed

½ tsp fennel seeds

2 tsp ground coriander

½ tsp ground cumin

¼ tsp turmeric

1 can chopped tomatoes, about 230 g

120 ml (4 fl oz) coconut milk

300 ml (10 fl oz) fish stock, bought chilled or made with a stock cube

2 tbsp fish sauce or light soy sauce

1 can sliced bamboo shoots, about 220 g, drained

675 g (1½ lb) thick skinless white fish fillet, such as cod, hake, haddock or hoki, cut into chunks

16 raw tiger prawns, peeled

juice of ½ lime

**To garnish**

2 spring onions, chopped

1 tbsp chopped fresh coriander

Preparation time: 10 minutes

Cooking time: about 20 minutes

1 Heat the oil in a large frying pan. Add the spring onions, chilli, celery and red pepper, and fry, stirring constantly, for 5 minutes or until the vegetables are slightly softened.

2 Stir in the garlic, fennel seeds, coriander, cumin and turmeric and cook for 1 minute. Add the tomatoes with their juice, the coconut milk, stock and fish sauce or soy sauce. Bring to the boil, then reduce the heat and cover the pan. Simmer for 5 minutes.

3 Stir in the bamboo shoots, white fish and prawns. Cover the pan again and simmer for 5–7 minutes or until the pieces of fish are just cooked and the prawns have turned pink. Stir in the lime juice.

4 Serve the braised fish at once, garnished with a sprinkle of chopped spring onions and fresh coriander.

**Plus points**

• Fennel and fennel seeds are said to aid digestion and help relieve stomach cramps. In India toasted fennel seeds are chewed to prevent bad breath.

• Some studies have shown that chillies can help to reduce blood cholesterol levels. There are also reports suggesting that eating chillies can help to protect against gastric ulcers by causing the stomach lining to secrete a mucus which coats the stomach, thus protecting it from damage by irritants such as aspirin or alcohol.

**Each serving provides**

kcal 330, **protein** 47 g, **fat** 10 g (of which saturated fat 5 g), **carbohydrate** 7 g (of which sugars 6 g), **fibre** 2.5 g

| | |
|---|---|
| ✓✓✓ | B$_{12}$, C |
| ✓ | iron, selenium, zinc |

### Some more ideas

● For a special meal, monkfish fillet can be used instead of the fish suggested in the main recipe. It takes slightly longer to cook, so increase the time in step 3 to 12–14 minutes.

● Chicken can be used instead of fish. Heat the oil and brown 4 halved, skinless boneless chicken breasts (fillets) for about 4 minutes on each side. Remove from the pan. Add the vegetables and soften as in step 1, then add

150 g (5½ oz) sliced mushrooms and cook for about 2 minutes. Return the chicken to the pan with the garlic and spices. Finish cooking as in the main recipe, using chicken stock and soy sauce instead of fish stock and sauce, and replacing the bamboo shoots with 1 can sliced water chestnuts, about 220 g, drained.

● Basmati rice with onion goes well with this dish. Soften 1 small onion in 15 g (½ oz) butter. Stir in 115 g (4 oz) basmati rice, then pour in

300 ml (10 fl oz) boiling water. Cover and cook over a low heat for about 10 minutes.

● Stir-fried noodles are also delicious as an accompaniment. Soak 250 g (8½ oz) dried medium Chinese egg noodles in boiling water for 5 minutes, stirring occasionally. Drain the noodles well. Heat 2 tsp toasted sesame oil in a wok or large frying pan and add the noodles. Toss well for 1 minute, then stir in 3 tbsp light soy sauce and a little chopped fresh coriander.

Fish

# Mini fish pizzas

Ciabatta rolls make an instant base for easy home-made pizzas. These are topped with a mixture of seafood and are given an authentic Italian flavour with red pesto and mozzarella. Serve with a crisp green leaf and vegetable salad for a nutritious fast meal.

## Serves 4

4 part-baked ciabatta rolls

4 tbsp red pesto

4 medium-sized tomatoes, each cut into 6 slices

1 can sweetcorn, about 200 g, well drained

125 g (4½ oz) mozzarella cheese, coarsely grated

1 can tuna in spring water, about 200 g, drained and flaked

100 g (3½ oz) cooked peeled prawns

100 g (3½ oz) squid rings

8 tsp extra virgin olive oil

salt and pepper

chopped parsley to garnish

Preparation time: 10 minutes
Cooking time: 10–12 minutes

1 Preheat the oven to 200°C (400°F, gas mark 6). Put a heavy baking sheet in the oven to heat up.

2 Split the rolls in half and spread the cut sides with the pesto, right to the edges. Arrange 3 slices of tomato on each half and sprinkle with the sweetcorn and grated mozzarella.

3 Divide the tuna, prawns and squid rings among the pizzas. Season with salt and pepper to taste and drizzle each pizza with 1 tsp of oil.

4 Put the pizzas on the hot baking sheet and bake for 10–12 minutes or until the cheese has just melted. Sprinkle with parsley and serve.

### Some more ideas

● Use a part-baked ciabatta loaf or 2 small part-baked French sticks, split horizontally, as the base for the pizzas.

● Another fast pizza is pitta bread topped with canned sardines and mackerel. Grill 4 large pitta breads lightly on both sides, then spread one side of each with 1 tsp tomato purée. Tear up about 8 large fresh basil leaves and sprinkle these over the tomato purée. Cut 2 tomatoes into thin wedges and scatter these on top with 125 g (4½ oz) mozzarella cheese, cut into slivers. Drain a can of sardines in olive oil, about 120 g, (keep the oil) and a can of mackerel fillets in brine, about 120 g. Roughly flake the sardines and mackerel and place on the pizzas with 100 g (3½ oz) cooked peeled

prawns. Season with salt and pepper to taste and drizzle 1 tsp of the reserved sardine oil over each pizza. Grill for 4–5 minutes. Garnish with more basil leaves and serve.

● Other canned fish can be used. Try anchovies, kipper fillets, sardines in tomato sauce, pilchards, crab, cockles or mussels.

## Each serving provides

kcal 633, **protein** 44 g, **fat** 30 g (of which saturated fat 9 g), **carbohydrate** 50 g (of which sugars 9 g), **fibre** 3 g

| | |
|---|---|
| ✓✓✓ | B₁₂, niacin, calcium, selenium |
| ✓✓ | A, B₁, B₆, E, copper, iron, zinc |
| ✓ | B₂, C, potassium |

### Plus points

● Prawns, like all shellfish, contain iodine, which is needed for the formation of thyroid hormones and the actual functioning of the thyroid gland.

● Canned tuna fish is a great storecupboard standby as it is so easy to use. Tuna canned in spring water or brine contains half the calories of tuna canned in oil.

● Sweetcorn provides a range of nutrients, including dietary fibre which is important to keep the digestive system functioning well.

Fish

# Trout with green beans and pesto

This casserole is simple but stylish, relying on an unusual but complementary blend of ingredients rather than complicated techniques for a superb result. Serve with fluffy mashed potatoes or boiled new potatoes.

### Serves 4

8 trout fillets, about 100 g (3½ oz) each

4 sprigs of fresh dill

250 g (8½ oz) green beans, halved

2 tbsp capers

200 ml (7 fl oz) dry white wine

300 ml (10 fl oz) hot fish stock, preferably home-made

4 tsp plain flour

2 tsp pesto

salt and pepper

sprigs of fresh dill to garnish

Preparation time: 10 minutes
Cooking time: about 15 minutes

---

### Each serving provides

kcal 310, **protein** 41 g, **fat** 8 g (of which saturated fat 4.5 g), **carbohydrate** 6 g (of which sugars 2 g), **fibre** 1.5 g

| | |
|---|---|
| ✓✓ | B$_{12}$, iron |
| ✓ | folate, selenium |

Fish

**1** Check the trout fillets for bones by running your fingers over the flesh. (Tweezers are useful for removing any stray bones, if necessary.) Lay the fillets skin side down and season them. Pull the fronds off the dill sprigs and sprinkle them over the fish. Roll up the fillets from tail to head end, with the skin on the outside, and set aside.

**2** Put the beans in a large, fairly shallow pan – a frying pan or sauté pan with a lid is ideal, but a flameproof casserole can also be used. Arrange the fish rolls, joins down, on top of the beans. Sprinkle on the capers and pour in the wine and fish stock. Bring the liquid almost to the boil, then reduce the heat and cover the pan. Simmer for 12–15 minutes or until the fish and beans are just tender.

**3** Mix the flour and pesto to a smooth paste. Use a draining spoon to transfer the fish rolls and beans to warm plates. Bring the cooking liquid to the boil. Whisk in half the pesto and flour paste until thoroughly combined with the sauce, then whisk in the remaining paste. Continue boiling, still whisking, for 2–3 minutes or until the sauce is lightly thickened.

**4** Taste the sauce and adjust the seasoning if necessary, then spoon it over the fish and beans. Garnish with sprigs of dill and serve.

### Plus points

● Trout is an oily fish, rich in omega-3 fatty acids, shown to help reduce the risk of heart attacks and stroke. They do so by thinning the blood, making it less likely to clot; lowering blood pressure and cholesterol levels; and encouraging the muscles lining the artery walls to relax, so improving blood flow to the heart. Omega-3 fatty acids also have an anti-inflammatory effect, which can help to relieve rheumatoid arthritis and the skin condition psoriasis. Other studies suggest that omega-3 fats may help to protect skin against damage from ultra-violet radiation and protect against skin cancer.

### Some more ideas

● The casserole can be cooked in the oven at 200°C (400°F, gas mark 6) for about 20 minutes. Use an ovenproof dish or casserole instead of the pan suggested in step 2.

● Fennel tastes good with the beans. Halve and thinly slice 1 bulb, then place it in the casserole before adding the beans. Caperberries can be used instead of the capers – they are larger and look rather like small green olives. They have a strong peppery flavour, which is delicious with fennel and fish.

● Vary the herbs according to taste and whatever is plentiful. Try parsley, chervil, chives or tarragon, or a mixture of these.

● Beurre manié, made with 4 tsp plain flour and 20 g (¾ oz) butter, can be used instead of the flour and pesto paste to thicken the sauce. Whisk in extra chopped fresh herbs for flavour before serving.

● For trout with leeks and thyme, flavour the fish rolls with fresh thyme leaves instead of dill. Heat the wine and stock in the casserole, then add 250 g (8½ oz) chopped leeks and 100 g (3½ oz) chopped celery. Place the trout on top, cover and simmer for 12–15 minutes. Remove the fish and vegetables. Thicken the sauce with beurre manié (see left) and add 2 skinned and chopped tomatoes, then pour the sauce over the fish.

# Sautéed tiger prawns with feta

In this quickly prepared dish, cubes of feta cheese are briefly marinated in fresh ginger juice and soy sauce, then added to a colourful sauté of sugarsnap peas, mushrooms, spring onions and tiger prawns. The sauté is served with rice cooked in vegetable stock.

**Serves 4**

2.5 cm (1 in) piece fresh root ginger, coarsely grated

2 tsp light soy sauce

170 g (6 oz) feta cheese, cut into 2 cm (¾ in) cubes

1½ tbsp sunflower oil

225 g (8 oz) long-grain rice

750 ml (1¼ pints) vegetable stock

1 bunch spring onions, sliced on the diagonal

225 g (8 oz) small button mushrooms, halved

170 g (6 oz) sugarsnap peas, cut in half lengthways

12 large raw tiger prawns, peeled

2 tbsp chopped fresh coriander

1 tbsp chopped parsley

2 tbsp sesame seeds

salt and pepper

sprigs of fresh coriander to garnish

Preparation and cooking time: 30 minutes

**Each serving provides**

kcal 445, **protein** 21 g, **fat** 18 g (of which saturated fat 7 g), **carbohydrate** 53 g (of which sugars 3.5 g), **fibre** 3 g

| | |
|---|---|
| ✓✓✓ | $B_{12}$, copper |
| ✓✓ | A, C, E, niacin, calcium, selenium, zinc |
| ✓ | $B_1$, $B_2$, $B_6$, folate, iron, potassium |

1 Put the ginger in a garlic press and squeeze out the ginger juice into a small bowl. Mix in the soy sauce. Add the cubes of feta and gently toss to coat. Set aside to marinate while you cook the rice.

2 Heat ½ tbsp of the oil in a large saucepan, add the long-grain rice and fry gently for 2–3 minutes, stirring, until the rice becomes translucent. Slowly pour in the vegetable stock, still stirring, then cover the pan with a tight-fitting lid. Leave to cook over a low heat for 12–15 minutes or until the stock has been absorbed and the rice is tender.

3 Meanwhile, heat the remaining 1 tbsp oil in a sauté pan or large non-stick frying pan. Add the spring onions and mushrooms, and sauté for 1 minute, stirring. Add the sugarsnap peas and prawns, and sauté for a further 2–3 minutes, stirring frequently, until the prawns are pink and cooked through and all the vegetables are tender but still crisp.

4 Stir in the feta cheese with its marinade and cook gently for about 30 seconds, just to heat through, turning the cheese carefully to prevent it from breaking up too much. Sprinkle over the chopped coriander and parsley and the sesame seeds, and season with pepper to taste. Toss gently to mix.

5 Spoon the prawn and feta sauté onto warmed serving plates and garnish with sprigs of fresh coriander. Fluff up the rice with a fork, season with salt and pepper to taste, and serve with the stir-fry.

**Plus points**

● Feta cheese was traditionally made just from sheep's milk, but today goat's or cow's milk is often included. Feta has a lower fat content than many other cheeses, such as Cheddar, Edam and Parmesan.

● Like all seafish, prawns contain iodine. This essential mineral is required for proper functioning of the thyroid gland.

● Although sesame seeds are not used in any great amount in this recipe, they do provide some calcium, adding to that contributed by the feta cheese.

Fish

### Some more ideas

● Instead of prawns, try 150 g (5½ oz) queen scallops or skinless salmon fillet, cut into 2 cm (¾ in) cubes. Use chopped fresh dill instead of coriander.

● For sautéed vegetables with Manchego cheese, drain 1 can of artichoke hearts in water, about 400 g; cut each artichoke into quarters and pat dry on kitchen paper. Heat 1 tbsp extra virgin olive oil in a large non-stick frying pan and sauté the artichokes until lightly browned. Remove and set aside. Add a further ½ tbsp extra virgin olive oil to the pan and sauté 170 g (6 oz) sliced baby leeks over a moderate heat for 1 minute. Add 1 large, seeded and sliced red pepper and 170 g (6 oz) thawed frozen broad beans. Cook for a further 3–4 minutes or until just tender. Return the artichoke quarters to the pan, together with 150 g (5½ oz) Manchego cheese, cut into 1 cm (½ in) cubes, 55 g (2 oz) pumpkin seeds, and salt and pepper to taste. Cook for a further 1–2 minutes, stirring gently, until all the vegetables are tender and the cheese is starting to melt. Serve hot, with the rice in the main recipe or with 8 large flour tortillas, warmed according to the packet instructions.

# Salmon with mango salsa

Here is a wonderful mixture of bright colours and zingy flavours, from the peppery salmon topping to the mustardy watercress and fragrant mango salsa with its surprise kick. This is vitality food – it looks great, is quick to make and is bursting with vitamins and minerals.

**Serves 4**

4 pieces of salmon fillet, 150 g (5½ oz) each

4 tsp mixed peppercorns (black, white, green and pink)

675 g (1½ lb) baby new potatoes, scrubbed, and halved if large

170 g (6 oz) watercress

**Mango salsa**

1 mango, about 400 g (14 oz)

3 spring onions, finely chopped

1–2 tsp pink peppercorns in brine, rinsed and roughly chopped

3 tbsp chopped fresh coriander

2 tbsp lime juice

2 tbsp extra virgin olive oil

Tabasco sauce to taste

Preparation and cooking time: 30 minutes

**Each serving provides**

kcal 500, **protein** 32 g, **fat** 24 g (of which saturated fat 5 g), **carbohydrate** 41 g (of which sugars 16 g), **fibre** 5 g

| ✓✓✓ | A, B₆, B₁₂ |
| --- | --- |
| ✓✓ | B₁, niacin, copper, iron, potassium, selenium |
| ✓ | B₂, E, folate, zinc |

1 Check the salmon fillets for any tiny pin bones and remove them with tweezers. Roughly crush the peppercorns in a pestle and mortar. Press them into the flesh side of the salmon. Set aside.

2 Put the potatoes in a saucepan, cover with boiling water and bring back to the boil. Reduce the heat and simmer for 10–12 minutes or until tender. At the same time, preheat a ridged cast-iron grill pan.

3 Meanwhile, make the salsa. Stone and peel the mango, and dice the flesh. Put into a large bowl and mix in the spring onions, pink peppercorns, coriander, lime juice, olive oil and a good dash of Tabasco sauce.

4 Brush the grill pan with a little oil if necessary, then put the salmon fillets in, skin side down. Cook over a moderately high heat for 4 minutes. Turn them over and cook for another 4 minutes or until the fish is cooked. Drain the potatoes.

5 Arrange the watercress and new potatoes on 4 serving plates. Place the salmon on top and serve with the mango salsa.

**Some more ideas**

● Instead of chopping the pink peppercorns, leave them whole in the mango salsa.

● The mango salsa is delicious with other oily fish, such as tuna, swordfish and mackerel.

● Top the salmon fillets with a horseradish crust instead of the peppercorns. Mix 2 tbsp creamed horseradish with 1 egg yolk and dip in the fish fillets, flesh side only. Mix 85 g (3 oz) fresh breadcrumbs with 1 tbsp chopped parsley and press the mixture onto the horseradish-coated fish. Heat 15 g (½ oz) butter and 1 tsp sunflower oil in a frying pan. Add the salmon, crust side down, and cook for 2 minutes. Turn the fish over and cook for a further 4–5 minutes. Serve on the potatoes and a mixture of cherry tomatoes and salad leaves, such as rocket and mizuna (a spiky, green Japanese salad leaf).

**Plus point**

● Salmon is rich in omega-3 fatty acids, a type of polyunsaturated fat thought to help protect against coronary heart disease and strokes by making blood less 'sticky' and therefore less likely to clot. A diet rich in omega-3 fatty acids may also be helpful in preventing and treating rheumatoid arthritis, because of the anti-inflammatory effect of the fatty acids.

Fish

# Quick-fried squid with chilli and fresh ginger

Rings of squid are briefly stir-fried with garlic, chilli and fresh colourful vegetables in this speedy supper dish. Take care not to overcook the squid as it has a tendency to toughen if cooked for too long.

## Serves 4

280 g (10 oz) basmati rice

2 tbsp sunflower oil

2 fresh red chillies, seeded and thinly sliced

2 garlic cloves, crushed

4 tsp finely grated fresh root ginger

1 orange pepper, seeded and diced

200 g (7 oz) baby corn, sliced at an angle

200 g (7 oz) small broccoli florets, halved

450 g (1 lb) fresh squid rings

5 tbsp light soy sauce

10 spring onions, thinly sliced

Preparation and cooking time: 30 minutes

**1** Bring a large saucepan of water to the boil, add the rice and cook for 10–12 minutes, or according to the packet instructions, until tender.

**2** Meanwhile, heat the oil in a wok or heavy-based frying pan and stir-fry the chillies, garlic and ginger for 2 minutes to release their flavour. Toss in the pepper, corn and broccoli florets, and stir-fry for 3–4 minutes or until the broccoli is almost tender.

**3** Add the squid and stir-fry for 1–2 minutes or until just firm and opaque. Spoon in the soy sauce and 2 tbsp water and scatter over the spring onions. Cook until bubbling, then serve immediately with the drained rice.

## Some more ideas

• To make quick-fried squid with tomatoes and black bean sauce, stir-fry 3 garlic cloves, crushed, with the chillies, then add the squid and stir-fry for 1 minute. Add 8 tomatoes, seeded and chopped, and 4 tbsp chopped fresh coriander with the spring onions, then stir in 8 tbsp black bean sauce instead of the soy sauce and water. Cook the mixture until bubbling, and serve immediately.

• As an alternative to the squid, try raw tiger or king prawns, peeled. Allow 4–5 per person, and stir-fry for 3–4 minutes or until they turn bright pink.

• Egg noodles make a good accompaniment instead of the rice.

### Each serving provides

kcal 453, **protein** 28 g, **fat** 9 g (of which saturated fat 1 g), **carbohydrate** 65 g (of which sugars 5 g), **fibre** 4 g

✓✓✓ $B_1$, $B_6$, $B_{12}$, C, E, niacin, copper, iron, selenium

✓✓ folate

✓ A, $B_2$, calcium, potassium, zinc

### Plus points

• Squid, or calamari, is an excellent source of low-fat protein and of vitamin $B_{12}$.

• Broccoli is an excellent source of beta-carotene, vitamin C and vitamin E – all powerful antioxidants that help to protect the body's cells against the damaging effects of free radicals.

Fish

# Steamed sea bass fillets with spring vegetables

Oriental steamer baskets are useful for this dish – you can stack them and steam everything together. The moist heat ensures that the fish doesn't dry out. If using a liquid fish stock base or a cube, make half strength stock as the marinade adds plenty of flavour.

**Serves 4**

1 tsp grated fresh root ginger

1 tbsp light soy sauce

½ tsp toasted sesame oil

1 garlic clove, finely chopped

1 tbsp dry sherry, dry white wine or vermouth

4 sea bass fillets, 3.5 cm (1¼ in) thick, about 140 g (5 oz) each

700 ml (24 fl oz) fish stock

200 g (7 oz) couscous

1 strip of lemon zest

225 g (8 oz) baby carrots

12 spring onions, trimmed to about 10 cm (4 in) long

200 g (7 oz) asparagus tips

2 tbsp chopped parsley

salt and pepper

Preparation and cooking time: 30 minutes

**Each serving provides**

kcal 320, **protein** 34 g, **fat** 5 g (of which saturated fat 1 g), **carbohydrate** 35 g (of which sugars 8 g), **fibre** 3 g

| | |
|---|---|
| ✓✓✓ | A, B₁₂ |
| ✓✓ | C, folate, calcium, iron |
| ✓ | B₁, B₆ |

1 First make the marinade. Combine the ginger, soy sauce, sesame oil, garlic and sherry, wine or vermouth in a bowl. Add the fish and turn to coat in the marinade. Set aside.

2 Bring 250 ml (8½ fl oz) of the stock to the boil in a saucepan that will accommodate the steamer basket(s). Put the couscous in a bowl and pour over the boiling stock. Cover and leave to stand for about 15 minutes or until the couscous has swelled and absorbed the liquid.

3 Pour the remaining stock into the saucepan. Add the lemon zest and bring to the boil. Add the carrots. Reduce the heat so the stock simmers.

4 Place the fish, skin side down, in a single layer in a steamer basket. Add the spring onions and asparagus tips, or put them in a second stacking steamer basket. Place the steamer basket(s) over the gently boiling stock and cover. Steam for 10–12 minutes or until the fish is opaque throughout and begins to flake, and the vegetables are tender.

5 When the couscous is ready, add the parsley and fluff the grains with a fork to mix the couscous and parsley. Season with salt and pepper to taste.

6 Lift the steamer basket(s) off the pan. Drain the carrots, reserving the cooking liquid. Arrange the fish, carrots and steamed vegetables on warm plates with the couscous. Discard the lemon zest from the cooking liquid. Moisten the fish, vegetables and couscous with a little of the liquid, and serve with any remaining liquid as a sauce.

**Plus points**

● White fish such as sea bass are low in fat and calories and they offer many B-complex vitamins. Sea bass is also a good source of calcium, an essential mineral with many important functions in the body, including keeping bones and teeth strong.

● The active ingredient in asparagus, called asparagine, has a strong diuretic effect. Herbalists recommend eating asparagus as a treatment for rheumatism, arthritis and the bloating associated with PMT.

Fish

### Some more ideas

● If you don't have a steamer, place the fish and vegetables in a colander, place inside a large pan and cover with a lid.

● Use salmon or cod fillets instead of sea bass. The cooking time may need to be reduced by a minute or 2 for thinner fish fillets; check for doneness after 8–9 minutes.

● For a simpler dish, omit the marinade and use water instead of fish stock. When the water comes to the boil, add 600 g (1 lb 5 oz) small new potatoes. Scatter 2 finely slivered small leeks and the finely grated zest of 1 lemon over the fish, then steam it over the potatoes. Meanwhile, cook 500 g (1 lb 2 oz) spinach until wilted; squeeze out excess water and chop.

Moisten with 4 tbsp single cream and season with salt and pepper to taste. Serve the fish on the creamed spinach, with the potatoes tossed with chopped fresh herbs.

● Instead of couscous, serve the fish with mashed potatoes. Use some of the fish cooking liquid instead of milk for mashing the potatoes and finish with a small knob of butter.

# Seared tuna and bean salad

Here, fresh tuna is quickly cooked in a hot pan so the outside is lightly browned, leaving the inside pink, moist and full of flavour, and then served on a cannellini bean and red pepper salad. Warm ciabatta bread, thickly sliced, is the best accompaniment.

**Serves 4**

400 g (14 oz) piece tuna steak, about 5 cm (2 in) thick

4 tbsp extra virgin olive oil

1 tbsp lemon juice, or to taste

1 garlic clove, crushed

1 tbsp Dijon mustard

1 can cannellini beans, about 410 g, drained and rinsed

1 small red onion, thinly sliced

2 red peppers, seeded and thinly sliced

½ cucumber, about 225 g (8 oz)

100 g (3½ oz) watercress

salt and pepper

lemon wedges to serve

Preparation and cooking time: 30 minutes

**Each serving provides**

kcal 380, protein 32 g, fat 17 g (of which saturated fat 3 g), carbohydrate 26 g (of which sugars 11 g), fibre 9 g

| | |
|---|---|
| ✓✓✓ | A, B$_6$, B$_{12}$, C, selenium |
| ✓✓ | B$_1$, niacin, iron |
| ✓ | E, folate, copper, potassium, zinc |

1 Brush a ridged cast-iron grill pan or heavy frying pan (preferably cast-iron) with a little oil and heat over a moderate heat. Season the tuna steak on both sides with coarsely ground black pepper.

2 Sear the fish in the hot pan over a moderately high heat for 4 minutes on each side – the outside should be browned and criss-crossed with dark lines from the grill pan, while the inside should be light pink in the centre. Take care not to overcook the tuna or it will become tough and dry. Remove from the pan and leave to rest while preparing the rest of the salad.

3 Mix together the oil, lemon juice, garlic and mustard in a salad bowl. Season with salt and pepper to taste and add more lemon juice, if needed. Add the cannellini beans, onion and peppers to the bowl. Cut the cucumber lengthways into quarters, then cut the quarters across into 1 cm (½ in) slices. Add them to the salad bowl together with the watercress. Toss the salad gently to mix.

4 Cut the tuna into slices about 1 cm (½ in) thick. Arrange the slices on top of the salad and spoon up a little of the dressing over the fish. Serve with lemon wedges.

**Another idea**

• For a warm chicken and bean salad, use 500 g (1 lb 2 oz) skinless boneless chicken breasts (fillets). Cook in the hot pan for 18–20 minutes, turning frequently, until the chicken is cooked through. Leave to cool while you make the salad. Instead of cannellini beans, watercress and cucumber, use 1 can borlotti beans, about 400 g, drained and rinsed, 100 g (3½ oz) baby leaf spinach or rocket, and 250 g (8½ oz) cherry tomatoes, halved, with the onion and peppers. Slice the chicken, arrange on the salad and spoon over the dressing.

**Plus points**

• The health benefits of eating watercress have been acknowledged for many centuries. Along with other dark green, leafy vegetables, it provides good amounts of several vitamins and minerals including vitamin C, vitamin E, carotenoid compounds and the B vitamins folate, niacin and vitamin B$_6$.

• Canned beans are a useful source of iron, and the vitamin C from the watercress and peppers will help enhance its absorption.

Fish

# Pasta and grains

Pasta, rice, and beans serve as the perfect background to many ingredients. They can create a heartening meal, an elegant dish, or a new culinary experience in next to no time. In this chapter you will find classic recipes, including Creamy goat's cheese tagliatelle with toasted hazelnuts and Asparagus risotto with truffle oil. And with dishes such as Cannelini bean burgers and Bulghur wheat pilaf providing tasty new vegetarian options, you will never be stuck for choice.

# Creamy goat's cheese tagliatelle with toasted hazelnuts

When you are hungry and in a hurry this pasta dish can be on the table in next to no time. You will even be able to put together a side salad and still be sitting down to eat within 20 minutes. Take care when melting the cheese to ensure that it does not get too hot.

**Serves 4**

300 g (10½ oz) tagliatelle
90 ml (3 fl oz) semi-skimmed milk
150 g (5½ oz) medium-fat soft goat's cheese
2 tsp finely chopped fresh tarragon
6 spring onions, finely sliced
2–3 tbsp finely chopped toasted hazelnuts
salt and pepper

Preparation time: 5 minutes
Cooking time: 10–12 minutes

1 Cook the pasta in boiling water for 10–12 minutes, or according to the packet instructions, until al dente.

2 Meanwhile, warm the milk in a saucepan over a low heat. Add the cheese, breaking it up as you add it to the milk, and stir until it has just melted. Do not allow the mixture to boil or the cheese will curdle.

3 Remove from the heat and stir in the tarragon and spring onions. Season to taste.

4 Drain the pasta well and transfer it to a serving dish. Add the goat's cheese sauce and mix well. Scatter the hazelnuts over the top and serve.

**Plus points**

• Goat's cheese provides useful amounts of protein, the minerals calcium and phosphorus, and the B vitamins $B_1$, niacin, $B_6$ and $B_{12}$. Using medium-fat goat's cheese keeps the fat content of the recipe down: it contains about half the fat of Cheddar.

**Some more ideas**

• For an almost-instant supper, use fresh pasta (which cooks more quickly than dried) and 250 g (9 oz) reduced-fat garlic and herb soft cheese instead of the goat's cheese and spring onions. Mix a dash of milk with the soft cheese, then toss it with the hot pasta.

• Toast 4 tbsp coarse breadcrumbs under the grill until crisp and golden, and scatter them over the pasta as a lower-fat alternative to the toasted hazelnuts.

**Each serving provides**

kcal 400, **protein** 16 g, **fat** 13 g (of which saturated fat 5 g), **carbohydrate** 60 g (of which sugars 4 g), **fibre** 3 g

| ✓✓ | $B_2$, $B_{12}$, niacin, calcium |
| --- | --- |
| ✓ | A, E, copper, selenium |

Pasta and grains

# Pasta with fresh sage, rocket and feta cheese

This quick dish can be served hot or cool. The pasta is topped with salty tasting feta cheese, which goes well with the pancetta, the Italian bacon, chickpeas and tomato in the sauce. Use a tubular or thick pasta shape that will complement the chunky sauce.

## Serves 4

400 g (14 oz) tubular pasta shapes, such as casarecce (slim rolls), penne or macaroni
50 g (1¾ oz) pancetta, finely chopped
2 garlic cloves, finely chopped (optional)
2 shallots, finely chopped
8 fresh sage leaves, shredded
1 can chickpeas, about 400 g, drained
1 can chopped tomatoes, about 400 g
pinch of sugar
50 g (1¾ oz) rocket, stalks removed if preferred
100 g (3½ oz) feta cheese, crumbled
pepper

Preparation time: 10 minutes
Cooking time: about 20 minutes

1 Cook the pasta in boiling water for 10–12 minutes, or according to the packet instructions, until al dente. Drain well.

2 While the pasta is cooking, heat a large frying pan over a moderately high heat. Add the pancetta, garlic, if using, shallots and sage, and cook, stirring frequently, for 6–8 minutes or until the pancetta is golden brown and the shallots are soft.

3 Add the chickpeas, tomatoes with their juice and the sugar, and bring to the boil. Reduce the heat and simmer for 10 minutes or until the sauce has thickened slightly. Season with pepper (there is no need for salt as feta cheese is quite salty).

4 Stir in the pasta until it is well coated with the sauce ingredients. Add the rocket and stir in lightly, then sprinkle with the feta cheese and serve.

## Some more ideas

● Use finely shredded radicchio or baby spinach instead of rocket. Adding the greens at the last minute preserves both their texture and vitamin content.

● To increase the fibre content, use wholemeal shapes or noodles. Wholemeal pasta will taste good with the rich sauce and sharp cheese.

● For a vegetarian dish, omit the pancetta and use 2 cans of chickpeas.

● Fresh sage has a natural affinity with beans, so try cannellini, flageolet, borlotti or butter beans instead of the chickpeas. Canned beans are quick and convenient, but dried beans, soaked and cooked, will have a better texture.

## Each serving provides

kcal 600, **protein** 26 g, **fat** 15 g (of which saturated fat 6 g), **carbohydrate** 96 g (of which sugars 6.5 g), **fibre** 8 g

| | |
|---|---|
| ✓✓ | C, E, niacin, calcium, iron, copper, selenium |
| ✓ | B₁, folate, potassium |

### Plus points

● Feta cheese is high in fat and salt, but because it has such a strong flavour, a little goes a long way. Like all cheese, it is a good source of protein, calcium and phosphorus, and it provides useful amounts of B vitamins and vitamin E.

Pasta and grains

# Stir-fried beef with fine noodles

Tangy tamarind and lemongrass infuse a Thai-inspired sauce for tender strips of beef and fine rice noodles. Chilli brings a little heat. With mange-tout and baby sweetcorn adding colour and crunch, this is a quick and easy dish that is a meal in itself.

**Serves 2**

1 tsp tamarind paste

3 tbsp boiling water

2 tbsp soy sauce

2 tsp toasted sesame oil

1 tbsp rice wine (sake or mirin) or sherry

100 g (3½ oz) fine rice noodles, such as vermicelli

1 tbsp sunflower oil

225 g (8 oz) lean rump steak, cut into strips

85 g (3 oz) onion, cut into wedges

2 tsp chopped lemongrass

1 fresh red chilli, seeded and chopped

2 large garlic cloves, crushed

85 g (3 oz) mange-tout, halved diagonally

6 baby sweetcorn, sliced

100 g (3½ oz) fresh shiitake or chestnut mushrooms, sliced

**To serve**

soy sauce

Preparation time: 20 minutes
Cooking time: 10 minutes

**Each serving provides**

kcal 460, **protein** 30 g, **fat** 15 g (of which saturated fat 3 g), **carbohydrate** 49 g (of which sugars 6.5 g), **fibre** 3 g

| | |
|---|---|
| ✓✓✓ | B$_{12}$, C, niacin, copper |
| ✓✓ | iron, zinc, potassium |
| ✓ | B$_1$, B$_2$, B$_6$ |

1 In a small bowl, combine the tamarind paste and boiling water and leave to soak for 10 minutes, stirring frequently to break down the paste. Mix the resulting tamarind liquid with the soy sauce, sesame oil and rice wine or sherry.

2 While the tamarind is soaking, soak the rice noodles in boiling water for 4 minutes, or according to the packet instructions. Then drain, rinse under cold running water and set aside to drain thoroughly.

3 Heat the sunflower oil in a wok or very large frying pan and stir-fry the beef over a high heat for about 3 minutes or until cooked. Use a draining spoon to remove the beef from the wok and set it aside.

4 Add the onion, lemongrass, chilli and garlic to the wok and stir-fry over a high heat for 1 minute. Add the mange-tout, sweetcorn and mushrooms, and continue stir-frying for 2 minutes.

5 Return the beef to the wok. Add the tamarind liquid and the noodles and stir for about 1 minute to heat through. Serve immediately, offering soy sauce for extra seasoning as required.

**Plus points**

● Mushrooms provide useful amounts of the B vitamins niacin and B$_2$. They are also a good source of copper, which is important for healthy bones and to help the body to absorb iron from food.

● Onions contain allicin, which has anti-fungal and antibiotic properties.

**Some more ideas**

● Use strips of chicken breast instead of beef.

● Other vegetables that work well in the stir-fry include strips of red or green pepper, sliced canned water chestnuts, chopped or shredded spring onions and bean sprouts.

Pasta and grains

# Penne with artichokes and olives

This light pasta dish is very fast to prepare as only the pasta needs to be cooked. Once al dente, it is simply tossed, still warm, with diced tomatoes, quartered artichoke hearts, black olives and a rich lemony dressing flavoured with sun-dried tomato paste and garlic.

**Serves 4**

400 g (14 oz) penne or other pasta shapes

500 g (1 lb 2 oz) ripe plum tomatoes, diced

4 spring onions, finely chopped

170 g (6 oz) artichoke hearts from a can or jar, drained and quartered

55 g (2 oz) stoned black olives

4 heaped tbsp Parmesan cheese shavings to garnish

**Tomato and oregano dressing**

3 tbsp extra virgin olive oil or oil from the jar of artichokes

grated zest and juice of 1 lemon

2 tbsp sun-dried tomato paste

2 garlic cloves, crushed

6 tbsp chopped fresh oregano

salt and pepper

Preparation and cooking time: 20–25 minutes

1 Cook the pasta in a large saucepan of boiling water for 10–12 minutes, or according to the packet instructions, until just al dente.

2 Meanwhile, mix together the tomatoes, spring onions, artichoke hearts and olives in a large serving bowl. In a separate small bowl, mix the oil with the lemon zest and juice, tomato paste, garlic, oregano, and salt and pepper to taste.

3 Drain the pasta and add to the large serving bowl. Drizzle over the dressing and toss well. Garnish with shavings of Parmesan (a swivel vegetable peeler is good for making these) and serve immediately while the pasta is still warm.

**Some more ideas**

● Vary the herbs: fresh basil is also delicious, as is flat-leaf parsley, or parsley mixed with other herbs such as a little finely chopped rosemary or sage.

● If you haven't any fresh herbs, add 1 tbsp pesto instead.

● For a mellower dressing, replace the lemon juice with 4 tsp balsamic vinegar.

● For a Sicilian-inspired pasta salad, omit the artichokes and use 85 g (3 oz) stoned black olives, 8 canned anchovy fillets, about 30 g (1 oz) in total, and 2 tbsp drained capers. Omit the sun-dried tomato paste from the dressing, and replace the oregano with 6 tbsp

chopped fresh tarragon or flat-leaf parsley.

● For a more traditional, softer pasta sauce, simmer the tomatoes, spring onions, artichoke hearts and olives in a saucepan for 5 minutes, then mix with the dressing ingredients.

● Instead of Parmesan, top the salad with crumbled feta cheese, diced brie or grated Lancashire or Cheshire cheese.

● Leftover pasta salad makes a good packed lunch the next day. Transfer to a well-sealed plastic container and pack in a cool bag with a mini frozen ice pack.

**Each serving provides**  Ⓥ

kcal 550, **protein** 20 g, **fat** 17 g (of which saturated fat 5 g), **carbohydrate** 83 g (of which sugars 8 g), **fibre** 5 g

| | |
|---|---|
| ✓✓ | A, C, calcium, iron |
| ✓ | B₁, B₆, E, folate, potassium, selenium, zinc |

**Plus points**

● Pasta is a healthy low-fat food – it's the rich buttery sauces that pile on the calories and fat. Opting for olive oil instead of butter, or, better still, using small amounts of oil in vegetable sauces, is the best way to keep saturated fat to a minimum.

● Adding fresh lemon juice to the dressing boosts the levels of vitamin C in this dish.

Pasta and grains

176

# Pasta with potato, beans and pesto

This is a traditional Ligurian dish that is usually made with potatoes, green beans and baby broad beans. Here, broccoli and courgettes boost the green vegetable content. The pesto sauce used to dress the pasta and vegetables packs a wonderful flavoursome punch.

**Serves 4**

600 g (1 lb 5 oz) small new potatoes, halved or quartered

225 g (8 oz) broccoli, cut into small florets

75 g (2½ oz) shelled broad beans, skinned if preferred, 340–400 g (12–14 oz) in pods

170 g (6 oz) fine green beans, topped and tailed

2 courgettes, cut into bite-sized chunks

300 g (10½ oz) tubular or hollow pasta shapes, such as casarecce (slim rolled lengths), gemelli (narrow spirals), orecchiette (little ears) or gnocchi (fluted shells)

sprigs of fresh basil to garnish

**Tomato pesto sauce**

4–5 garlic cloves, coarsely chopped

2 tbsp pine nuts

100 g (3½ oz) fresh basil leaves

55 g (2 oz) Parmesan cheese, freshly grated

4 tbsp extra virgin olive oil

2 ripe tomatoes, diced

salt

Preparation time: 10 minutes
Cooking time: about 20 minutes

1 Cook the potatoes in boiling water for about 15 minutes or until they are tender, but not soft. Add the broccoli, broad beans, green beans and courgettes, and simmer all together for a further 5 minutes.

2 Meanwhile, cook the pasta in boiling water for 10–12 minutes, or according to the packet instructions, until al dente.

3 Make the pesto sauce while the vegetables and pasta are cooking. Pound the garlic with a pinch of salt and the pine nuts in a mortar using a pestle. Add the basil and continue pounding until the ingredients form a green paste, then work in the Parmesan cheese and oil. Finally, work in the tomatoes. Alternatively, the pesto can be made in a food processor or blender: put all the ingredients, except the oil, in the container and whiz to a paste, then gradually add the oil through the feed tube with the motor running.

4 Drain the pasta and vegetables and toss both together. Top with the pesto, garnish with sprigs of basil, scattering them over the top, and serve immediately.

**Some more ideas**

• For a more concentrated basil flavour, omit the tomato and Parmesan from the pesto sauce. Toss the pesto with the pasta and vegetables, and serve topped with dollops of soft mild goat's cheese.

• For a Sicilian-style pesto, use blanched almonds instead of the pine nuts. Cut them into fine slivers and add to the pounded mixture.

• To boost the flavour, especially when fresh basil is not at its best, add a few sprigs of fresh mint, flat-leaf parsley and/or rocket to the pesto.

**Plus points**

• Garlic helps to reduce high cholesterol levels and inhibit blood clotting, thereby reducing the risk of heart attack and stroke.

• Pine nuts are an excellent source of zinc, which is crucial in helping to protect the body against infection.

**Each serving provides**

kcal 660, **protein** 25 g, **fat** 24 g (of which saturated fat 5.5 g), **carbohydrate** 90 g (of which sugars 7 g), **fibre** 9 g

| | |
|---|---|
| ✓✓✓ | C, calcium |
| ✓✓ | A, B₁, B₆, E, folate, niacin, copper, iron, potassium |
| ✓ | selenium |

Pasta and grains

**179**

# Chilli prawns with rice sticks

Rice sticks are flat noodles made from rice flour, available from Oriental food stores. With a light texture, they are perfect for stir-fries. Here, fine asparagus, succulent tiger prawns and crunchy water chestnuts are cooked quickly with the tender noodles.

**Serves 4**

200 g (7 oz) rice sticks

2 tbsp sunflower oil

200 g (7 oz) raw tiger prawns, peeled

3 garlic cloves, cut into fine shreds

1 fresh red chilli, halved, seeded and thinly sliced

1 tbsp finely chopped fresh root ginger

100 g (3½ oz) extra fine asparagus, cut into 5 cm (2 in) lengths

150 g (5½ oz) trimmed sugarsnap peas, cut into shreds

1 can water chestnuts, about 225 g, drained and halved

4 spring onions, cut into strips

2 tsp ground coriander

4 tbsp fish sauce

1 tbsp clear honey

1½ tsp cornflour

15 g (½ oz) fresh coriander, finely chopped

fresh coriander to garnish (optional)

Preparation time: 15 minutes
Cooking time: 10 minutes

**Each serving provides**

kcal 345, **protein** 14.5 g, **fat** 6 g (of which saturated fat 0.5 g), **carbohydrate** 58 g (of which sugars 7 g), **fibre** 1.5 g

| | |
|---|---|
| ✓✓✓ | B$_{12}$, C |
| ✓✓ | copper |
| ✓ | iron, selenium |

1 Cook or soak the noodles according to the packet instructions. Drain well and set aside.

2 Heat 1 tbsp oil in a wok or large frying pan, then stir-fry the prawns for just a few minutes, until they turn from blue-grey to pink. Use a draining spoon to transfer the prawns to a plate.

3 Add the remaining oil to the wok and heat briefly, then add the garlic, chilli and ginger. Stir for a few seconds to flavour the oil, but take care not to let the flavourings burn.

4 Toss the asparagus, sugarsnap peas and water chestnuts into the wok. Stir-fry for about 3 minutes or until the asparagus and sugarsnaps start to soften. Add the spring onions and ground coriander and stir to mix.

5 Mix the fish sauce, honey and cornflour with 2 tbsp water, then pour into the wok and stir gently until boiling and thickened.

6 Return the prawns to the wok and add the noodles and chopped coriander. Toss gently until the ingredients are evenly combined and everything is hot. Serve immediately, garnished with coriander leaves, if liked.

**Plus points**

● Prawns are low in fat, but high in protein. They contain useful amounts of many of the B vitamins, particularly vitamin B$_{12}$, essential for the formation of red blood cells and for maintaining a healthy nervous system. Prawns are also a good source of the antioxidant selenium.

**Another idea**

● Use 2 skinless boneless chicken breasts (fillets) instead of the prawns; cut them into thin strips. Instead of the asparagus, sugarsnap peas and water chestnuts, use 1 seeded and diced red pepper, 125 g (4½ oz) sliced baby corn and 1 can bamboo shoots, about 225 g, drained and cut into shreds. Substitute Chinese five-spice powder and fresh basil for the ground and fresh coriander.

Pasta and grains

180

# Hong Kong-style chow mein with pork and green vegetables

A mixture of green vegetables adds colour, crispness and food value to this simple noodle stir-fry with pork and dried mushrooms. Chinese egg noodles are prepared very quickly – they only need brief soaking – so this dish can be made in less than 30 minutes.

### Serves 4

25 g (scant 1 oz) dried Chinese mushrooms or shiitake

chicken or vegetable stock (optional – see method)

340 g (12 oz) Chinese egg noodles

2 tbsp sunflower oil

1 large garlic clove, crushed

1 tbsp finely chopped fresh root ginger

1 fresh red or green chilli, seeded and finely chopped, or to taste

2 tsp five-spice powder

200 g (7 oz) pork fillet, trimmed and cut into strips

2 green peppers, seeded and thinly sliced

100 g (3½ oz) small broccoli florets

2 celery sticks, thinly sliced

2 tbsp soy sauce

1 tbsp rice wine (sake or mirin) or dry sherry

100 g (3½ oz) bean sprouts

2 tbsp finely chopped fresh coriander

2 tsp toasted sesame oil

fresh coriander leaves to garnish

Preparation time: about 20 minutes
Cooking time: about 6 minutes

1 Place the mushrooms in a small bowl and pour in enough boiling water to cover them. Leave to soak for 10 minutes. Line a sieve with muslin or kitchen paper and place it over a bowl, then pour the mushrooms and the liquid they have soaked in through the sieve. Measure the strained liquid and make it up to 100 ml (3½ fl oz) with chicken or vegetable stock if necessary, then set aside. Discard any tough stalks from the mushrooms, slice them and set aside.

2 While the mushrooms are soaking, place the noodles in a large mixing bowl and pour in enough boiling water to cover them generously. Leave to soak for 4 minutes, or according to the packet instructions, until tender. Drain well and set aside.

3 Heat a wok or large frying pan over a high heat. Add 1 tbsp of the sunflower oil and, when it is hot, stir in the garlic, ginger, chilli and five-spice powder. Stir-fry for 30 seconds, taking care not to let the flavourings burn.

4 Add the strips of pork and continue stir-frying for about 2 minutes or until they are cooked through. Use a draining spoon to remove the pork from the wok and set it aside.

5 Add the remaining oil to the wok and heat until it is almost smoking. Stir in the peppers, broccoli, celery and mushrooms, and stir-fry for 2 minutes. Stir in the mushroom liquid, soy sauce and rice wine or sherry, then return the pork to the wok. Continue cooking, stirring constantly, for about 1 minute or until the pork is reheated.

6 Stir in the noodles, then the bean sprouts and toss together briefly, just long enough to heat the ingredients without softening the bean sprouts, as they should retain their crunch.

7 Stir in the chopped coriander and sprinkle with the sesame oil. Serve the chow mein immediately, garnished with coriander leaves.

### Plus points

• The average fat content of lean pork is just 3.5% (3.5 g per 100 g), much the same as that contained in chicken breast, which (without skin) contains 3.2 g per 100 g. Pork is also a good source of zinc, and it provides useful amounts of iron and the B vitamins, particularly $B_1$, $B_6$, $B_{12}$ and niacin.

Pasta and grains

**Each serving provides**

kcal 488, **protein** 17 g, **fat** 13 g (of which saturated fat 3 g), **carbohydrate** 73 g (of which sugars 3 g), **fibre** 2.5 g

| | |
|---|---|
| ✓✓✓ | C |
| ✓✓ | $B_1$, $B_{12}$, niacin |
| ✓ | $B_6$, folate, iron, potassium, zinc |

**Some more ideas**

● Replace the pork with skinless boneless chicken breasts (fillets), cut into thin slices, or peeled raw tiger prawns.

● Use wheat-free Chinese rice noodles for anyone on a gluten-free diet.

● For a delicious vegetarian version, omit the pork fillet and add 300 g (10½ oz) mange-tout or sugarsnap peas. Baby sweetcorn, halved lengthways, sliced carrots, chopped French beans, cauliflower florets and sliced fresh mushrooms are also all suitable.

# Pasta with two-cheese sauce

After a busy day, this is one of the quickest options for a nutritious meal – the cheese mixture is prepared in the time it takes the pasta to cook. When you add the hot pasta to the Parmesan and ricotta, the heat melts them, producing an instant creamy sauce.

## Serves 4

400 g (14 oz) fusilli (spirals) or other pasta shapes

225 g (8 oz) frozen peas

45 g (1½ oz) Parmesan cheese, freshly grated

2 tbsp extra virgin olive oil

150 g (5½ oz) ricotta cheese

finely torn fresh basil or oregano

salt and pepper

Preparation and cooking time: 15 minutes

**1** Cook the pasta in boiling water for 7 minutes. Add the peas, return the water to the boil and continue cooking for 3–5 minutes, or according to the pasta packet instructions, until the pasta is al dente and the peas are cooked.

**2** Meanwhile, put the Parmesan cheese into a large serving bowl, add the olive oil and beat until a thick paste forms. Add the ricotta cheese and beat until well blended. Season with salt and pepper to taste.

**3** Drain the pasta, reserving about 6 tbsp of the cooking water. Immediately add the hot pasta to the cheese mixture and stir until the pasta is well coated. Add the reserved cooking water to thin the sauce.

**4** Adjust the seasoning, if necessary, and sprinkle generously with fresh basil or oregano. Serve at once.

### Some more ideas

• All kinds of vegetables can be used in this dish. If they are fresh, chop or slice them small enough so that they cook in the same time that it takes to cook the pasta. Try broccoli florets, grated carrots, green beans or sweetcorn kernels.

• Stir in grated raw courgettes or carrots at the end of step 3. Raw vegetables are particularly high in fibre and vitamins.

• Sun-dried tomatoes, well drained and cut into thin strips, can be added to the cheese sauce.

• For a Mediterranean-style dish of pasta and broad beans with a quick cheese sauce, replace the peas with frozen or fresh broad beans. Mash 100 g (3½ oz) drained feta cheese, then beat in 50 g (1¾ oz) soft goat's cheese to make a thick paste. Stir in a little of the pasta cooking water to thin the sauce, if necessary, and season with salt, pepper and a little freshly grated lemon zest. Stir in finely chopped fresh dill just before serving.

### Plus points

• Parmesan cheese, traditionally served with so many pasta dishes, is very high in fat. Here only a small amount is used for its distinctive flavour, and it is combined with ricotta cheese which is relatively low in fat – ricotta contains 11 g fat per 100 g (3½ oz), while the same weight of full-fat soft cheese has 47 g fat.

• Peas are a good source of fibre and they supply vitamin C, folate, iron and zinc. Peas also contribute B vitamins, in particular $B_1$, and their protein content is high for a vegetable that also provides a useful amount of folate.

## Each serving provides

kcal 535, **protein** 22 g, **fat** 15 g (of which saturated fat 6 g), **carbohydrate** 81 g (of which sugars 4 g), **fibre** 6 g

✓✓  calcium, copper, iron, zinc

✓  A, $B_1$, $B_{12}$, folate, niacin, selenium

Pasta and grains

# Spaghetti with chickpeas, spinach and spicy tomato sauce

Here's a colourful and easy vegetarian dish that makes a satisfying main course all on its own. It's a delicious way to mix pasta and beans, in this case chickpeas, for a good balance of protein and starchy carbohydrate.

**Serves 4**

2 tbsp extra virgin olive oil

1 onion, chopped

1 garlic clove, crushed

1 celery stick, finely chopped

1 can chopped tomatoes, about 400 g

340 g (12 oz) spaghetti

2 cans chickpeas, about 410 g each, drained and rinsed

½ tsp Tabasco sauce, or to taste

170 g (6 oz) baby spinach leaves

salt and pepper

55 g (2 oz) pecorino cheese, freshly grated

fresh flat-leaf parsley leaves to garnish

Preparation and cooking time: 20–25 minutes

**Each serving provides**  Ⓥ

kcal 582, **protein** 27 g, **fat** 15 g (of which saturated fat 4 g), **carbohydrate** 89 g (of which sugars 9 g), **fibre** 10 g

| | |
|---|---|
| ✓✓✓ | A |
| ✓✓ | C, E, folate, niacin, calcium, copper, iron, potassium, zinc |
| ✓ | B₁, B₆ |

1 Heat the olive oil in a heavy-based saucepan, add the onion and garlic, and cook over a moderate heat for 3–4 minutes, stirring occasionally, until softened.

2 Add the celery and fry, stirring, for 1–2 minutes, then stir in the chopped tomatoes with their juice and bring to the boil. Reduce the heat and simmer gently, stirring occasionally, for about 15 minutes or until thick.

3 Meanwhile, cook the spaghetti in a large pan of boiling water for 10–12 minutes, or according to the packet instructions, until al dente.

4 When the sauce is cooked, stir in the chickpeas and Tabasco sauce. Add the spinach leaves and simmer for 1–2 minutes, stirring, until the spinach wilts. Season with salt and pepper to taste.

5 Drain the spaghetti and toss with the chickpeas and tomato sauce. Scatter over the parsley leaves, and serve immediately, sprinkled with the pecorino cheese.

**Some more ideas**

• For tagliatelle with cannellini beans, use tagliatelle or fettuccine instead of spaghetti, and replace the chickpeas with canned cannellini or haricot beans. Instead of spinach, add 200 g (7 oz) cooked asparagus spears, cut into 2.5 cm (1 in) lengths, to the sauce. Just before serving, stir in 85 g (3 oz) thin strips of trimmed Parma ham; omit the pecorino cheese.

• Grill 4 lean rashers of back bacon until crisp and golden, then drain well and chop roughly. Stir into the tomato sauce with the chickpeas. Reduce the pecorino cheese to 30 g (1 oz).

**Plus points**

• Despite its name, the chickpea is not really a pea but a seed. Chickpeas contain good amounts of iron, manganese and folate, and are richer in vitamin E than most other pulses.

• Pasta, like bread and potatoes, has a reputation for being fattening, but in fact it is healthily low in fat – it's butter, cheese and rich sauces that add on the calories and fat.

• By cooking the spinach leaves in the sauce very briefly, just to wilt them, all their juices and the maximum nutrients are retained.

# Sun-dried tomato and bean risotto

Moist risotto served with a simple side salad makes a satisfying meal, and the risotto can be endlessly varied – all sorts of vegetables (fresh, frozen, canned or dried) can be used. To achieve the perfect texture, use risotto rice such as arborio and add the hot stock in stages.

**Serves 4**

1 tbsp extra virgin olive oil

1 large onion, chopped

2 garlic cloves, crushed

300 g (10½ oz) risotto rice

85 g (3 oz) sun-dried tomatoes (dry-packed), coarsely chopped

240 ml (8 fl oz) dry white wine

1.2 litres (2 pints) hot vegetable stock, preferably home-made

225 g (8 oz) frozen broad beans

55 g (2 oz) Parmesan cheese, freshly grated

30 g (1 oz) pine nuts

salt and pepper

12 large fresh basil leaves, freshly shredded, to garnish

Preparation time: 5 minutes
Cooking time: 25 minutes

**Each serving provides** Ⓥ

kcal 610, **protein** 17 g, **fat** 25 g (of which saturated fat 5 g), **carbohydrate** 67 g (of which sugars 5 g), **fibre** 4 g

| | |
|---|---|
| ✓✓ | A, C, E, folate, niacin, calcium |
| ✓ | B₁, B₆, B₁₂, copper, potassium, zinc |

**1** Heat the oil in a large saucepan. Add the onion and garlic and fry over a moderate heat for 5 minutes, stirring frequently, until the onion softens and begins to colour.

**2** Stir in the rice and sun-dried tomatoes, making sure the grains are coated in the oil, then pour in the wine. Bring to the boil, stirring occasionally.

**3** Pour in half the hot stock and bring back to the boil, then reduce the heat and simmer, stirring frequently, for 10 minutes. Add the broad beans and half the remaining hot stock. Bring back to the boil again, then continue to simmer for about 10 minutes, adding the remaining stock in one or two stages as the rice absorbs the liquid.

**4** The risotto is ready when the rice is tender but the grains are still whole, and the broad beans are cooked. It should be moist and creamy.

**5** Add the Parmesan cheese and pine nuts with seasoning to taste and stir to mix. Serve at once, sprinkled with shredded basil.

**Some more ideas**

• To use fresh broad beans instead of frozen, allow 1 kg (2¼ lb) in pods. Shell them and add with the first batch of stock in step 3.

• Replace the broad beans with 300 g (10½ oz) baby spinach leaves, stirring them into the cooked risotto just before the Parmesan cheese. This way, the spinach is freshly wilted and full flavoured when served.

• Add 3 tbsp pesto with the last of the stock and omit the Parmesan, pine nuts and basil.

• For a mushroom risotto, omit the broad beans and use chicken stock instead of vegetable stock. Add 1 tsp fresh thyme leaves with the first addition of stock. Just before the risotto has finished cooking, fry 450 g (1 lb) mixed fresh mushrooms, halved or sliced if large, in 30 g (1 oz) butter or 2 tbsp olive oil over a high heat for 3–4 minutes or until lightly browned. Stir the mushrooms and their juices into the risotto with the Parmesan. For an even richer mushroom flavour, add 1 tbsp finely chopped dried porcini mushrooms with the wine.

**Plus points**

• Rice is one of the most important staple crops, the very basis of life for millions of people worldwide. Polishing the grains to produce the familiar white varieties partially removes B vitamins; however, in this recipe, both broad beans and pine nuts provide B₁ and niacin.

• Along with other beans and pulses, broad beans are high in protein and low in fat, and offer good amounts of dietary fibre.

# Smoked fish paella

One of the reasons the Mediterranean diet is considered healthy is that it features dishes like this one from Spain, based on rice cooked in olive oil with lots of vegetables and a modest amount of protein. The chorizo sausage here adds an authentic Spanish flavour.

**Serves 4**

900 ml (1½ pints) vegetable or fish stock

large pinch of saffron threads

50 g (1¾ oz) thin chorizo sausage

400 g (14 oz) undyed smoked haddock fillet, skinned

2 tbsp extra virgin olive oil

1 large onion, finely chopped

2 large garlic cloves, crushed, or 1 tbsp bottled chopped garlic in oil, drained

250 g (8½ oz) green beans, cut into bite-sized pieces

250 g (8½ oz) paella or other short-grain rice

150 g (5½ oz) frozen peas

salt and pepper

finely chopped parsley to garnish

Preparation time: 10 minutes
Cooking time: 20 minutes

**Each serving provides**

kcal 465, **protein** 28 g, **fat** 13 g (of which saturated fat 1 g), **carbohydrate** 58 g (of which sugars 4 g), **fibre** 4 g

| | |
|---|---|
| ✓✓ | B₁₂, folate, iron, selenium |
| ✓ | B₁, B₆, C, niacin, calcium, potassium |

1 Bring the stock to the boil in a pan over a high heat. Add the saffron threads, reduce the heat and leave to simmer gently while preparing the other ingredients.

2 Remove the thick skin from the chorizo sausage and thinly slice the sausage. Cut the haddock into large chunks. Heat the olive oil in a 30 cm (12 in) round, shallow flameproof casserole, paella pan or frying pan. Add the chorizo, onion, garlic and green beans and fry for 2 minutes, stirring occasionally.

3 Add the rice and stir until all the grains are coated with oil. Add the saffron-flavoured stock and stir. Season with salt and pepper to taste. Bring to the boil, then reduce the heat to low and simmer for 3 minutes.

4 Gently stir in the haddock pieces and peas. Simmer for 20 minutes or until all the liquid has been absorbed and the rice is tender. Stir halfway through cooking, taking care not to break up the haddock too much. Sprinkle with parsley and serve.

**Some more ideas**

● For a smoked ham and vegetable paella, omit the haddock and chorizo sausage and instead use 300 g (10½ oz) smoked ham, cut into cubes. Instead of green beans, use 2 sliced celery sticks and 300 g (10½ oz) chopped runner beans. In step 4, stir in 1 can red kidney beans or pinto beans, about 400 g, drained and rinsed.

● Use fresh haddock fillet instead of smoked.

**Plus points**

● Frozen peas couldn't be quicker or easier to use, and the good news is that they are just as nutritious as fresh peas. Research comparing the level of vitamin C in fresh and frozen vegetables found that, in many cases, frozen vegetables contain higher levels of vitamin C than fresh. The longer fresh vegetables are stored, the greater the vitamin loss will be, but frozen vegetables maintain their vitamin levels throughout storage – frozen peas retain 60–70% of their vitamin C content.

● Smoked haddock, like other fish, is an excellent low-fat source of protein. It is also an excellent source of iodine, and a useful source of potassium and vitamin B₆.

Pasta and grains

**191**

# Asparagus risotto with truffle oil

Not only is risotto satisfying and delicious, it is a great vehicle for whatever fresh vegetables are in season. It needs plenty of stirring, but takes only minutes to become perfectly cooked and creamy. Truffle oil is a luxurious finishing touch for this risotto.

**Serves 4**

2 tbsp extra virgin olive oil

1 red onion, chopped

3 garlic cloves, chopped

350 g (12½ oz) risotto rice

250 ml (8½ fl oz) dry white wine

about 700 ml (24 fl oz) boiling vegetable
  stock

300 g (10½ oz) asparagus, cut into small
  pieces

1 tsp truffle oil

4 tbsp freshly grated Parmesan cheese

15 g (½ oz) softened butter, divided into
  4 portions

2–3 tbsp snipped fresh chives

salt and pepper

Preparation and cooking time: 30 minutes

**1** Heat the oil in a heavy-based pan and lightly sauté the onion and garlic for 2–3 minutes or until softened. Add the rice and cook over a moderately high heat for 1–2 minutes, stirring, until the rice is lightly toasted and golden brown in places.

**2** Pour in the wine and stir until the rice has absorbed it. Add a small amount of stock and stir until it is absorbed. Continue gradually adding the stock, letting each amount be absorbed before adding the next, stirring frequently.

**3** When the rice is almost al dente (after about 15 minutes), stir in the asparagus. Cook for a further 5 minutes or until the asparagus is tender and the rice is completely cooked. Continue adding stock during this time. The finished risotto should have a slightly soupy, almost creamy texture.

**4** Remove from the heat. Season with salt and pepper to taste, and stir in the truffle oil and grated Parmesan. Spoon into warmed bowls, top each serving with a portion of butter and a sprinkling of chives, and serve.

**Some more ideas**

• When baby leeks are in season, make the risotto with 3–4 baby leeks, coarsely chopped, and 5 shallots, chopped, instead of asparagus.

• For a porcini and pea risotto with Parma ham, break up 10 g (¼ oz) dried porcini, rinse well to remove grit and add with the wine. In step 3, stir in 250 g (8½ oz) frozen petit pois in place of the asparagus. Omit the truffle oil and, instead of butter, garnish with 50 g (1¾ oz) Parma ham, cut into thin shreds.

• For a non-vegetarian dish, you can use chicken stock instead of vegetable stock.

**Each serving provides** ⓥ

kcal 575, **protein** 17 g, **fat** 18 g (of which saturated fat 6 g), **carbohydrate** 80 g (of which sugars 4 g), **fibre** 3 g

| | |
|---|---|
| ✓✓ | A, B₁, B₆, C, folate, calcium, copper, iron, zinc |
| ✓ | E, niacin, potassium, selenium |

**Plus points**

• Asparagus has been cultivated for over 2000 years and has been used medicinally since the 16th century. It is a rich source of many of the B vitamins, especially folate. A good intake of folate is important during the early stages of pregnancy to prevent birth defects such as spina bifida.

• The starch in rice is digested and absorbed slowly by the body, thereby providing a steady release of glucose into the blood, which is helpful in keeping blood sugar at a constant level.

Pasta and grains

# Cannellini bean burgers

These nutritious vegetarian burgers are tasty enough to appeal to everyone. They hold their shape well yet remain wonderfully moist when grilled. A cherry tomato and basil salad is the perfect complement for this quick main meal.

**Serves 4**

5 tsp extra virgin olive oil
1 small onion, finely chopped
1 carrot, coarsely grated
2 tsp sun-dried tomato paste
2 cans cannellini beans, about 410 g each, drained and rinsed
55 g (2 oz) fresh white breadcrumbs (made by grating the bread)
55 g (2 oz) mature Cheddar cheese, grated
2 tbsp chopped parsley
4 large wholemeal baps
salt and pepper
frisée to garnish

**Cherry tomato salad**

1 tbsp extra virgin olive oil
1 tsp lemon juice
340 g (12 oz) cherry tomatoes, a mixture of red and yellow if possible, quartered
1 tbsp torn or shredded fresh basil

Preparation time: 20 minutes
Cooking time: 8–10 minutes

**Each serving provides** Ⓥ

kcal 500, **protein** 22 g, **fat** 15 g (of which saturated fat 5 g), **carbohydrate** 75 g (of which sugars 11 g), **fibre** 14 g

| | |
|---|---|
| ✓✓✓ | A, selenium |
| ✓✓ | B₁, C, niacin, calcium, copper, iron, zinc |
| ✓ | B₂, B₆, E, folate, potassium |

1 Heat 3 tsp of the oil in a non-stick frying pan, add the onion and cook for 5 minutes, stirring frequently, until softened. Add the grated carrot and cook for a further 2 minutes, stirring. Remove from the heat and stir in the tomato paste.

2 Preheat the grill to moderate. Tip the cannellini beans into a bowl and mash with a potato masher to break them up roughly. Add the cooked vegetables, breadcrumbs, cheese, parsley, and salt and pepper to taste.

3 Use your hands to mix all the ingredients together, then divide into 4 portions. Shape each into a large burger, about 10 cm (4 in) in diameter and 2.5 cm (1 in) thick.

4 Lightly brush the burgers on both sides with the remaining 2 tsp olive oil and place on the rack of the grill pan. Cook for 4–5 minutes on each side or until slightly crisp and hot all the way through.

5 Meanwhile, make the salad by whisking together the oil, lemon juice and seasoning to taste in a bowl. Add the tomatoes and basil.

6 Split the baps in half using a serrated knife. If liked, toast under the grill with the burgers for the last 2–3 minutes of cooking. Place the bean burgers inside and serve, with the tomato salad and a garnish of frisée.

**Some more ideas**

• For spicy bean burgers, replace the tomato paste with 1½ tsp of your favourite curry paste.
• Make soya bean and olive burgers. Cook a bunch of finely chopped spring onions and 1 seeded and finely chopped fresh red chilli in the 3 tsp oil for 3–4 minutes to soften, then stir in 1 grated courgette and cook for 2 more minutes; omit the tomato paste. Mash 2 cans soya beans, about 410 g each, drained and rinsed. Add the cooked vegetables together with 55 g (2 oz) chopped stoned black olives, a dash of soy sauce, 2 tbsp chopped fresh coriander and seasoning to taste. Shape into 8 burgers and brush with the remaining 2 tsp oil. Grill for 3–4 minutes on each side. Serve in halved pitta breads, allowing 2 burgers per person, and add 450 g (1 lb) plum tomatoes and ½ cucumber, both sliced.

**Plus points**

• Not only are cannellini beans packed with protein, they also contain many minerals, including iron, potassium, phosphorus and manganese.
• Cheese is a very nutritious food to include in the diet. In general, the harder, more dense cheeses such as Cheddar contain more protein, calcium, phosphorus and B vitamins than softer cheeses.

Pasta and grains

# Bulghur wheat pilaf

The combination of grains and beans is common to all cuisines with a tradition of vegetarian meals. In this delicious one-pot main dish, ground coriander and cinnamon and dried apricots add a Middle Eastern flavour.

**Serves 4**

2 eggs

2 tbsp sunflower oil

1 large onion, finely chopped

2 large garlic cloves, crushed

1½ tsp ground coriander

1 tsp ground cinnamon

1 tsp turmeric

pinch of crushed dried chillies (optional)

1 can butter beans, about 400 g, drained and rinsed

100 g (3½ oz) ready-to-eat dried apricots

300 g (10½ oz) bulghur wheat

150 g (5½ oz) thin green beans, halved

salt and pepper

fresh coriander leaves to garnish

Preparation and cooking time: 30 minutes

**Each serving provides** Ⓥ

kcal 485, **protein** 18 g, **fat** 11 g (of which saturated fat 2 g), **carbohydrate** 81 g (of which sugars 13 g), **fibre** 7 g

| | |
|---|---|
| ✓✓ | E, copper, iron |
| ✓ | A, B₁, B₂, B₁₂, folate, calcium, potassium |

1 Place the eggs in a saucepan of cold water, bring to the boil and boil gently for 10 minutes. Drain the eggs and cool under cold running water. Set aside.

2 While the eggs are cooking, heat the oil in a large flameproof casserole. Add the onion and garlic and fry for 3 minutes, stirring occasionally. Stir in the ground coriander, cinnamon, turmeric and chillies, if using. Stir for a further minute.

3 Add the butter beans and apricots, and stir to coat them with the spices. Stir in the bulghur wheat and green beans, then pour in enough water to cover by about 2 cm (¾ in). Season with salt and pepper to taste. Bring to the boil, then reduce the heat to its lowest setting. Cover and simmer for 20 minutes or until all the liquid has been absorbed.

4 While the stew is cooking, shell and slice the eggs. Fluff the bulghur wheat with a fork and adjust the seasoning, if necessary. Serve hot, garnished with the egg slices and sprinkled with coriander leaves.

**Plus points**

● Bulghur wheat is a good low-fat source of starchy (complex) carbohydrate. It contains useful amounts of some of the B vitamins, particularly B₁, as well as copper and iron.

● Ready-to-eat dried apricots are a versatile and nutritious ingredient and it is well worth keeping a packet in your storecupboard. They are ideal for quick snacks, and they can be added to breakfast cereals, baked goods, stews and casseroles. They provide beta-carotene, which is converted into vitamin A in the body, and are a useful source of iron, calcium and fibre.

**Another idea**

● Couscous, like bulghur wheat, is a great low-fat source of starchy carbohydrate. To make a couscous pilaf, fry 1 large diced red pepper with the onion and garlic. Instead of green beans, use 140 g (5 oz) carrots, chopped, adding them with the spices. In step 3, stir in 200 g (7 oz) couscous, 100 g (3½ oz) raisins, or a mixture of raisins and sultanas, and a can of chickpeas, about 400 g, drained. Add enough water to cover the ingredients by about 1 cm (½ in) and simmer, covered, for 15 minutes. Fluff the couscous with a fork, adjust the seasoning and stir in 200 g (7 oz) baby spinach leaves. Sprinkle with chopped parsley or fresh coriander and serve.

Pasta and grains

# Couscous and flageolet niçoise

This is a bright, cheery salad with a real Mediterranean feel and flavour. Couscous is mixed with pale green flageolet beans, then tossed with fresh green beans, tomatoes and cucumber in a piquant dressing made with sun-dried tomatoes.

**Serves 4**

250 g (8½ oz) couscous

400 ml (14 fl oz) boiling water

1 tbsp extra virgin olive oil

1 tsp dried herbes de Provence

140 g (5 oz) green beans

½ cucumber

2 cans flageolet beans, about 410 g each, drained and rinsed

1 small red onion, finely chopped

200 g (7 oz) cherry tomatoes, cut in half

2 hard-boiled eggs, cut into quarters

8 anchovy fillets, drained and halved lengthways

75 g (2½ oz) black olives

**Sun-dried tomato dressing**

juice of 1 large lemon

2 tbsp extra virgin olive oil

1 tbsp finely chopped sun-dried tomatoes packed in oil

salt and pepper

Preparation time: 30 minutes

## Each serving provides

kcal 424, **protein** 16 g, **fat** 18 g (of which saturated fat 3 g), **carbohydrate** 51 g (of which sugars 7 g), **fibre** 7 g

| | |
|---|---|
| ✓✓ | B₁, B₁₂, C, E, iron |
| ✓ | A, B₂, B₆, folate, niacin, calcium, copper, potassium, selenium, zinc |

1 First make the dressing. Combine the lemon juice, oil, sun-dried tomatoes and pepper to taste in a screwtop jar, cover and shake well to mix. Set aside.

2 Put the couscous into a large mixing bowl and pour over the boiling water. Stir in the olive oil and dried herbs, then cover and leave for 5 minutes or until the couscous has absorbed all the water. Uncover, stir to separate the grains and leave to cool.

3 Meanwhile, steam the green beans for 3–4 minutes or until tender but still crisp. Drain, then refresh under cold running water. Cut in half.

4 Cut the cucumber into thick slices, then cut each slice into 4 wedges. Stir the cucumber into the couscous, together with the flageolet beans, green beans, onion and tomatoes. Add the dressing and toss gently until well mixed. Taste and add salt and pepper, if necessary (remember that the anchovies and olives will be salty).

5 Transfer the salad to a serving bowl. Garnish with the hard-boiled egg quarters, anchovies and black olives, and serve.

**Some more ideas**

● For a vegetarian dish, simply omit the anchovies.

● Make a butter bean couscous salad, using 2 cans butter beans, about 410 g each, drained and rinsed, instead of flageolet beans. Replace the green beans with 2 large peppers, 1 red and 1 green, seeded and cut into thin strips. Make the dressing with 1 tbsp pesto, the juice of 1 lemon and 1 tbsp extra virgin olive oil. To garnish, instead of eggs, anchovies and olives, grill 100 g (3½ oz) lean back bacon, then drain well and crumble it over the salad.

**Plus points**

● Couscous, made from semolina, is the staple food in many North African countries. Like other cereals, it is low in fat and high in starchy carbohydrate.

● Eggs are an excellent source of vitamin B₁₂, which is vital for the growth and division of cells and for red bloodcell formation.

● Anchovies, like all oily fish, are a source of vitamin D, esssential for maintaining strong, healthy bones, and vitamin A, required for healthy vision and skin.

**Pasta and grains**

# Wholewheat and vegetable pan-fry with teriyaki tofu

Here pre-cooked wholewheat grains are cooked in stock, then tossed with fresh ginger and Oriental vegetables to make the perfect partner for Japanese-style marinated tofu. This is a delicious, nutritious dish made in minutes.

**Serves 4**

600 ml (1 pint) vegetable stock
200 g (7 oz) pre-cooked wholewheat grains
2 garlic cloves, crushed
1 tbsp finely grated fresh root ginger
2 tbsp dark soy sauce
1 tbsp mirin
1 tbsp sunflower oil
1 tbsp clear honey
1 tsp Chinese five-spice powder
1 packet tofu, about 285 g, cut into bite-sized triangles

**Vegetable pan-fry**

2 tbsp sunflower oil
2 garlic cloves, crushed
1 tbsp finely grated fresh root ginger
1 large red pepper, seeded and cut into long matchsticks
1 leek, cut into long matchsticks
250 g (8½ oz) bean sprouts

Preparation and cooking time: 30 minutes

**Each serving provides** ⓥ

kcal 375, **protein** 16 g, **fat** 13 g (of which saturated fat 2 g), **carbohydrate** 50 g (of which sugars 12 g), **fibre** 6 g

| | |
|---|---|
| ✓✓✓ | A, C, E, calcium, copper |
| ✓✓ | B₁, niacin, iron |
| ✓ | B₆, folate, potassium, zinc |

1 Pour the vegetable stock into a saucepan and bring to the boil. Add the wholewheat grains and simmer for 15–20 minutes or until they are tender and the stock has been absorbed.

2 Meanwhile, for the teriyaki tofu, mix together the garlic, ginger, soy sauce, mirin, sunflower oil, honey and five-spice powder in a bowl. Add the tofu and turn until all the pieces are coated in the mixture. Set aside to marinate while cooking the vegetables.

3 Heat the oil in a wok or large frying pan, add the garlic and ginger, and stir-fry for a few seconds. Add the red pepper and leek strips, and stir-fry for 3–4 minutes or until softened. Stir in the bean sprouts and stir-fry for 3 minutes.

4 Add the wholewheat grains to the wok. Hold a sieve over the wok and tip the tofu mixture into it, straining the marinade into the wok. Toss until the wholewheat grains and marinade are mixed with the vegetables. Gently toss in the tofu and cook for 1–2 minutes longer or until heated through. Serve immediately.

**Another idea**

• To make a Mediterranean wholewheat and vegetable pan-fry, mix together 2 crushed garlic cloves, 8 finely chopped sun-dried tomatoes packed in oil, drained, 1 tbsp oil from the jar of tomatoes, and 10 shredded fresh basil leaves from a 15 g packet (reserve the rest). Add the tofu and set aside to marinate. In step 3, omit the ginger, leek and bean sprouts, and stir-fry 1 thinly sliced large onion and 2 courgettes, cut into strips, with the red pepper and garlic. Add the wholewheat grains, 55 g (2 oz) black olives, the remaining shredded basil, and the tofu and tomato mixture. Heat through, stirring and tossing, and serve.

**Plus points**

• Wholewheat grains are low in fat and high in starchy carbohydrate. Because the whole of the grain is eaten, they are also a good source of dietary fibre.

• Soya beans are rich in isoflavones, a hormone-like substance. They function in various ways, including improving the balance of cholesterol in the blood, and helping to fight against heart disease.

• Bean sprouts, like other sprouted seeds, are rich in B vitamins and vitamin C.

Pasta and grains

# Vegetables

Vegetables can be so much more than just accompaniments to the main dish. The juicy flavours of ripe vegetables are a delicious way to boost your vitamin and nutrient intake. In this chapter you will find familiar recipes with tasty variations, such as a Speedy two-bean chilli and Caribbean butternut squash and sweetcorn stew. You can also try out some entirely new dishes, including the famous Mediterranean dish known as Chakchouka.

# Speedy two-bean chilli

Here's a hearty and satisfying chilli – without the carne (meat) – that can be made in minutes. This version combines two varieties of beans with sweetcorn in a rich tomato sauce flavoured with herbs and fresh chilli. Serve with boiled rice or warm crusty bread.

**Serves 4**

2 tbsp extra virgin olive oil

1 large onion, halved and sliced

1 fresh red chilli, seeded and chopped

1 can chopped tomatoes, about 400 g

1 tbsp chilli sauce

2 tbsp tomato ketchup

600 ml (1 pint) hot vegetable stock, preferably home-made

1 tbsp chopped parsley

1 tbsp chopped fresh oregano

1 can red kidney beans, about 400 g, drained and rinsed

1 can cannellini beans, about 400 g, drained and rinsed

200 g (7 oz) frozen sweetcorn

salt and pepper

**To serve**

150 g (5½ oz) fromage frais

2 tbsp snipped fresh chives

fresh oregano leaves to garnish

Preparation time: 5 minutes

Cooking time: 25 minutes

**1** Heat the oil in a large frying pan. Add the onion and chilli, and fry over a moderate heat for 5 minutes, stirring occasionally, until the onion is lightly browned.

**2** Stir in the tomatoes with their juice, the chilli sauce, ketchup, stock, parsley and oregano, with seasoning to taste. Bring to the boil, then reduce the heat and simmer for 10 minutes, stirring occasionally.

**3** Add the kidney and cannellini beans and the sweetcorn. Simmer for a further 10 minutes.

**4** Meanwhile, mix the fromage frais with the snipped chives. Taste the chilli for seasoning and adjust if necessary. Serve the chilli sprinkled with the oregano leaves and offer the fromage frais mixture separately.

**Some more ideas**

● Serve the chilli with baked potatoes, with couscous or with warmed flour tortillas.

● Turn the bean mixture into vegetarian chilli burgers: cook the onion and chilli as in the main recipe, then place in a food processor. Omit the tomatoes and stock, but add all the remaining ingredients to the processor. Add 1 egg yolk and 200 g (7 oz) fresh breadcrumbs. Process until smooth, then divide into 8 portions. Shape into burgers and chill for at least 1 hour. Coat the burgers with more fresh breadcrumbs, pressing them on neatly – you will need about 75 g (2½ oz). Brush each burger with a little extra virgin olive oil and cook on a griddle or in a non-stick frying pan for 10 minutes on each side. Alternatively, cook under the grill preheated to moderate.

**Each serving provides**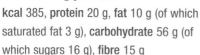

kcal 385, **protein** 20 g, **fat** 10 g (of which saturated fat 3 g), **carbohydrate** 56 g (of which sugars 16 g), **fibre** 15 g

| | |
|---|---|
| ✓✓ | B₁, B₂, B₆, B₁₂, C, E, folate, niacin, iron |
| ✓ | A, calcium, copper, potassium, selenium, zinc |

**Plus points**

● Pulses have a lot going for them. They are a cheap source of protein, a good source of B-group vitamins and, when sprouted, are an excellent source of vitamin C. In addition, kidney beans and cannellini beans provide more than 3 times the amount of fibre found in many vegetables.

Vegetables

# Tacos with salsa and guacamole

Quick and easy to make, this filling and colourful main course is low in saturated fat but high in flavour. It is a great recipe to tempt even the most ardent of meat-eaters into enjoying a vegetable-based meal.

**Serves 4**

**Aubergine and squash filling**

2 tbsp extra virgin olive oil

1 onion, finely chopped

1 aubergine, about 280 g (10 oz), cubed

1 butternut squash, about 675 g (1½ lb), halved, seeded, peeled and cubed

1 large courgette, about 170 g (6 oz), cubed

¼ tsp chilli powder

½ tsp ground cumin

1 garlic clove, crushed

1 can tomatoes, about 400 g

salt and pepper

**Guacamole**

1 large ripe avocado

juice of ½ lime

**Tomato salsa**

3 ripe tomatoes, diced

½ red onion, finely chopped

4 tbsp chopped fresh coriander

**To serve**

8 taco shells, about 85 g (3 oz) in total

150 g (5½ oz) plain low-fat yogurt

pinch of paprika

lime wedges

sprigs of fresh coriander to garnish

Preparation time: 10 minutes

Cooking time: 20 minutes

1 Heat the oil in a large saucepan, add the onion and aubergine, and fry for 5 minutes over a high heat, stirring frequently, until the vegetables are lightly browned.

2 Add the butternut squash and courgette, then stir in the chilli powder, cumin and garlic. Pour in the canned tomatoes with their juice, and add seasoning to taste. Bring to the boil, breaking up the tomatoes with a wooden spoon. Cover the pan and simmer for about 15 minutes, stirring occasionally, until the squash is just tender. Check occasionally to ensure that there is enough liquid in the pan and add a little water, if necessary, to prevent the vegetables from sticking.

3 Meanwhile, preheat the oven to 180°C (350°F, gas mark 4). To make the guacamole, halve and stone the avocado, scoop out the flesh into a bowl and mash it with the lime juice. Mix together all the ingredients for the salsa in a separate bowl. Set the guacamole and salsa aside.

4 Put the taco shells on a baking tray and warm them in the oven for 3–4 minutes. Transfer the taco shells to warmed serving plates. Fill with the aubergine mixture. Top with guacamole, yogurt and salsa, then sprinkle with paprika. Garnish with lime wedges and coriander sprigs, and serve.

**Plus points**

● Avocados are high in calories, mainly from the monounsaturated fat they contain. This is the same type of fat that makes olive oil so highly recommended for the prevention of coronary heart disease. Avocados are also rich in vitamin E, an important antioxidant.

● When they were first introduced to Europe, tomatoes were the focus for suspicion, being known as love apples and thought to have aphrodisiac properties. We now know that they do have benefits for the heart, but not in the romantic sense.

**Each serving provides** Ⓥ

kcal 335, **protein** 9 g, **fat** 16 g (of which saturated fat 3 g), **carbohydrate** 40 g (of which sugars 19 g), **fibre** 8 g

| | |
|---|---|
| ✓✓✓ | A, C, E |
| ✓✓ | folate, calcium, potassium |
| ✓ | B₁, B₂, B₆, niacin, copper, iron, zinc |

Vegetables

### Some more ideas

- This vegetable filling is also delicious rolled up in warmed flour tortillas. It will fill 8 tortillas, each about 15 cm (6 in) in diameter and weighing about 200 g (7 oz) in total.

- As an alternative to guacamole, put 1 can red kidney beans, about 215 g, drained and rinsed, in a food processor or blender with the juice of ½ lime; ½ small red onion, coarsely chopped; 1 tomato, chopped; 1 garlic clove, chopped; and 3 tbsp chopped fresh coriander. Whiz until creamy. Add seasoning to taste.

- Use quartered chestnut mushrooms in place of the courgette.

- If you do not want to heat the oven just for warming the taco shells, preheat the grill, then turn it off a few seconds before warming the taco shells in the hot grill compartment.

# Caribbean butternut squash and sweetcorn stew

Butternut squash has a lovely firm texture, ideal for cooking in stews. Combined with black-eyed beans, sweetcorn and red pepper it makes a fast, nutritious supper dish that is perfect for cold winter days. Serve with boiled rice or warm crusty bread.

**Serves 4**

1 tbsp extra virgin olive oil

1 onion, sliced

2 garlic cloves, crushed

1 butternut squash, about 675 g (1½ lb), peeled and cut into 1 cm (½ in) cubes

1 red pepper, seeded and sliced

1 bay leaf

1 can chopped tomatoes, about 400 g

1 can black-eyed beans, about 410 g, drained and rinsed

1 can sweetcorn kernels, about 200 g, drained

300 ml (10 fl oz) vegetable stock

1 tbsp Worcestershire sauce, or to taste

1 tsp Tabasco sauce, or to taste

1 tbsp dark muscovado sugar

1–2 tsp balsamic vinegar

chopped parsley to garnish

Preparation and cooking time: 30 minutes

**Each serving provides**

kcal 335, **protein** 15 g, **fat** 4 g (of which saturated fat 1 g), **carbohydrate** 62 g (of which sugars 21 g), **fibre** 9 g

| | |
|---|---|
| ✓✓✓ | A, B$_6$, C, folate |
| ✓✓ | B$_1$, E, copper, iron, potassium |
| ✓ | calcium, zinc |

1 Heat the oil in a large saucepan and add the onion, garlic, butternut squash, red pepper and bay leaf. Stir well, then cover the pan and allow the vegetables to sweat for 5 minutes, stirring occasionally.

2 Add the tomatoes with their juice, the black-eyed beans and sweetcorn, and stir to mix. Add the stock, Worcestershire sauce, Tabasco sauce, sugar and vinegar and stir again. Cover and simmer for 15 minutes or until the squash is tender.

3 Sprinkle the parsley over the stew and serve at once.

**Some more ideas**

● Give the stew an Indian flavour. Soften the sliced onion and garlic in the olive oil for 2–3 minutes, then stir in 2 tbsp medium balti paste. Add the butternut squash with 150 g (5½ oz) thickly sliced baby corn. Cover and cook for 5–6 minutes. Replace the black-eyed beans with borlotti beans, adding them with the canned tomatoes and stock (omit the sweetcorn kernels). Garnish with 2 tbsp chopped fresh coriander instead of parsley, and serve with boiled jasmine rice or warm naan bread.

● For a vegetarian alternative, use mushroom ketchup instead of Worcestershire sauce.

**Plus points**

● There are over 25 species of pumpkin and squash, some of which have been cultivated for 9000 years. All varieties are rich in beta-carotene and contain useful amounts of vitamin C.

● If you have the time, leave the freshly crushed garlic cloves to stand for 10 minutes or so before starting to cook. Researchers at Penn State University in the USA have found that this maximises the formation and retention of cancer-fighting compounds.

Vegetables

# Penne primavera

This classic Italian dish is intended to make the most of freshly picked young spring produce. With today's choice of vegetables in supermarkets, the selection can be varied all year, and the recipe can also be made as a 'storecupboard supper' with frozen vegetables.

**Serves 4**

340 g (12 oz) penne or other pasta shapes

170 g (6 oz) young asparagus

170 g (6 oz) green beans, trimmed and cut into 3 cm (1¼ in) lengths

170 g (6 oz) shelled fresh peas

1 tbsp extra virgin olive oil

1 onion, chopped

1 garlic clove, chopped

85 g (3 oz) pancetta, chopped

115 g (4 oz) button mushrooms, chopped

1 tbsp plain flour

240 ml (8 fl oz) dry white wine

4 tbsp single cream

2 tbsp chopped mixed fresh herbs, such as parsley and thyme

salt and pepper

Preparation time: 15 minutes
Cooking time: 15 minutes

**1** Cook the pasta in boiling water for 10–12 minutes, or according to the packet instructions, until al dente. Drain well.

**2** While the pasta is cooking, cut the asparagus into 3.5 cm (1½ in) lengths, keeping the tips separate. Drop the pieces of asparagus stalk, the green beans and peas into a saucepan of boiling water. Bring back to the boil and cook for 5 minutes. Add the asparagus tips and cook for a further 2 minutes. Drain thoroughly.

**3** Heat the oil in a saucepan. Add the onion and cook for 3–4 minutes or until softened. Add the garlic, pancetta and mushrooms, and continue to cook, stirring occasionally, for a further 2 minutes.

**4** Stir in the flour, then gradually pour in the wine and bring to the boil, stirring. Simmer until the sauce is thickened. Stir in the cream and herbs with seasoning to taste. Add the vegetables to the sauce and heat gently for 1–2 minutes, without boiling.

**5** Divide the pasta among 4 serving bowls and spoon the sauce over the top. Serve immediately.

**Some more ideas**

● For a vegetarian version, omit the pancetta and add 170 g (6 oz) shelled young broad beans, cooking them with the asparagus stalks and the green beans. Once drained, the skins may be slipped off the broad beans, if preferred. Add 4 shredded fresh sage leaves with the parsley and thyme, or try tarragon for a slightly aniseed flavour.

● Omit the pancetta and instead serve sprinkled with freshly grated Parmesan cheese – about 45 g (1½ oz) in total for the 4 portions.

● Use frozen peas instead of fresh, adding them with the asparagus tips.

**Each serving provides**

kcal 560, **protein** 20 g, **fat** 17 g (of which saturated fat 6 g), **carbohydrate** 77 g (of which sugars 5.5 g), **fibre** 7 g

| | |
|---|---|
| ✓✓✓ | C |
| ✓✓ | B₁, folate, niacin, copper, iron |
| ✓ | A, potassium, selenium |

**Plus points**

● Asparagus is an excellent source of folate and the green spears are a good source of vitamin C. The beta-carotene content makes asparagus a useful source of vitamin A, and it also offers useful vitamin E.

● Peas provide good amounts of the B vitamins $B_1$, niacin and $B_6$. They also provide dietary fibre, particularly the soluble variety, some folate and vitamin C.

Vegetables

# Potato, corn and pepper frittata

Known in Italy as frittata, or in Spain as tortilla, flat omelettes can be served hot or cold with salad. The delicious version here can be kept for a day in the refrigerator, but remove it about 30 minutes before serving as it tastes best at room temperature.

**Serves 4**

675 g (1½ lb) potatoes, peeled, quartered lengthways and thinly sliced across

1 red, yellow or orange pepper, seeded and chopped

2 tbsp extra virgin olive oil

1 onion, halved and thinly sliced

250 g (9 oz) frozen sweetcorn, thawed

6 eggs

4 tbsp finely chopped parsley

salt and pepper

Preparation time: 10 minutes
Cooking time: about 20 minutes

**Each serving provides** Ⓥ

kcal 380, **protein** 18 g, **fat** 17 g (of which saturated fat 4 g), **carbohydrate** 42 g (of which sugars 4 g), **fibre** 4 g

| | |
|---|---|
| ✓✓✓ | C |
| ✓✓ | B₁, B₆, B₁₂, E, iron |
| ✓ | A, B₂, niacin, copper, potassium, selenium, zinc |

1 Put the potatoes in a saucepan, cover with boiling water and bring back to the boil. Reduce the heat, then add the chopped peppers and simmer for 3 minutes or until the potatoes are just starting to cook. Drain well, cover and keep hot.

2 Heat a 25 cm (10 in) non-stick frying pan over a high heat. Add the oil to the pan and swirl it around. When the oil is hot, reduce the heat to moderate, add the onion and fry, stirring often, for 3 minutes or until softened.

3 Add the potatoes, chopped pepper and sweetcorn and continue frying for about 8 minutes, stirring and turning the vegetables, until the potatoes are tender. Remove from the heat.

4 In a large bowl, beat the eggs with the parsley and seasoning to taste. Use a draining spoon to add the vegetables to the eggs, stirring them in thoroughly. (If any vegetables have stuck to the bottom of the pan, thoroughly clean and dry the pan before heating it with an additional 1 tbsp oil; however, this should not be necessary with a reliable non-stick pan.)

5 Replace the frying pan, with the oil remaining from cooking the vegetables, over a moderate heat. When the pan is hot, pour in the egg mixture, spreading out the vegetables evenly. Cook the omelette, shaking the pan frequently, for 3–4 minutes or until the edges are set and the top is beginning to look set.

6 Meanwhile, preheat the grill to the hottest setting. Place the frittata under the grill for about 2 minutes or until the eggs are just set. Pierce the top of the mixture with a knife to check that the omelette is cooked through.

7 Remove the pan from under the grill and leave the frittata to set for 2 minutes, then slide it onto a serving plate. Serve hot or at room temperature, cut into wedges.

**Plus points**

• Sweetcorn is a useful source of dietary fibre – important for keeping the digestive system in good working order – and it also offers vitamins A, C and folate. Although some vitamins are lost in canned sweetcorn, they are retained in the frozen vegetable.

• Potatoes and peppers contribute vitamin C to this dish. In addition, potatoes offer starchy carbohydrates, which should make up at least half of the daily calorie intake in a healthy diet.

Vegetables

### Some more ideas

● Take a tip from Spanish tapas bars and serve frittata at room temperature, cut into bite-sized pieces, as an alternative to salty or high-fat fried snacks with drinks.

● For a fennel and courgette frittata, replace the pepper, onion and sweetcorn with 1 bulb of fennel, thinly sliced; 85 g (3 oz) mushrooms, thinly sliced; and 1 courgette, cut in half lengthways and thinly sliced across. Fry these

vegetables in the hot oil for 3 minutes before adding the part-cooked potatoes.

● For a simple pepper and potato frittata, use 3 peppers (any colour) and 2 onions, and omit the sweetcorn.

# Eggs with spicy peas and lentils

A little spice can turn a few everyday ingredients into something special. This simple, satisfying dish provides a wealth of vital vitamins and minerals and the right balance of essential protein and fibre. Serve with basmati rice and/or warm naan bread.

**Serves 4**

1 tbsp sunflower oil

1 onion, chopped

2 garlic cloves, sliced

2.5 cm (1 in) piece of fresh root ginger, peeled and finely chopped

2 tbsp garam masala

1 tbsp tomato purée

450 g (1 lb) broccoli or cauliflower, or a mixture of the two, cut into small florets

450 ml (15 fl oz) vegetable stock, preferably home-made

55 g (2 oz) red lentils, rinsed

6 eggs

225 g (8 oz) frozen peas

3 tbsp chopped fresh coriander

coarsely grated zest of 1 lime (optional)

salt and pepper

**To garnish**

lime wedges

sprigs of fresh coriander

Preparation time: 10 minutes

Cooking time: 20 minutes

**Each serving provides** Ⓥ

kcal 310, **protein** 24 g, **fat** 15 g (of which saturated fat 3 g), **carbohydrate** 20 g (of which sugars 6 g), **fibre** 6 g

| | |
|---|---|
| ✓✓✓ | B₁₂, C, folate, iron |
| ✓✓ | A, B₁, B₂, B₆, E, niacin, copper, zinc |
| ✓ | calcium, potassium, selenium |

1 Heat the oil in a saucepan and fry the onion, garlic and ginger for 3 minutes. Stir in the garam masala and tomato purée. Cook for 1 minute, then add the broccoli or cauliflower and seasoning to taste. Pour in the stock. Bring to the boil, then add the lentils. Cover the pan, reduce the heat and simmer for 15 minutes, stirring occasionally.

2 Meanwhile, put the eggs in a pan of cold water, bring just to the boil and boil gently for 6 minutes. Drain and rinse them under cold water, gently cracking the shells. Peel off the shells, taking care as the eggs will not be completely hard.

3 Add the eggs, whole, and the peas to the lentil mixture and stir gently. Bring back to simmering point, then cover the pan again and cook for about 5 minutes. By this time the peas should be cooked and the spicy sauce thickened with the softened lentils.

4 Remove the eggs with a spoon and cut them in half. Divide the spicy vegetable mixture among 4 plates. Mix the chopped coriander with the grated lime zest, if using, and sprinkle over the vegetables. Top each plate with 3 egg halves. Garnish with lime wedges and sprigs of coriander, and serve immediately.

**Plus points**

● The combination of spices in garam masala not only adds a distinctive flavour to Indian cooking, but has also been shown to possess natural preservative properties. These help to prevent bacterial growth in dishes that include it as an ingredient. (But foods should still be stored safely if they are not to be eaten immediately after cooking.)

**Some more ideas**

● This dish works well with frozen vegetables – mixed vegetables, broad beans, sweetcorn and green beans are all suitable.

● Replace the lentils with chickpeas. Drain 1 can chickpeas, about 400 g, and coarsely mash them, then add to the vegetable mixture in step 1. Reduce the quantity of stock to 300 ml (10 fl oz).

● A creamy sauce complements eggs. Try swirling 150 ml (5 fl oz) plain low-fat yogurt into the vegetable mixture once the eggs have been removed from the pan.

● Instead of adding boiled eggs, serve poached eggs on top of the spicy vegetable mixture.

Vegetables

# Hot conchiglie with grilled pepper and tomato dressing

Grilling green peppers gives them a slightly smoky taste and makes it easy to slip off their skins. They give a great flavour to the diced tomato and Kalamata olive dressing in this speedy dish. Serve it for a light lunch or supper, with a simple green salad.

**Serves 4**

3 green peppers

450 g (1 lb) ripe tomatoes

3 garlic cloves, finely chopped

1 tbsp red wine vinegar

1 tsp crushed dried red chillies (optional)

4 tbsp extra virgin olive oil

10 Kalamata or other black olives, stoned and halved

3 tbsp finely chopped fresh basil

3 tbsp finely chopped rocket

400 g (14 oz) conchiglie (pasta shells), or other shapes such as penne

salt and pepper

rocket leaves to garnish (optional)

Preparation time: 15 minutes
Cooking time: 10–12 minutes

1 Preheat the grill to high and grill the green peppers, turning occasionally, until the skin is blistered and blackened all over. Place the peppers in a polythene bag and leave until they are cool enough to handle and the skins are loosened.

2 Peel and seed the peppers, then cut them into bite-sized pieces. Cut the tomatoes into similar-sized pieces and mix them with the peppers. Add the garlic, wine vinegar, chilli flakes (if using), olive oil, olives, basil and rocket, and mix well. Set the dressing mixture aside to marinate while you cook the pasta.

3 Cook the pasta in boiling water for 10–12 minutes, or according to the packet instructions, until al dente. Drain and toss with the marinated pepper and tomato dressing. Garnish with rocket leaves, if liked, then serve immediately.

**Plus points**

• Green peppers are an excellent source of vitamin C, which is important for maintaining and healing the body's immune system. Even when grilled, useful amounts of the vitamin remain. Peppers also provide good amounts of vitamin A (through beta-carotene).

• Basil is believed by some to aid digestion and, as a natural tranquilliser, it is said to calm the nervous system. It is also thought to be helpful in treating a cold.

**Another idea**

• Add a can of chickpeas, about 400 g, drained, to the marinating peppers and tomatoes.

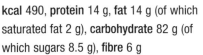

**Each serving provides**

kcal 490, **protein** 14 g, **fat** 14 g (of which saturated fat 2 g), **carbohydrate** 82 g (of which sugars 8.5 g), **fibre** 6 g

✓✓✓ C

✓✓ E, niacin, copper, selenium

✓ A, B$_1$, B$_6$, folate, iron, potassium

Vegetables

# Pappardelle with aubergine

A good tomato sauce can turn a plate of pasta and aubergine into a delicious dish. The inspiration comes from Catania in Sicily, where aubergine and tomato pasta is known as pasta alla Norma, in honour of the town's famous son, Bellini, and his opera, *Norma*.

**Serves 4**

6 tsp extra virgin olive oil

1 aubergine, unpeeled, cut crossways into 3–5 mm (⅛–¼ in) slices

3–4 garlic cloves, thinly sliced

2 cans chopped tomatoes, about 400 g each

400 g (14 oz) pappardelle or other wide flat noodles

2 tbsp tomato purée

¼ tsp sugar, or to taste

¼ tsp dried oregano, or to taste

salt and cayenne pepper

100 g (3½ oz) goat's cheese, sliced

15 g (½ oz) chopped parsley or torn fresh basil leaves to garnish

Preparation and cooking time: 25 minutes

**Each serving provides** ⓥ

kcal 500, **protein** 18 g, **fat** 12 g (of which saturated fat 4 g), **carbohydrate** 85 g (of which sugars 10 g), **fibre** 6 g

| | |
|---|---|
| ✓✓ | C, E, copper, iron |
| ✓ | A, B₁, B₆, B₁₂, folate, niacin, calcium, potassium, selenium, zinc |

1 Heat a ridged cast-iron grill pan, then brush with 2 tsp of the olive oil. Arrange the aubergine slices in the pan and cook for 3–4 minutes. Brush the top side of the slices with another 2 tsp oil and turn them over. Cook for another 3–4 minutes or until tender and browned. Remove from the heat and cover lightly with a piece of foil to keep warm.

2 While the aubergine is cooking, heat the remaining 2 tsp olive oil in a heavy-based frying pan. Add the garlic and cook for 1–2 minutes or until just turning golden (do not let it brown or burn). Add the tomatoes with their juice. Cook over a high heat for 4–5 minutes, then reduce the heat to moderate and cook for a further 4–5 minutes, stirring ocasionally, until reduced to a thick sauce.

3 Meanwhile, cook the pappardelle in boiling water for 10–12 minutes, or according to the packet instructions, until al dente.

4 Add the tomato purée, sugar and oregano to the tomato sauce. Season with salt and cayenne pepper to taste. Keep warm.

5 Drain the pasta, turn it into the sauce and lightly toss together to mix. Serve the pasta with the aubergine and goat's cheese, garnished with parsley or basil.

**Another idea**

• Try farfalle with grilled vegetables and green herb pesto. Arrange 1 courgette, cut into diagonal slices, 1 red or yellow pepper, seeded and sliced, 1 red onion, cut into wedges, 2 large ripe tomatoes, cut into wedges, and 12–16 tiny portabellini mushrooms or button mushrooms on a baking tray. Brush them with 1 tsp extra virgin olive oil, and grill under a moderate heat until tender and lightly browned in places. Meanwhile, make the pesto. In a food processor or blender, purée 170 g (6 oz) cooked spinach, squeezed dry, with 1 peeled garlic clove, 50 g (1¾ oz) mixed fresh herbs (primarily basil, with some chives, marjoram and flat-leaf parsley) and 2 tbsp extra virgin olive oil until smooth. Add the juice of ½ lemon and season with salt to taste. Cook 400 g (14 oz) farfalle (pasta bows); drain and toss with the pesto. Pile the grilled vegetables on top and sprinkle with 45 g (1½ oz) freshly grated Parmesan cheese.

**Plus point**

• Aubergine is a satisfyingly filling vegetable that is low in calories and fat. Grilling or baking is a healthy way to cook aubergine, which is renowned for absorbing large amounts of fat when fried.

Vegetables

# Chakchouka

This dish is popular all over the Mediterranean and there are many variations. Basically it is a tomato-based vegetable stew, like a ratatouille, with eggs poached right in the mixture. Serve it for a sustaining lunch with garlic and rosemary focaccia or olive ciabatta.

**Serves 2**

1 tbsp extra virgin olive oil

1 small onion, roughly chopped

2 garlic cloves, crushed

1 red pepper, seeded and thinly sliced

1 green pepper, seeded and thinly sliced

400 g (14 oz) large ripe tomatoes, roughly chopped

2 tbsp tomato purée

¼ tsp crushed dried chillies (optional)

1 tsp ground cumin

pinch of sugar

4 eggs

salt

sprigs of fresh flat-leaf parsley to garnish

Preparation and cooking time: 30 minutes

**1** Heat the oil in a deep, heavy-based frying pan. Add the onion, garlic, and red and green peppers, and cook gently for 5 minutes or until softened.

**2** Stir in the tomatoes, tomato purée, chillies, if using, cumin, sugar, and salt to taste. Cover and cook gently for about 5 minutes or until the mixture is thick and well combined.

**3** Make 4 hollows in the vegetable mixture using the back of a wooden spoon, then break an egg into each hollow. Cover the pan again and cook gently for 6–8 minutes or until the eggs are just set.

**4** Serve immediately, straight from the pan, garnishing each plate with sprigs of parsley.

**Some more ideas**

● Add 55 g (2 oz) stoned black olives or chopped sun-dried tomatoes to the vegetable mixture.

● Instead of the chillies, add 1 tsp harissa sauce, or to taste.

● To make an omelette-like chakchouka, after breaking the eggs into the mixture, stir them gently to mix up the whites and yolks.

● For chakchouka with aubergine and mushrooms, replace the red and green peppers with 1 aubergine, cut into small chunks. In step 2, use 1 can chopped tomatoes, about 400 g, with the juice, instead of fresh tomatoes and add 170 g (6 oz) chopped button or chestnut mushrooms. Omit the chillies and cumin, and instead flavour with 1 tsp fennel or caraway seeds. Cover and cook gently for 15 minutes before breaking the eggs into the mixture.

**Each serving provides** ⓥ

kcal 321, **protein** 19 g, **fat** 20 g (of which saturated fat 5 g), **carbohydrate** 18 g (of which sugars 17 g), **fibre** 6 g

| | |
|---|---|
| ✓✓✓ | A, B$_{12}$, C, E, copper |
| ✓✓ | B$_1$, B$_2$, B$_6$, folate, niacin, iron, potassium, zinc |
| ✓ | calcium, selenium |

**Plus points**

● Eggs are a useful source of vitamin A, but it is a myth that a darker-coloured yolk has a higher content of this vitamin (as carotene). The coloration is due to pigments found in grass and other food the chicken eats.

● Tomatoes are rich in the antioxidants vitamin C, beta-carotene and lycopene. Antioxidants help to protect the body's cells against the damaging effects of free radicals.

Vegetables

# Moroccan-style pumpkin and butter beans

Middle Eastern spices flavour this casserole, which is full of vegetables and other fibre-rich ingredients. It is great for a cook-ahead meal as the flavours mature and improve if the casserole is chilled overnight, then thoroughly reheated for serving. Try it with couscous.

**Serves 4**

600 ml (1 pint) boiling water

1 vegetable stock cube, crumbled, or
  2 tsp vegetable bouillon powder or paste

½ tsp turmeric

½ tsp ground coriander

pinch of ground cumin

200 g (7 oz) leeks, halved lengthways and
  sliced

225 g (8 oz) parsnips, cut into 1 cm (½ in)
  cubes

600 g (1 lb 5 oz) piece of pumpkin, peeled,
  seeded and cut into 1 cm (½ in) cubes

400 g (14 oz) yellow or green courgettes,
  sliced

1 red pepper, seeded and chopped

100 g (3½ oz) ready-to-eat dried apricots,
  chopped

1 can butter beans, about 400 g, drained

pinch of crushed dried chillies, or to taste
  (optional)

salt and pepper

**To garnish**

30 g (1 oz) pine nuts

chopped parsley or fresh coriander

Preparation time: about 10 minutes
Cooking time: about 20 minutes

1 Pour the boiling water into a flameproof casserole. Stir in the stock cube, powder or paste, the turmeric, ground coriander and cumin. Add the leeks and parsnips and bring to the boil. Reduce the heat to moderate, cover the pan and simmer the vegetables for 5 minutes.

2 Add the pumpkin, courgettes and red pepper to the pan, then bring the stock back to the boil. Stir in the apricots, butter beans and chilli flakes, if using, adding more to taste for a spicier result. Season with salt and pepper. Reduce the heat, cover the pan and simmer for 10 minutes or until all the vegetables are tender.

3 Meanwhile, toast the pine nuts in a non-stick frying pan over a moderate heat, stirring constantly, until just beginning to brown and giving off their nutty aroma. Tip the pine nuts onto a board and chop them coarsely.

4 Taste the casserole and adjust the seasoning, if necessary, then ladle it into 4 deep bowls. Sprinkle with the chopped pine nuts and parsley or fresh coriander and serve.

**Plus points**

● Pumpkin is a rich source of beta-carotene and other carotenoid compounds. Save and roast or toast the seeds as a snack, as they provide good amounts of protein and zinc.

● Dried apricots are an excellent source of beta-carotene and a useful source of calcium.

● Parsnips provide useful amounts of potassium, folate and vitamin $B_1$.

**Each serving provides**  Ⓥ

kcal 250, **protein** 12 g, **fat** 7 g (of which saturated fat 1 g), **carbohydrate** 35 g (of which sugars 21 g), **fibre** 11 g

| | |
|---|---|
| ✓✓✓ | A, C, iron |
| ✓✓ | $B_1$, $B_6$, folate |
| ✓ | calcium |

Vegetables

### Some more ideas

● This casserole is delicious ladled over couscous. Place 340 g (12 oz) couscous in a heatproof bowl. Add salt to taste and pour in 600 ml (1 pint) boiling water to cover. Cover the bowl and leave to stand for about 5 minutes or until all the water has been absorbed and the couscous is plumped up and tender. Add 15 g (½ oz) butter and fluff up the couscous with a fork to separate the grains.

● Try other vegetables with the pumpkin – for example, broccoli florets can be added with the pumpkin instead of the courgettes. The distinctive flavour of turnips is also good with the other vegetables.

● For a fresh, peppery flavour, garnish the casserole with 55 g (2 oz) grated red radishes or large white radish (mooli).

# Desserts

You might think that fast, healthy puddings are unlikely to extend beyond plain yogurt or fruit salad, but you would be wrong. This selection of quick puddings are all perfect for a sweet burst at the end of the meal. Satisfy your craving with Chocolate and hazelnut soufflés or Plums en papillote with honey, or even try something a bit different with Cherry brandy clafoutis or Peach and blackberry filo pizzas.

<br />

# 30 minutes

# Chocolate and hazelnut soufflés

These luscious soufflés are surprisingly easy to prepare and make an impressive special occasion dessert, with far less fat than the traditional version. For best results, use a good-quality chocolate.

**Serves 6**

2 tsp unsalted butter
30 g (1 oz) amaretti biscuits, finely crushed
240 ml (8 fl oz) semi-skimmed milk
few drops of pure vanilla extract
3 tbsp cornflour
55 g (2 oz) ground hazelnuts
100 g (3½ oz) good plain chocolate (at least 70% cocoa solids), broken into small pieces
2 egg yolks
1 tbsp hazelnut or almond liqueur
4 egg whites
pinch of cream of tartar or salt
85 g (3 oz) caster sugar
500 g (1 lb 2 oz) strawberries, halved
1 tbsp icing sugar for dusting (optional)

Preparation time: 15 minutes
Cooking time: 15 minutes

**Each serving provides**  Ⓥ
kcal 340, **protein** 8 g, **fat** 16 g (of which saturated fat 5 g), **carbohydrate** 44 g (of which sugars 34 g), **fibre** 1.5 g

| | |
|---|---|
| ✓✓✓ | C |
| ✓✓ | B₂, B₆, E |
| ✓ | calcium, copper, iron |

Desserts

**226**

1 Preheat the oven to 180°C (350°F, gas mark 4). Grease six 200 ml (7 fl oz) ramekins or ovenproof cups with the butter and coat with amaretti biscuit crumbs, turning the dishes to cover the insides evenly.

2 Put the milk and vanilla extract into a saucepan and bring just to the boil. Remove from the heat. Put the cornflour and ground hazelnuts in a mixing bowl and whisk in a little of the hot milk, a spoonful at a time, to make a thick paste. Slowly whisk in enough of the remaining milk to make a smooth, thick liquid, then whisk in the remainder. Pour the mixture back into the saucepan and bring to the boil, stirring. Boil gently for 2–4 minutes or until thickened.

3 Remove from the heat and add the chocolate. Cover the pan and leave to stand for 1–2 minutes or until the chocolate has melted. Stir to combine well. Whisk in the egg yolks, one at a time, and then the hazelnut or almond liqueur.

4 Put the egg whites in a large, clean, greasefree bowl with the cream of tartar or salt. Using an electric mixer or balloon whisk, whisk the egg whites until they form soft peaks, then add the sugar a spoonful at a time, whisking well. Continue whisking until glossy and forming stiff peaks.

5 Stir a spoonful of the egg whites into the chocolate mixture to lighten it, then pour this mixture over the rest of the whites. Using a large rubber spatula or metal spoon, gently fold together until just combined. (Don't worry about a few white streaks.)

6 Scrape the soufflé mixture into the prepared dishes or cups and bake for 15 minutes or until puffed and lightly browned on top. Set the ramekins or cups on individual plates with the strawberries and, if you wish, dust each soufflé lightly with icing sugar. Serve immediately.

**Plus points**

● None of us needs to feel guilty about the occasional indulgence – as long as the rest of the diet is healthy. According to the organisation ARISE (Research into the Science of Enjoyment), there is scientific evidence that eating chocolate can be good for you. Studies suggest that people who indulge once in a while tend to be more relaxed and happier, and medical evidence shows that happy people live longer.

## Some more ideas

- Instead of amaretti biscuits, you can use finely crushed digestive biscuits.
- Use ground almonds instead of hazelnuts and almond liqueur instead of hazelnut; coffee liqueur could be substituted for either.
- For a lower-fat version, omit the egg yolks and increase the liqueur to 2 tbsp.
- Make a berry soufflé omelette to serve 4. Sprinkle 400 g (14 oz) sliced strawberries or

whole raspberries with 1–2 tbsp caster sugar and leave to macerate while you make the omelette. Preheat the grill to moderate. Separate 3 large eggs and beat the yolks with 2 tbsp caster sugar until thick and light in colour. Stir in 2 tbsp milk or orange liqueur and ¼ tsp pure vanilla extract. Whisk the egg whites until they form stiff peaks. Fold the egg yolk mixture gently into the whites. Melt 2 tsp butter in a non-stick frying pan, about 25 cm (10 in) in

diameter, with a heatproof handle (alternatively, wrap the handle with foil). Scrape the egg mixture into the frying pan and smooth the top. Cook over a low heat, without stirring, for 4–5 minutes or until the omelette is browned on the base. Put under the grill for 1½–2 minutes or until lightly browned on top and puffed up. Slide onto a warm plate and cut into quarters. Serve with the fruit spooned over.

- Substitute brandy for the liqueur.

# Flambéed Asian pears with orange

A delicious yet simple dessert, this is ready in just 25 minutes. Flaming the brandy burns off the alcohol, leaving a wonderful flavour which complements the oranges and pears. Even after cooking, Asian pears retain their pleasant, crunchy texture.

**Serves 4**

2 Asian pears

juice of ½ lemon

3 oranges

30 g (1 oz) butter

3 tbsp soft brown sugar

3 tbsp brandy

2 tbsp coarsely chopped pistachios

sprigs of fresh lemon balm to decorate

Preparation time: 15 minutes

Cooking time: 10 minutes

1 Peel, quarter and core the Asian pears. Cut them into slices and sprinkle with the lemon juice to prevent them from turning brown.

2 Peel the oranges, removing all the white pith. Cut them across into neat slices.

3 Melt the butter in a frying pan. Add the sugar and stir until dissolved. Add the pear slices and cook gently for about 3 minutes on each side or until they are just tender but still quite firm. Add the orange slices for the last minute of cooking, turning them to coat well with the juices in the pan.

4 Using a draining spoon, remove the pears and oranges to a shallow serving dish and keep warm. Boil the juices remaining in the pan to reduce a little, then pour over the fruit. Pour the brandy into the frying pan, heat it and set alight. Pour over the fruit.

5 Serve on warmed plates, sprinkled with the pistachios and decorated with lemon balm.

**Some more ideas**

● Use sliced dessert pears instead of Asian pears. They will need only about 2 minutes cooking on each side to make them tender.

● Use Poire Williams liqueur or Cointreau instead of brandy.

● Replace the pears with apples, cut in rings. Cox's are particularly good prepared this way. Flambé with Calvados and sprinkle with chopped toasted hazelnuts.

**Plus points**

● Oranges are justly famous for their vitamin C content (54 mg per 100 g/3½ oz). This is one of the 'water-soluble' vitamins, which cannot be stored by the body, so it is essential that fruit and vegetables containing vitamin C are eaten every day. As scientists have increasingly recognised, this vitamin helps to prevent a number of degenerative diseases such as heart disease and cancer, through its powerful antioxidant activity.

**Each serving provides**    Ⓥ

**kcal** 200, **protein** 3 g, **fat** 9 g (of which saturated fat 4 g), **carbohydrate** 24 g (of which sugars 23 g), **fibre** 3 g

✓✓  C

✓  E, folate

Desserts

# Summer fruit fool

A quick pudding to rustle up at a moment's notice, this can be made with almost any fruit in season. The usual whipped double cream in fruit fool is replaced here with a mixture of low-fat yogurt and whipping cream, yet this is still a wonderfully rich and creamy dessert.

**Serves 4**

300 g (10½ oz) mixed soft fruit, such as raspberries, blackberries, blueberries or currants

55 g (2 oz) caster sugar

150 ml (5 fl oz) whipping cream

grated zest of ½ orange

150 g (5½ oz) plain low-fat bio yogurt

finely shredded orange zest to decorate (optional)

Preparation time: 20 minutes, plus cooling and chilling

1 Reserve about 55 g (2 oz) of the mixed fruit for decoration. Put the remaining mixed fruit in a saucepan with 2 tbsp water. Bring just to the boil, then reduce the heat and cook gently for 5 minutes or until soft and very juicy. Stir in the sugar.

2 Remove from the heat and leave to cool slightly. Pour into a food processor or blender and purée. Press the purée through a sieve to remove all the pips. Alternatively, just press the fruit through a sieve to purée it. Set aside to cool completely.

3 Whip the cream with the grated orange zest until thick. Add the yogurt and lightly whip into the cream, then mix in the cooled fruit purée.

4 Spoon into 4 dessert dishes or goblets. Chill well before serving, decorated with the reserved berries and orange zest, if using.

**Some more ideas**

• For gooseberry fool, replace the soft fruit with 450 g (1 lb) gooseberries (don't reserve any for decoration) and increase the caster sugar to 115 g (4 oz). Cook the gooseberries for about 15 minutes or until softened. This gooseberry fool will serve 6.

• For a strawberry fool, slice 225 g (8 oz) ripe strawberries, reserving 4 whole ones for decoration, and sprinkle with the sugar. Leave for 30 minutes or until the juices are running from the fruit, then purée. Add to the cream and yogurt mixture. Serve decorated with the reserved strawberries, quartered or sliced.

• For a guava fool, roughly chop 225 g (8 oz) ripe guavas, with their skins, and purée in a food processor or blender with 45 g (1½ oz) sugar. Press through a sieve, then taste the purée and add a little more sugar if it isn't sweet enough. Fold into the cream and yogurt mixture with 1 tbsp orange liqueur. Guava is an excellent source of vitamin C.

## Plus points

• Yogurt is a good source of calcium. Throughout life, but particularly during adolescence and pregnancy, it is important for women to get enough calcium to keep bones healthy and prevent osteoporosis later.

• The mixed soft fruit are all rich in the antioxidant vitamin C, and their natural acidity helps to prevent the loss of this vitamin during the cooking. To retain as much vitamin C as possible, the sugar is added after the fruit is softened.

**Each serving provides**

kcal 230, **protein** 3 g, **fat** 15 g (of which saturated fat 9 g), **carbohydrate** 22 g (of which sugars 22 g), **fibre** 2 g

| | |
|---|---|
| ✓✓✓ | C |
| ✓✓ | A |
| ✓ | B₂, calcium |

Desserts

# Glazed banana pain perdu

Based on two nursery favourites – 'eggy bread' and banana sandwiches – this more glamorous version is bound to become a favourite. Other fruit, such as strawberries and pears, can be used to ring the changes, with brioche slices or other bread as the base.

**Serves 4**

2 eggs

4 tbsp semi-skimmed milk

1 tsp honey

large pinch of ground cinnamon

8 small slices Granary bread

2 tsp sunflower oil

2 large bananas

**To glaze**

3 tbsp icing sugar

pinch of ground cinnamon

**To decorate**

icing sugar

fresh mint leaves

Preparation time: 5 minutes

Cooking time: 5–7 minutes

**1** Preheat the grill. In a shallow dish, gently whisk together the eggs, milk, honey and cinnamon.

**2** Trim the top and bottom crusts off the bread, if very crusty.

**3** Heat a non-stick frying pan and brush with a little of the oil. Quickly dip each piece of bread in the egg mixture to moisten on both sides, then put it into the hot pan. Cook for 1–2 minutes or until pale golden brown on both sides. You may need to cook the bread slices in two batches, brushing the pan with a little more oil when necessary. As the bread is done, transfer to the grill pan.

**4** Peel the bananas and cut into thin diagonal slices, arranging them on the bread slices to cover generously. Mix the icing sugar with the cinnamon and sprinkle over the bananas. Place under the grill to melt the sugar and glaze the fruit.

**5** Sprinkle a little icing sugar over a few mint leaves and use to decorate the pain perdu. Serve immediately.

**Some more ideas**

- Try slices of sweet brioche loaf, topped with sliced strawberries spiced with a sprinkling of ground ginger.
- Spiced fruit breads make delicious pain perdu. Top with peach or pear slices spiced with a little freshly grated nutmeg.
- Leftover day-old bread is the best to use for this recipe as it absorbs the egg slightly better than very fresh, moist bread.

**Plus points**

- Bread has suffered in the past from a false reputation of being 'fattening' and its positive features have been overlooked. Even white bread provides some dietary fibre, and by law it is fortified with vitamins and minerals, including calcium and $B_1$.
- Eggs provide high-quality protein as well as iron and the fat-soluble vitamins A and E. Although eggs contain cholesterol, the hazards of eating eggs have often been exaggerated. Normally, dietary cholesterol has little effect on blood cholesterol levels.

**Each serving provides** Ⓥ

kcal 300, **protein** 10 g, **fat** 7 g (of which saturated fat 2 g), **carbohydrate** 53 g (of which sugars 26 g), **fibre** 3 g

| | |
|---|---|
| ✓✓✓ | $B_{12}$ |
| ✓✓ | E, folate, niacin |
| ✓ | $B_1$, $B_2$, $B_6$, calcium, copper, zinc |

Desserts

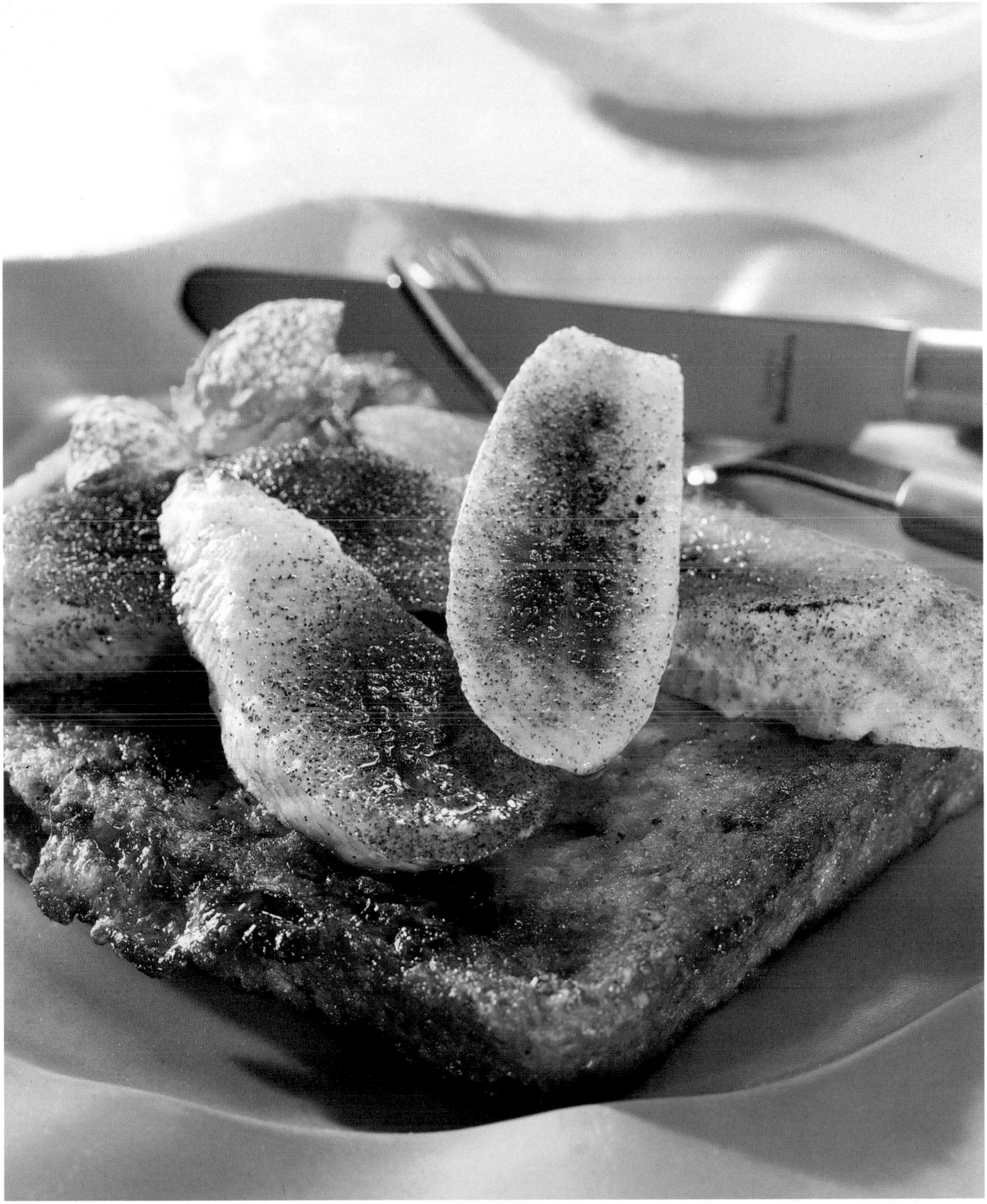

# Apple-berry soufflé omelette

This light, sweet omelette should be cooked just before serving, but can be prepared up to the end of step 2 an hour ahead. It's a simple yet delectable pudding to make in late summer/early autumn.

### Serves 2

2 crisp dessert apples, such as Cox's

55 g (2 oz) blackberries

½ tsp ground allspice

1½ tbsp caster sugar

2 eggs, separated

finely grated zest of ½ orange

½ tsp pure vanilla extract

15 g (½ oz) unsalted butter

1 tsp demerara sugar

2 tbsp Greek-style yogurt

Preparation time: 15 minutes
Cooking time: 5–8 minutes

1 Peel, core and thickly slice the apples. Put into a small saucepan and add the blackberries, allspice and 1 tbsp of the caster sugar. Cover and heat gently for 2–3 minutes, shaking the pan occasionally, until the fruit juices run and the sugar has dissolved. Remove from the heat and keep warm.

2 Put the egg yolks, remaining ½ tbsp caster sugar, the orange zest and vanilla extract in a bowl, and whisk together until smooth and thick.

3 In a separate, clean bowl, whisk the egg whites until they form soft peaks. Using a large metal spoon, fold the whites into the yolk mixture.

4 Preheat the grill to moderately hot. Melt the butter in a 20 cm (8 in) frying pan with a heatproof handle. Tip in the egg mixture, spreading it evenly, and cook gently for 2–3 minutes or until set and golden on the base.

5 Place the pan under the grill and cook for 1–2 minutes or until the omelette is puffed up and just set on top. Remove from the heat and turn up the grill to high.

6 Spoon the fruit mixture on top of the omelette and fold it over in half. Sprinkle with the demerara sugar and grill for about 30 seconds or until the sugar caramelises. Cut the omelette in half and serve immediately, topped with the yogurt.

### Some more ideas

● For a cherry soufflé omelette, replace the apples and blackberries with 150 g (5½ oz) stoned red cherries. Poach with 1 tbsp caster sugar and a star anise or bay leaf until the juices run. Make the omelette as in the main recipe, but replacing the vanilla extract with pure almond extract.

● Make a caramelised apple soufflé omelette. Melt 15 g (½ oz) unsalted butter, add 2 sliced dessert apples and sprinkle with 15 g (½ oz) light soft brown sugar. Sauté for 4–5 minutes, stirring, until tender and caramelised. Sprinkle with the grated zest of 1 lemon, then use to fill the omelette made as in the main recipe.

### Plus points

● Blackberries and other blue or purple-coloured fruits get their colour from flavonoids, powerful antioxidants that help to protect against coronary heart disease.

● The use of dessert apples instead of a cooking variety means that they need only light cooking and therefore not only retain their shape and texture but also much of their nutritive value too.

● The sodium content of unsalted butter is only 11 mg per 100 g (3½ oz), compared with salted butter which has a content of 750 mg per 100 g (3½ oz).

### Each serving provides Ⓥ

kcal 309, **protein** 10 g, **fat** 16 g (of which saturated fat 8 g), **carbohydrate** 33 g (of which sugars 33 g), **fibre** 3 g

| | |
|---|---|
| ✓✓✓ | B₁₂ |
| ✓✓ | A |
| ✓ | B₂, C, E, folate, niacin, calcium, copper, iron, selenium, zinc |

Desserts

# Grilled fruit brochettes

Cooking fruit on skewers, just long enough to heat the fruit and slightly caramelise its sugars, is an easy way to enjoy fresh fruit. If you are having a barbecue, cook the brochettes over the fire – take care not to char them or leave them too long in the smoke.

**Serves 4**

½ medium-sized ripe pineapple

2 just ripe, firm bananas

2 ripe but firm pears

4 ripe but firm fresh figs

2 ripe but firm peaches

juice of 1 lemon

4 tsp sugar

Cape gooseberries to decorate

**Raspberry-orange coulis**

225 g (8 oz) raspberries

grated zest and juice of ½ orange

1½ tbsp sugar, or to taste

Preparation time: 20 minutes

Cooking time: 6–7 minutes

**1** Soak 8 bamboo skewers in cold water for 20 minutes.

**2** Meanwhile, make the coulis. Purée the raspberries with the orange zest and juice and the sugar in a blender or food processor. If you like, sieve the purée to remove the raspberry pips. Taste the coulis and add a little more sugar, if necessary. Set aside.

**3** Preheat the grill. Prepare the pineapple, bananas, pears, figs and peaches, peeling as necessary and cutting into attractive bite-sized pieces. Thread the fruit onto the soaked skewers, alternating them to make a colourful arrangement.

**4** Sprinkle the kebabs with half of the lemon juice and sugar. Grill them for 3–4 minutes or until lightly tinged with brown, then turn over, sprinkle with the remaining lemon juice and sugar and grill for a further 3 minutes or until the second side is lightly browned and caramelised a little.

**5** While the kebabs are being grilled, pull back the papery skins on the Cape gooseberries to form a star-like flower round the fruit.

**6** Place 2 fruit kebabs on each plate, drizzle round the coulis, decorate with Cape gooseberries and serve hot.

**Plus points**

● This delicious recipe provides useful amounts of important antioxidant vitamins – plenty of vitamin C from the raspberries and the orange and lemon juices, and vitamin A converted from the beta-carotene in the peaches. As the fruit is heated for only a very short time, most of the vitamin C is retained.

● There is plenty of dietary fibre – both soluble and insoluble – in this array of fruit, and this is essential to keep the digestive tract healthy. Insoluble fibre provides bulk and prevents constipation. The soluble fibre found in fruit can be fermented by bacteria in the gut, producing substances that help to protect against bowel cancer.

**Some more ideas**

● Use nectarines instead of peaches.

● Use apples when peaches are not in season.

● Serve the fruit kebabs raw, just the fresh fruit skewers resting in a pool of the coulis.

**Each serving provides** Ⓥ

kcal 220, **protein** 3 g, **fat** 1 g (of which saturated fat 0.2 g), **carbohydrate** 54 g (of which sugars 53 g), **fibre** 7 g

✓✓✓ C

✓ B$_1$, niacin, copper, potassium

Desserts

# Sparkling peach dessert

For an almost instant dessert at the height of summer, top ripe, juicy peaches with raspberry sorbet, ice-cold sparkling wine (Champagne is especially good) and a sprinkling of chopped toasted nuts. If time allows, chill the wine glasses or dessert dishes first.

**Serves 4**

4 ripe peaches

4 scoops of raspberry sorbet, about 250 g (8½ oz) in total

8 tbsp sparkling white wine, well chilled

4 tbsp chopped toasted almonds

Preparation time: 10 minutes

1 Rinse the peaches and pat dry on kitchen paper. Halve each fruit and discard the stones. Using a small sharp knife, dice the flesh, then divide it among 4 wine glasses or dessert dishes.

2 Rinse an ice-cream scoop with hot water and use to scoop up the sorbet. Put a scoop on top of the peach in each glass.

3 Add 2 tbsp of sparkling wine to each glass, then sprinkle with the toasted almonds. Serve immediately.

**Some more ideas**

• If peaches are unavailable, ripe nectarines make a good substitute.

• When soft fruit is at its best, make a sparkling berry dessert. Use 300 g (10½ oz) strawberries, halved, or a mixture of raspberries and blueberries. You can use fruits of the forest sorbet instead of raspberry, or frozen vanilla yogurt or fruits of the forest yogurt.

• Replace the almonds with 4 tbsp chopped toasted hazelnuts.

• Instead of sparkling wine (or even Champagne), use a dessert wine such as Beaume de Venise.

• For a non-alcoholic alternative to sparkling wine, add 1 tbsp undiluted elderflower cordial to each serving.

**Plus points**

• Peaches are an excellent source of vitamin C (1 medium-sized peach provides around three-quarters of the recommended daily amount). They also provide useful amounts of fibre and are low in calories.

• Although sorbets can be quite high in calories because of the sugar they contain, they are much lower in fat than ice cream.

**Each serving provides**

kcal 225, **protein** 5 g, **fat** 8 g (of which saturated fat 1 g), **carbohydrate** 30 g (of which sugars 30 g), **fibre** 3 g

✓✓✓ C

✓✓  E

✓   $B_2$, copper

Desserts

# Peach and blackberry filo pizzas

These simple, attractive tarts have a crisp filo pastry base and a luscious fresh fruit topping. Filo pastry is made with very little fat, and most of it you add yourself when you brush the sheets sparingly with butter.

**Serves 4**

10 sheets filo pastry, about 30 x 20 cm (12 x 8 in) each, thawed if frozen

30 g (1 oz) unsalted butter, melted

2 tsp ground almonds or hazelnuts

4 peaches, about 115 g (4 oz) each

150 g (5½ oz) blackberries

2 tbsp vanilla caster sugar

**To serve (optional)**

Greek-style yogurt

Preparation time: 15 minutes
Cooking time: 15 minutes

1 Preheat the oven to 200°C (400°F, gas mark 6).

2 Place a sheet of filo on the work surface and brush very lightly all over with melted butter. Top with another sheet and brush with butter. Layer on 3 more filo sheets, brushing with butter each time, and finally brush the top surface. Using a saucer measuring about 13 cm (5½ in) as a guide, cut out 2 discs from the layered filo. Transfer to a baking tray. Repeat with the remaining filo pastry and butter to make 4 layered discs in total.

3 Sprinkle each filo disc with ½ tsp of the ground almonds or hazelnuts, then set aside.

4 Cut the peaches in half, twist apart and remove the stones. Slice the peaches thinly. Place the peach slices on the filo pastry discs, arranging them so they leave a little of the pastry edge uncovered all round. Divide the blackberries among the pizzas. Sprinkle 1½ tsp sugar over each pizza.

5 Bake for 15 minutes or until the pastry is golden brown and the peaches are very tender and lightly caramelised. Transfer to individual plates and serve at once, with Greek-style yogurt, if liked. These filo pizzas are best served within 15 minutes of coming out of the oven as the pastry will quickly lose its crispness.

**Plus points**

● Even though the filo pastry is brushed with butter, the quantity used here is small compared to that normally used in similar filo preparations, and the total fat content is lower than tarts made with shortcrust.

● Peaches are a good source of carbohydrate, with virtually no fat. Fresh peaches are also low in calories, with an average peach containing only 30 kcal.

● Blackberries provide lots of vitamins C and E, as well as being rich in bioflavonoids that work with vitamin C as antioxidants to boost immunity.

**Each serving (pizza alone) provides**
kcal 200, **protein** 3 g, **fat** 9 g (of which saturated fat 3 g), **carbohydrate** 27 g (of which sugars 18 g), **fibre** 3 g

✓✓  C, E

Desserts

## Some more ideas

● Use raspberries instead of blackberries, and nectarines instead of peaches.

● To make pear pizzas, replace the peaches and blackberries with 2 dessert pears, peeled, cored and sliced. Toss the slices with 1 tsp ground coriander before arranging on the filo discs and baking.

● For even quicker preparation, use peeled and sliced fruit preserved in alcohol. Particularly delicious are well-drained peaches in brandy, with fresh blackberries or raspberries.

● For a more conventional tart shape, trim the filo discs to 11 cm (4½ in) and press them into shallow, non-stick Yorkshire pudding tins. Bake as above, but watch that the edges do not burn.

● Vanilla-flavoured caster sugar, sold in supermarkets and delicatessens, adds extra flavour. If you can't find any, make your own by submerging a split vanilla pod in a bag of caster sugar for at least a week. Alternatively, toss the peach slices with ground cinnamon or ground mixed spice and then use plain caster sugar for the glaze.

● When berries are out of season, use well-drained preserved stem ginger, finely chopped – 2–3 tsp for each filo pizza.

Desserts

# Raspberry and vanilla risotto

This sweet and creamy fruit risotto is a delicious way of introducing more grain into your diet. The fresh raspberries colour the pudding a lovely pale pink, as well as adding a refreshing sweetness.

## Serves 6

1 litre (1¾ pints) semi-skimmed milk

1 vanilla pod, split open in half

140 g (5 oz) risotto rice

1 strip lemon zest

3 tbsp golden caster sugar or light soft brown sugar

6 tbsp flaked almonds

200 g (7 oz) fresh raspberries

6 tbsp single cream

vanilla pods to decorate (optional)

Preparation and cooking time: 30 minutes

1 Pour the milk into a heavy-based saucepan and add the vanilla pod. Sprinkle in the rice, stirring constantly. Bring to the boil over a moderate heat, stirring, then reduce the heat so the mixture is gently simmering.

2 Add the lemon zest and sugar. Cook, stirring frequently, for 15–18 minutes or until the rice is suspended in the sauce and is tender, and the liquid is thick and creamy.

3 Meanwhile, put the almonds in a small non-stick frying pan and toast over a low heat for 4–5 minutes or until they are lightly browned.

4 When the risotto has finished cooking, remove the vanilla pod and lemon zest. Stir in half of the raspberries. Remove from the heat and continue stirring for 1–2 minutes or until the fruit softens and begins to turn the risotto pink.

5 Spoon the raspberry risotto into 6 warmed bowls and drizzle 1 tbsp cream over each serving. Sprinkle the almonds over the top and add the remaining berries. Decorate with vanilla pods, if wished, and serve at once – the risotto thickens as it cools.

### Another idea

● Make a sweet pudding with quinoa, an ancient grain used by the Incas. Available from healthfood shops, quinoa is rich in nutrients and has a high amino acid content. Rinse 125 g (4½ oz) quinoa and drain well, then toast in a frying pan, without any fat, for about 4 minutes, stirring frequently. It will become a deeper golden colour and pop regularly. Sprinkle the quinoa into the hot milk (heated without the vanilla pod), stirring. When the milk boils, reduce the heat so the mixture is bubbling very gently. Cover and cook for 10 minutes. Instead of flaked almonds, use 45 g (1½ oz) ground almonds and stir them into the quinoa. Continue cooking for about 20 minutes or until most of the milk has been absorbed, stirring occasionally. (The quinoa will retain a slight crunchy texture and have a lovely toasted flavour.) Stir in 1 tbsp clear honey with half of the raspberries, or serve them all on top of the pudding.

### Each serving provides Ⓥ

kcal 320, **protein** 11 g, **fat** 14 g (of which saturated fat 4 g), **carbohydrate** 38 g (of which sugars 19 g), **fibre** 2 g

✓✓  C, E, calcium

✓  B₂, B₁₂, copper, iron, zinc

### Plus point

● Almonds are a good source of vitamin E, which helps to protect against heart disease. They also contribute useful amounts of phosphorus, copper and magnesium.

Desserts

# Plums en papillote with honey

En papillote is a method of cooking food in parcels of paper, thus sealing in all the juices. When the parcels are opened, a wonderful spicy perfume is released. Use baking parchment for the parcels as its coating is more moistureproof than greaseproof paper.

**Serves 4**

8 large dessert plums, stoned and thickly
 sliced
30 g (1 oz) unsalted butter
2 cinnamon sticks, halved
8 whole cloves
4 tbsp acacia honey, or another clear variety
1 large orange

**To serve**

4 scoops vanilla frozen yogurt or ice-cream
3 tbsp coarsely chopped pecans
extra honey for drizzling (optional)

Preparation time: 10 minutes
Cooking time: 20 minutes

1 Preheat the oven to 200°C (400°F, gas mark 6).

2 Take 4 large squares of baking parchment and in the centre of each put a quarter of the plum slices and butter, a piece of cinnamon stick and 2 whole cloves. Drizzle 1 tbsp of honey over each portion of plums.

3 Use a citrus zester to take fine shreds of zest from the orange, or thinly pare off the zest with a vegetable peeler and then cut it into fine shreds. Squeeze the juice from the orange. Add a quarter of the orange zest and juice to each portion of plums, sprinkling the zest and juice over the fruit evenly.

4 For each parcel, bring two opposite sides of the paper together over the fruit filling and fold two or three times. Fold over the other ends twice, then tuck them underneath, to make a neatly sealed parcel.

5 Place the parcels on a baking tray and bake for 20 minutes. The paper parcels will puff a little and brown slightly, and the fruit mixture inside will be bubbling hot.

6 Place the parcels on individual serving plates, carefully open up each one and top with a scoop of frozen yogurt or ice-cream. Sprinkle with the pecans and drizzle with extra honey, if you like. Serve immediately.

**Some more ideas**

● For pineapple and banana en papillote, replace the plums and spices with 1 small ripe pineapple, peeled, cored and chopped, and 4 bananas, thickly sliced. Add 2 star anise to each parcel, then drizzle with the honey and orange zest and juice.

● Maple syrup makes a toffee-flavoured alternative to honey.

● You can use foil for the parcels rather than baking parchment, but transfer the fruit compote to bowls for serving.

**Plus points**

● Plums contain a useful amount of vitamin E, an important antioxidant that helps to protect against degenerative diseases associated with ageing.

● Pecans, like other nuts, are rich in fat (70 g per 100 g/3½ oz), but little of this is saturated. They also provide generous amounts of vitamin E.

● Yogurt, along with other dairy products, is a valuable source of calcium. This mineral is essential for the structure of bones and teeth, which contain 99% of all calcium in the body. But calcium is also important in a number of other vital processes, including blood clotting and the proper functioning of muscles and nerves.

**Each serving provides** Ⓥ

kcal 270, **protein** 3 g, **fat** 14 g (of which saturated fat 5 g), **carbohydrate** 35 g (of which sugars 34 g), **fibre** 3 g

| | |
|---|---|
| ✓✓ | C, E |
| ✓ | A, calcium, copper, potassium |

Desserts

# Drop scones

Drop scones, also called Scotch pancakes, are easy and fun to make, and perfect for tea or even as a simple dessert. Served with creamy fromage frais and sweet, succulent berries, they are quite irresistible.

### Makes about 24 drop scones

125 g (4½ oz) self-raising flour

2 tsp caster sugar

1 egg, beaten

1 tbsp melted unsalted butter

150 ml (5 fl oz) semi-skimmed milk

4 tsp sunflower oil

**To serve**

100 g (3½ oz) blueberries

1 tsp clear honey

100 g (3½ oz) raspberries

200 g (7 oz) fromage frais

Preparation time: 10 minutes
Cooking time: 15–20 minutes

**1** Put the flour in a bowl and stir in the sugar. Make a well in the centre, and add the egg, melted butter and a little of the milk. Gradually stir the flour into the liquids and add the remaining milk a little at a time, to make a fairly thick, smooth batter.

**2** Heat a large shallow dish in a low oven, then turn off the heat and line the dish with a tea-towel (this is for keeping the cooked drop scones warm). Heat a griddle or large, heavy-based frying pan over a moderate heat and grease it with 1 tsp of the oil.

**3** Using a dessertspoon, pour the batter from the pointed end (rather than the side of the spoon) to make neat, round drop scones. Depending on the size of the griddle, you should be able to cook 4–6 scones at once, but make sure you leave enough space round them so you can turn them easily. Cook for about 2 minutes or until almost set and bubbles are breaking on the surface; the scones should be golden brown underneath.

**4** Using a palette knife, turn the scones over and cook for a further 1–2 minutes or until golden brown on the other side. Transfer to the prepared dish, wrap in the tea-towel and keep warm while you cook the remaining scones. Grease the griddle lightly with 1 tsp oil before cooking each batch.

**5** Place the blueberries in a bowl and stir in the honey. Add the raspberries and lightly crush the fruit, leaving some berries whole. Serve the scones warm with the honeyed berries and the fromage frais.

### Some more ideas

● Instead of serving the drop scones with fromage frais and crushed fruit, top each one with a dab of Greek-style yogurt and a little jam.

● To make apple drop scones, stir 1 cored and finely diced dessert apple into the batter with a pinch of ground cloves. Serve the scones dusted with a little sifted icing sugar.

● To make savoury Parmesan and herb drop scones, instead of caster sugar add 1 tbsp snipped fresh chives, 1 tbsp chopped fresh oregano and 2 tbsp freshly grated Parmesan cheese to the flour. Serve the drop scones topped with a little soft cheese and halved cherry tomatoes.

### Plus points

● Home-made drop scones contain less fat and sugar than bought scones, and serving them with fromage frais instead of butter keeps the total fat content low.

● Milk is a good source of calcium, essential for healthy bones and teeth. It also supplies protein, and vitamins $B_2$ and $B_{12}$

### Each scone provides     ⓥ

kcal 55, **protein** 2 g, **fat** 2 g (of which saturated fat 1 g), **carbohydrate** 6 g (of which sugars 2 g), **fibre** 0.5 g

✓     $B_{12}$

Desserts

# Cherry brandy clafoutis

Clafoutis is a classic French dessert in which fruit is baked in a sweetened batter. Both canned and fresh fruit are suitable, so this is an ideal dessert to make with whatever is in season – or even from storecupboard ingredients when time is short.

**Serves 4**

2 cans stoned cherries in syrup, about
   425 g each
2 tbsp brandy
75 g (2½ oz) plain flour
55 g (2 oz) light muscovado sugar
250 ml (8½ fl oz) semi-skimmed milk
3 eggs
1 tsp pure vanilla extract
icing sugar to dust (optional)

Preparation time: 10 minutes
Cooking time: 20 minutes

1 Preheat the oven to 200°C (400°F, gas mark 6). Drain the cherries, then tip them onto kitchen paper and pat dry.

2 Divide the cherries equally among four 300 ml (10 fl oz) individual flan dishes, or other ovenproof dishes, spreading them in an even layer. Drizzle the brandy over the cherries. Set aside.

3 Sift the flour into a bowl and add the sugar. In a jug, beat the milk and eggs with the vanilla extract, then whisk into the flour mixture to make a smooth batter. Alternatively, combine the ingredients in a food processor and process until smooth.

4 Pour the batter slowly over the fruit. Bake for 20 minutes or until lightly set and pale golden. Dust with icing sugar, if you like, and serve warm.

**Some more ideas**

● Bake in one dish, if you prefer. Use a 25 cm (10 in) round china flan dish and bake for 20–25 minutes.

● Use fresh sweet cherries, stoned, rather than canned cherries.

● When fresh peaches are in season, replace the canned cherries with 4 ripe but firm peaches, peeled and sliced, and use peach schnapps instead of the brandy. Flavour the batter with 1 tsp mixed spice instead of vanilla, adding the spice to the flour. Peaches provide twice as much fibre, 10 times the amount of vitamin A and 30 times the amount of vitamin C per 100 g (3½ oz) as cherries.

● To reduce the fat a little more use skimmed milk rather than semi-skimmed.

● The tiny black seeds scraped from half a vanilla pod can be used as an alternative to the vanilla extract.

**Plus points**

● Cherries not only provide delicious flavour and fibre, but also vitamin $B_1$, essential for proper functioning of the nervous system, and a small amount of iron.

● If you were to use skimmed milk in the batter instead of semi-skimmed, to reduce the fat content, this would not affect the amount of calcium provided (calcium is particularly important for maintaining healthy bones). It's worth remembering, though, that reducing the fat will also reduce the amount of fat-soluble vitamins, so this is not recommended for children under the age of 2 (and possibly up to age 5, according to the child's general appetite and diet).

---

**Each serving provides**                    Ⓥ

kcal 380, **protein** 11 g, **fat** 6 g (of which saturated fat 2 g), **carbohydrate** 74 g (of which sugars 59 g), **fibre** 2 g

---

✓✓   $B_{12}$

✓   A, $B_1$, $B_2$, $B_6$, folate, niacin, calcium, iron

---

Desserts

# Cranberry and banana rice pudding

This could be called a sweet risotto as it uses risotto rice – the starchy grains are ideal as they create a creamy-textured milk pudding. Rather than sweetening it with lots of sugar, it is simmered with dried bananas and cranberries, both of which add natural sweetness.

**Serves 4**

1 litre (1¾ pints) semi-skimmed milk
140 g (5 oz) risotto rice
1 vanilla pod, split open in half
30 g (1 oz) light muscovado sugar
55 g (2 oz) dried cranberries
55 g (2 oz) small dried bananas, sliced
scented geranium leaves to decorate
    (optional)

**To serve**
berry coulis or other fruit coulis

Preparation time: 5 minutes
Cooking time: 15–20 minutes

**1** Pour the milk into a heavy-based saucepan and add the rice, vanilla pod, sugar, cranberries and bananas. Stir to mix. Bring to the boil over a moderate heat, stirring constantly, then turn the heat down so the mixture is gently simmering. Cook, stirring frequently, for 15 minutes or until the pudding has a creamy consistency and the rice is tender.

**2** Remove the vanilla pod from the pudding. Spoon the rice pudding into the centre of 4 large flat soup plates. Drizzle with a few spoonfuls of the coulis and decorate with scented geranium leaves, if liked. Serve the remainder of the coulis separately.

**Some more ideas**

• You can make the rice pudding ahead of time to serve later, but you will need to add extra milk when reheating to return the pudding to its creamy consistency.

• For a creamy cinnamon and sultana rice pudding, replace the dried cranberries and banana with 75 g (2½ oz) sultanas and use a cinnamon stick instead of the vanilla pod. Serve with a tangy apricot coulis made by puréeing a well-drained can of apricot halves in apple and apricot juice, about 410 g, adding enough of the juice to make a smooth sauce.

**Plus points**

• Milk is one of our most nourishing foods. It is rich in calcium, which is essential for healthy teeth and bones, and is also a good source of protein.

• Unless catering for children under the age of 2, who always require full-fat milk, it is a good idea for everyone following a healthy diet to switch to semi-skimmed milk to reduce their intake of saturated fats.

• Cranberries, bananas and rice all boost the carbohydrate content of this dessert, and add a variety of vitamins as well.

**Each serving (with coulis) provides**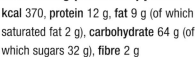
kcal 370, **protein** 12 g, **fat** 9 g (of which saturated fat 2 g), **carbohydrate** 64 g (of which sugars 32 g), **fibre** 2 g

| | |
|---|---|
| ✓✓✓ | C |
| ✓✓ | calcium, potassium |
| ✓ | B$_{12}$ |

Desserts

**251**

# Index

Titles in *italics* are for recipes in 'Some More Ideas'.

**Fast Healthy Food** was published by
The Reader's Digest Association Limited, London,
from material first published in the Reader's Digest Eat Well, Live Well series

**Project Editor**
Rachel Warren Chadd

**Art Editor**
Jane McKenna

**Assistant Editor**
Rachel Weaver

**Reader's Digest, General Books, London**

**Editorial Director**
Cortina Butler

**Art Director**
Nick Clark

**Executive Editor**
Julian Browne

**Development Editor**
Ruth Binney

**Managing Editor**
Alastair Holmes

**Picture Resource Manager**
Martin Smith

**Style Editor**
Ron Pankhurst

First edition Copyright © 2003
The Reader's Digest Association Limited,
11 Westferry Circus, Canary Wharf, London E14 4HE

We are committed to both the quality of our products and the service
we provide to our customers. We value your comments, so please feel
free to contact us on 08705 113366 or via our web site at:
**www.readersdigest.co.uk**
If you have any comments or suggestions about the content of our books,
email us at **gbeditorial@readersdigest.co.uk**

Copyright © 2003 Reader's Digest Association Far East Limited
Philippines Copyright © 2003 Reader's Digest Association Far East Limited

Reprinted 2003

**Reader's Digest production**
Book production manager: Fiona McIntosh
Pre-press accounts manager: Penelope Grose

Origination: Colour Systems Limited, London
Printing and Binding: Toppan Printing Company, Hong Kong

ISBN 0 276 42748 3
Book code 400-150-02

Visit our web site at www.readersdigest.co.uk